D1033934

JACK AND DORIS SMOTHERS SERIES
in Texas History, Life, and Culture, No. Thirty-one

THE

TRIALS

OF

THE MURDER CASE THAT SHOOK
THE TEXAS PRISON SYSTEM

EROY

BROWN

MICHAEL **BERRYHILL**

UNIVERSITY OF TEXAS PRESS
Austin

Publication of this work was made possible in part by support from the J. E. Smothers, Sr., Memorial Foundation and the National Endowment for the Humanities.

Requests for permission to reproduce material
from this work should be sent to:
    Permissions
    University of Texas Press
    P.O. Box 7819
    Austin, TX 78713-7819
    www.utexas.edu/utpress/about/bpermission.html

The paper used in this book meets the minimum requirements
of ANSI/NISO Z39.48-1992 (R1997) (Permanence of Paper). ∞

Library of Congress Cataloging-in-Publication Data

Berryhill, Michael.
    The trials of Eroy Brown : the murder case that shook
the Texas prison system / Michael Berryhill. — 1st ed.
       p. cm. — (Jack and Doris Smothers series in Texas
history, life, and culture ; no. 31)
    Includes bibliographical references and index.
    ISBN 978-0-292-72694-9 (cloth : alk. paper)
    ISBN 978-0-292-73876-8 (e-book)
    1. Brown, Eroy. 2. Prison homicide—Texas—Case studies.
3. Prison administration—Corrupt practices—Texas—Case studies.
4. Trials (Murder)—Texas. I. Title.
    HV9475.T4B47 2011
    364.152'3092—dc23   2011021428

FRONTISPIECE: Eroy Brown. Photograph by Michael O'Brien.

For Lynn, who made it possible.

In memory of Molly Ivins, who always said it was a great story.

The historian's task is not to disrupt for the sake of it, but it is to tell what is almost always an uncomfortable story and explain why the discomfort is part of the truth we need to live well and live properly. A well-organized society is one in which we know the truth about ourselves collectively, not one in which we tell pleasant lies about ourselves. ||| TONY JUDT

If you put good people in a bad place, do the people triumph or does the place corrupt them? ||| PHILIP ZIMBARDO, *THE LUCIFER EFFECT*

CONTENTS

The visiting rules at the Federal Correctional Institution at Victorville, California, are strict: no cameras, no recorders, no cell phones, no scanty clothing, no hats, no do-rags, no billfolds, no car keys. For most visitors, no notebooks or pens, either, but I have been allowed to bring one of each. I left three pages of typed questions in the rental car. One condition of my visit was "no extraneous paperwork."

It was the Saturday before Easter, 2010, and it had taken several weeks to arrange an interview with Eroy Edward Brown. The visitors' center is a concrete-block room the size of a high school gym, with a video camera stuck in the highest corner. The guards, dressed in blue, watch the visitors and the inmates from a platform. The inmates, dressed in khaki, emerge from the back corner of the room, where two bright murals have been painted. One depicts a mountain lake with swans in the foreground. The other features a mob of cartoon characters to amuse the visiting children: Mighty Mouse, SpongeBob SquarePants, Batman, Superman, the Simpsons. Two ogres, Shrek and his wife, dominate the center of the mural, cuddling their green baby.

Eroy Brown emerges from the corner, looking around for me. It had been ten years since we last visited at the federal prison in Beaumont. His head is now completely shaved and gleaming. His close-cropped beard has gone salt and pepper. He wears a gray long-john shirt under his short-sleeved khaki shirt, sharply creased khaki trousers, and thick black work shoes. He had requested to be moved to Victorville from Beaumont.

"Beaumont has all the most dangerous men in America," he says.

Although he has uneventfully spent the last twenty-five years in federal prisons, Texas parole officials would probably argue that Eroy Brown is one of those dangerous men he wants to get away from. That has to do with something that happened thirty years ago, when in an instant he chose to defend himself against a Texas warden who had pointed a gun at his head. At least, that's the story Eroy Brown told, and the story thirty-five of thirty-six jurors believed. After studying the case for the past ten years, I believe him, too.

Brown's capital charges filled Texas newspapers and airwaves during the early 1980s, the same time that Texas inmates won a massive civil rights trial in federal court and changed the way their prisons were run. In that case, *Ruiz v. Estelle*, or more simply, *Ruiz*, a federal judge believed that inmates were telling the truth about the unrelenting cruelty of the Texas prison system. The major studies of the *Ruiz* case mention Eroy Brown in passing, a sentence here, a paragraph there, an endnote.[1] Brown's case replayed many of the issues that had been tried in *Ruiz*. That a black inmate could kill two white officials and not be convicted of murder shocked the prison system and marked the end of Jim Crow justice in Texas.

Prison officials never got over Brown's exoneration. In his memoir, former Texas warden Jim Willett recalled being present when Brown was brought to the prison hospital with a gunshot in his foot.

"He looked scared," Willett wrote. "Later I learned more of the sad story. In the Ellis farm shop, farm manager Billy Moore had a problem with inmate Brown—a problem serious enough that Moore called the warden for help. The two men attempted to handcuff Brown, who somehow grabbed Pack's pistol. In the scuffle, Brown apparently shot and killed Moore, then overtook Warden Pack and drowned him in the nearby creek. How the prisoner himself came to be shot remained a mystery.

"When Brown's trial came to court, I sat in the gallery with other prison employees, all of us there on our own time. When Brown was acquitted of murder charges, the verdict hit us like a kick in the stomach. We were numb. We watched justice lurch horribly awry, and we were angry."[2]

Another former Texas warden, Lon Glenn, wrote in his history of Texas prisons that Brown "had obtained a pistol from the warden's car while being transported." Brown's lawyer, "a controversial minority senator from Houston," "put every convict who had ever had a grudge against the warden or TDC on the stand to cry and whine about how brutal the system had been to them."

"For those of us who understand the realities of the Texas prison system," Glenn wrote, "this was a clear case of injustice. We were left knowing that a multiple-offender convict with a rap sheet a yard long had killed two good men and gotten away with it. It made me want to throw up."[3]

Brown has spent the last twenty-five years in prison for being an accessory to a convenience store robbery in 1984 that netted twelve dollars and a couple of candy bars. He was given ninety years as a habitual criminal. The two accomplices who testified against him got nothing.

For his own protection, he has served his time in federal, not Texas, prisons. But his fate still rests with the Texas parole board. Brown almost got parole in 2000, until someone reminded the board about his past. What he is really in prison for, he believes, is not for being a robber, but for defending himself against two Texas prison officials in 1981.

Brown seemed more expansive than last time I talked to him, when he was more guarded and cool. He resembles the actor Danny Glover a bit—a darker, contemplative Danny Glover, who smiles reflexively as he talks, and continually chews a plastic toothpick.

He feels the oppression of being in prison all these years. He has hepatitis C, probably from his heroin addiction as a young man. He says his mental health is "average," and though he is indignant about why he is in prison, he maintains a cheerful demeanor.

"I really need a single cell," he says, but none are to be had. "This is bad on me, an old man like me. I'm a sleepwalker. I fight in my sleep. When I had problems at TDC, it was sleepwalking. I would fall out of my bunk."

He would like to work. He has trained as a welder and in industrial sewing, and took classes in WordPerfect. Victorville had a program armoring Humvees for the army, and Brown had hoped to be using his welding skills, but with the recession, the program has been cut back.

Unlike Texas prisons, which never pay inmates for their labor, federal prisons pay inmates a small wage. He says he made $140 a month sewing uniforms in Beaumont. In the 1980s a proposal to pay Texas inmates a dollar a day, with fifty cents to go to a victim relief fund, was shot down.[4] He doubts Texas will ever pay an inmate for his work. "Nah," he says, "they'll never do that."

He's hoping for a parole and a short chance at a working life. He'll be sixty-five if he serves all his time and is released in 2017. "Maybe someone might hire me at fifty-nine," he said, "but at sixty-five? Right now I could get in five or six years. But if they hold me 'til I'm sixty-five, I'll be dependent on the state. And for what?"

He answered his question the first time I asked him about his situation: "They are still retaliating."

But what happened that April day in 1981? And most of all, what does it mean? This is hardly a case of simple injustice on the part of jurors. It was a tragedy that needn't have happened, but it also became a signal moment in the history of prison civil rights, revealing everything that can go wrong in prisons.

1

A FISHING TRIP TO ELLIS PRISON

On the first Saturday of April 1981, two men woke up in darkness in East Texas and drove a hundred miles south to go fishing at a prison. This was not as strange as it may sound. Prisons were a world unto themselves in East Texas, a part of the state more like the Old South than the West. There were a dozen prisons in East Texas then, most of them within a short drive of Huntsville, the headquarters of the Texas Department of Corrections (TDC). Another six were situated near Houston, in Brazoria and Fort Bend counties. Several had been built on former plantations where slaves had worked. Usually they backed up on rivers that formed a natural barrier to escape.

The two men were driving to see Billy Max Moore, the farm manager of Ellis prison. Richard Pustka, a close friend of Moore, was an assistant warden at Coffield prison in Tennessee Colony, a village just outside Palestine. Pustka was riding with Billy Moore's younger brother, Benny, a contract electrician for the prison complex in Tennessee Colony. The drive from Palestine follows the Trinity River through the piney woods of East Texas to Crockett. State Highway 19 drops through the towns of Lovelady and Trinity, then crosses the Trinity River at the little town of Riverside. From there it is only five miles east to the country lane that leads to Ellis prison, a dozen miles north of Huntsville. During the early 1960s, eight hundred convicts spent two years building it on the old Smithers plantation, a little more than 11,670 acres of bottomlands that lie along the Trinity River.

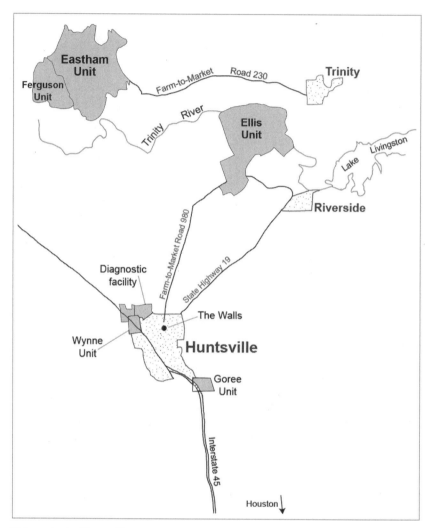

Prisons in the Huntsville area.

Although the TDC had been ordered to desegregate, the plantation mentality still prevailed. The last old-time black work songs were recorded at Ellis in 1965. With racial integration, the TDC gradually broke up the black field squads. The young black inmates, inspired by the civil rights movement, weren't about to sing slave songs.

About half the inmates were black, and they were still called "boys" and "niggers" and "old things." Many prison officials denied that the use of racial epithets was condoned or even practiced, but that was just a lie.[1] What did the outside world know or need to know of their world? They were doing a difficult and unappreciated job for very little money. To maintain order, they had to work men hard in the fields.

Most of the officials were proud of the paternalistic way in which they ran the prisons. In 1982 an assistant warden at Ellis told a *Life* magazine reporter that he decided the prison needed a gospel group and picked it from a field squad working with the heavy hoes called aggies. "Well," he said, "I just walked out there in the middle of a line of aggies and picked seven of the sorriest niggers I could find. Sunday comes, though, and can those boys sing."[2]

While inmates performed stoop labor in the fields, this was mostly to keep them in line. Fields were plowed and hay was mown with tractors. The Ellis farm raised cotton, row crops, vegetables, hogs, and beef. There was a dairy operation, an egg-production barn, a syrup mill to process sugar cane, and a cotton gin. Ellis was a mechanized, self-sustaining plantation worth several million dollars a year.

As the farm manager, Billy Max Moore was in charge of it all. Moore had grown up in the small town of Troupe in East Texas. After working in the oil fields in the early 1960s, he became a game warden in Crockett. Things didn't go well for Moore with Texas Parks and Wildlife. He had a reputation for letting people off for game violations in exchange for money. Moore's first marriage broke up.

While he was still a game warden, he courted his second wife, Lola. She was young, divorced, and the mother of two. He had introduced himself to her one night at a restaurant in Woodville, her hometown. He was, by many accounts, a charming man, the classic good old boy with a likeable grin. He was narrow-hipped with a big belly and chest and a head of thick, dark hair. Lola wasn't quite sure about him, but she gave him her number. A year and a half later he phoned her for a date. It was mid-December and they sat up all night, parked in a truck deep in the woods, and talked, while he listened for the gunshots of poachers. He had a keen ear for distant gunshots. They dated all through deer season and into the spring and married in June 1967.

Moore soon found a new job as a tractor supervisor at one of the oldest prison farms in the system, Eastham. Eastham was thirty miles north of Huntsville, and like Ellis, it backed up to the Trinity River. During the summer Moore would work in the fields from five in the morning until eight at night. He liked the work, and when friends and relatives came to visit, he showed off the Eastham crops as if they were his own.

After a couple of years, Moore had become a good family man. He would come home and fill up the truck with children and friends and drive to the little town of Lovelady for ice cream. During the winters, when farming was less intense, he took his children hunting and fishing, and on the weekends grilled venison.

Other prisons called Moore to help them deal with poachers. He loved following the tracking dogs. If there was an escape, Moore grabbed his slicker and shotgun and raced off in his truck. Sometimes he would be gone for days, and often he would be the one to catch the escapee.

In the spring of 1979 Moore won a commendation from the director of the prison system, Jim Estelle. A farmer who lived near Eastham had phoned for help. An escaped mental patient, armed with a shotgun and a knife, was holding his family hostage in a trailer next to the farmhouse. A few TDC guards were outside trying to figure out what to do when Moore arrived. "What are we waiting for?" he said, and he charged into the trailer, knocked the man down, and took away his weapons. That was typical, Lola Moore said of her husband, that was Billy.

"Billy never saw danger," Lola Moore said. "He was very tough. The only weakness he ever had was for his family, if someone was sick or had died. He feared no one. I can't tell you how many times he had a gun poked in his stomach tracking down poachers out at Eastham, but he always stared the men down. As far as danger was concerned, Billy's instinct was always to walk towards it, not away."[3]

Shortly after Moore charged the hostage-taker, he was promoted to farm manager at Ellis.

Moore's cousin, Ray Hill, also remembered him. Hill had served time for burglary during the 1960s and '70s. Moore had inmate welders use prison materials and tires to make cattle trailers that he then sold, Hill said. Moore had offered one to Hill's father, but he had turned him down, Hill said. Shortly after Hill got out of prison in 1978, he saw Moore at a family reunion. Moore was wistful, he recalled. He wished that, like Hill, he could get out of prison too, but he was chained to the paycheck.[4]

That was a common refrain of correctional officers. They were serving life in prison, too, at the rate of eight to twelve hours a day. Hill developed a theory about prison culture. From the outside it might appear that there are two cultures, one for the inmates and one for the guards. But there is only one culture in prison, Hill says. Inmates and guard share the same slang, the same workplace, the same food, and the same recreation. The keepers and the kept are one society, each dependent on the other and, in important ways, identical.

At seven o'clock on April 4, Pustka and Benny Moore pulled up to Billy Moore's house outside the main building at the Ellis Unit. Lola told them her husband had already gone fishing. Pustka and Benny Moore drove to the picket tower and introduced themselves to the guard. There were six such towers at Ellis. The picket guard cannot be approached in person. He lowers a bucket on a rope to haul up the identification of visitors. Law enforcement officials who enter the prison are supposed to put their guns in the bucket, and the picket hauls them up to the tower for safekeeping.

Pustka and Moore told the picket officer that they were headed to the pond below the syrup mill to go fishing with Billy Moore.[5] A few miles southeast of the Ellis farm, the Trinity River is dammed, forming Lake Livingston, a ninety-thousand-acre reservoir stocked with striped bass and catfish by Billy Moore's former employer, Texas Parks and Wildlife. The free world offered plenty of nearby places to fish, but Billy Moore and his friends and brother preferred the three-hundred-acre reservoir of the Ellis farm, an almost square, treeless pond surrounded on three sides by a levee.

Pustka and Benny Moore drove around the building and turned down a dirt road. They could see Billy Moore's pickup sitting on the corner of the levee. He and a game warden named Billy Platt were fishing from the aluminum skiff Moore kept at the pond. Moore brought the boat to shore and the two men got in and threw out their lines. It was a tiny boat with a small outboard motor, almost too small for four men. The morning was warm and humid, and clouds were building up.

Moore was not wearing a gray uniform, but "free-world" clothes: dark brown jeans with a leather Western belt, a short-sleeved khaki shirt with white snap buttons, a straw Resistol hat, and white leather sneakers with two brown stripes on the sides.

Some of the trusties—inmates who had earned the confidence of prison authorities by their good behavior—were also enjoying the day. The white "dog boy," who trained the tracking hounds to pursue escapees, was fishing at the pond. So were a couple of black trusties. A black trusty came riding by on Billy Moore's colt, which he was training to handle livestock. The trusty stopped the colt and visited a moment. How was the horse doing, Moore asked. He's doing good, the inmate said. Well, handle him easy, Moore said. Handle him easy.

The men had been fishing for an hour when a green Plymouth sedan came up the levee. Moore's new boss, Warden Wallace Pack, was driving. Moore brought the boat to shore and the four men exchanged pleasantries. Pack had been on the job less than three weeks.

Pack was fifty-nine years old and only a year from retirement when he accepted the job. He had been born in Bryan, a conservative small town adjoining College Station and Texas A&M University. Unlike many wardens, who had gone to the TDC straight out of high school, Pack had served in the army. He didn't enter the TDC until 1961, when he was thirty-five. His first assignment was to the Wynne Unit in Huntsville, where he remained for nineteen years. Pack had proven his mettle at Wynne, which held psychiatric patients. He was known as a man who could deal with difficult people. His colleagues at Wynne and some inmates used a prison cliché about him: "Firm but fair." At least two said he had chewed them out for talking abusively to inmates. They said he was a deeply religious man who encouraged inmates to stay in touch with their families. After a divorce, in 1965 he married a widow with three children. In 1973 he was baptized at the Cook Springs Baptist Church.

Pack and his wife, Faye, had built a home in Wheelock, a tiny town of a few dozen houses at the intersection of two farm-to-market roads fifteen miles north of Bryan. They spent their weekends there, away from the pressures of the Wynne Unit. Pack was thinking of retiring to Wheelock. Faye had already moved there. But the director of the prison system, Jim Estelle, had been persuasive. He had appealed to Wallace Pack's loyalty, and to his sense of membership in the TDC family. Wheelock and retirement would have to wait.

Pack had been given control of the toughest, most troubled prison in Texas. Since Ellis had opened in 1963, the TDC had deliberately filled it with repeat offenders. A third of the inmates were serving life sentences and would have to serve twenty years before being considered for parole. Facing such long sentences, many inmates at Ellis felt they had nothing left to lose. Ellis was overcrowded and understaffed.

Conditions were so bad in Texas prisons that three months earlier, in December 1980, a federal judge had declared them unconstitutional. For years Texas inmates had been complaining about harsh treatment, and for years Texas prison officials had denied there were any problems except those generated by malcontents and troublemakers. But the testimony had been alarming. When the case went to trial in October 1978, several hundred Ellis inmates went on a work stoppage that lasted three weeks. The strike spread to other prisons before it died out. At Ellis, hundreds of inmates were crammed three to a tiny cell, with one man sleeping on the floor, usually with his head next to the toilet. Inmates were seething with expectations. They hoped the federal government was going to change the way Texas prisons were run.

Pack had replaced Billy McMillan, who quit the TDC after twenty-three years to join the Walker County sheriff's department. McMillan had spent two years as warden of Ellis. His predecessor, Oscar Savage, had lasted only a year on the job.[6] McMillan said he was burnt out and frustrated by problems he couldn't do anything about, especially the paperwork filed by litigious inmates. McMillan had stayed on at the warden's house on the Ellis grounds, but that arrangement was coming to an end that Saturday.[7] While Pack was exchanging pleasantries at the pond, his wife was moving into the warden's house. That morning he had kissed Faye goodbye, and promised to meet her at noon when the moving van arrived.

Like Moore, Pack wore free-world clothes: a blue-gray polyester suit with a faint pinstripe from a men's store in Waco, a long-sleeved white shirt with a wine-colored tie patterned with blue diamonds, and black lace-up shoes. A felt Western hat rested on the front passenger seat of his car.

It was not surprising that Pack was working. Saturdays were visiting days, and sometimes a warden could solve problems with inmates and their families. A Texas warden was always on call. The most important thing Pack could do was to be seen. That let everybody know that a new man was running things, and he was watching what was going on. Pack had already uncovered some problems both in the mess hall and in the fields. He had also noticed problems with the bookkeeping and proper reporting of the crops. One of his central tasks was managing Billy Moore, the agriculture boss. Moore ran the farm, but the job of running Ellis prison belonged to one man: Wallace Pack.

Around nine o'clock it started raining, so the four men quit fishing. They sat in their trucks on the top of the levee for a while, and then drove a mile north to the tractor shop and drank coffee for half an hour. The shop consisted of two long narrow sheds, each with eighteen open bays to shelter the farm machinery. At the end of the sheds were enclosed shops for tools and offices. There was an old refrigerator with a freezer and a place to cook. Coffee was always available.

After the rain stopped, the four fishermen drove past the shooting range to the hog pens where Harmon Creek ran. They threw a cast net into the creek and caught some minnows. The game warden left to run an errand in Livingston. Pustka and the Moore brothers returned to the pond. The rain had wet the grass and filled the ditches. It was too wet to plow, and the tractor drivers came into the shop for lunch. Only a handful of trusties and a couple of farm supervisors were working that Saturday.

One of them was Eroy Edward Brown, a trusty who ran the tire shop for Billy Moore. He was thirty years old and had spent most of his young manhood in Texas prisons. His skin was so dark that his features disappeared in his prison mug shots. He was of medium height, with a small waist and strong arms and shoulders thickened by wrestling tractor tires all day.

After a long series of run-ins with the Waco juvenile authorities, Brown first entered the TDC in 1968, having pled guilty to burglary. He was seventeen. He served three years and was paroled to Waco, where he fitfully worked and acquired a heroin addiction. He returned to prison in 1974 for having burgled a Waco department store for twenty-seven dollars' worth of men's socks. He was nearing the end of his third sentence, as an accomplice to the armed robbery of a Fort Worth motel. He had never been tried for his crimes. He always pled guilty.

Brown came to Ellis in 1977, just before it phased out its segregated field squads. The black line squads always got the worst fields, Brown thought. For six months he picked cotton and chopped cane and stripped it and sent it to the syrup mill. He knew that if he behaved himself in the field he could get promoted to an easier job. During his earlier stints at Darrington and Ferguson prisons, he had driven tractors, and soon was driving one at Ellis. When the trusty who ran the implement shed went home, Brown got his job. Brown filled ammonia tanks with fertilizer, fixed flats, and changed tires on the farming implements and tractors.

He lived in Ellis dormitory D10, one of several Quonset huts the TDC had built outside the back gate to relieve the overcrowding at Ellis. These dorms, or "tanks," were filled with bunk beds lined up end to end. These were for "outside" trusties.

Outside trusties could spend time on the farm, away from the crowded, dangerous tanks and cell blocks. They had refrigerators and stoves in the work buildings where they could make lunch. They caught rabbits in the fields. They baited fish traps with chicken gizzards and had a tractor driver drop them in the Trinity River.

Eroy Brown had never succeeded in the free world, but at Ellis he did work that kept the plantation functioning. He was due for parole in three months and he was looking forward to his freedom.

When Billy Moore came to run the farm in 1979, he had made it clear that he was in charge. Brown didn't think Moore was such a bad guy. But he came in stealing and hustling, getting oil changes and lube jobs for himself and his friends and stealing tires that he had Brown mark down on the farm inventory.

Brown had not met the new warden at Ellis, Wallace Pack. No one at Ellis seemed to know much about him, except that he was rumored to have been tough on the mentally retarded convicts who were kept at the Wynne prison.

Brown had been an outside trusty three times in prison and he knew how to do time. His motto was the convict's motto: "I ain't got nothing to do with nobody." He kept his mouth shut.

But on this Saturday morning, Brown was goofing off with another convict. He was cleaning out the bus used to haul the trusties from the back gate to their jobs at the farm buildings, and he was complaining about not getting a furlough. A year before he had been granted a furlough for the funeral of his father, his namesake, Eroy Edward Harris, a man he had barely known. He had gone to Waco, had seen a girlfriend, and enjoyed his freedom.

With the overcrowding of Texas prisons, furloughs were in the news. There was talk of creating work programs for well-behaved convicts to relieve the overcrowding, and to create some rehabilitative alternatives to the maximum-security prisons that were all Texas had ever built.

Brown did not know why he had been turned down for a furlough. He had worked hard at Ellis and had stayed out of trouble. He had done what he was told by the white men who ruled him, even helping them steal tires and car parts and commit other types of petty graft. But he violated his convict's code when he complained to his work partner in a woeful, loud voice: "After all I done for Billy Moore, I don't see why I can't get no furlough."

Brown didn't see him, but the tractor supervisor, a boss named Bill Adams, was standing in the back of the shop, listening. Adams didn't like the tone of that phrase, "after all I done for Billy Moore," and wanted to know what Brown was doing "running his head." Brown tried to explain that he meant no harm. Adams told him he must be drunk or stoned, running his head like that, and to get in the truck. They were going to see Billy Moore about this. Adams knew Moore was fishing at the pond. He had come by the farm shop that morning to drink coffee.

In an earlier era, Adams might have let Brown's comment go. Who would listen to a convict anyway? But for the past several years, civil rights lawyers and FBI agents had been combing through the Texas prisons, talking to convicts about prison brutality. The TDC was in an uproar about civil rights.

Adams was not about to let a convict mouth off. Brown didn't think Adams had much use for Billy Moore, anyway. Now Adams could hand off a problem to Moore, even if it was his day off and he was fishing with his friends and brother. Adams told the livestock supervisor, Charles Spivey, to follow him to the reservoir, a little more than a mile away. Billy Moore could deal with Eroy Brown.

2

DEATH AT TURKEY CREEK

The three men had been fishing for about thirty minutes after the noon whistle went off, when two white TDC stake-bed pickups drove slowly up the levee and stopped. Bill Adams drove the lead truck. The stock supervisor, Charles Spivey, followed him. Sitting beside Adams was Eroy Brown, dressed in the coarse white cotton pants and white shirt of a Texas inmate. His name was stamped in black letters above the shirt pocket.

Adams hollered out the window: "Billy, I need to see you a minute." Moore pointed and said, "I'll meet you-all at the truck." Adams said, "No, I need to see you now, if I can." They paddled to the corner of the reservoir. Billy Moore stepped out of the boat and walked up the levee to confer with Adams.

The two men talked a moment and then Moore walked around the truck and got in on the passenger side. Brown was in the middle and the talk got louder. Pustka and Benny Moore were still sitting in the boat. Pustka couldn't hear what was said but he could tell they were fussing. Then they saw Moore get out of the truck and heard him tell Brown: "Don't you be calling me *man*! You know better than that."

Moore walked around the truck to the driver's side and called down to Pustka and his brother, "You-all go on back fishing. I'll be back in a little bit." Adams got out of the truck and Billy Moore took over the driving. Both pickups backed slowly down the levee to the east corner, where there was room to turn around. Benny Moore turned on the boat's motor and sped across the pond with Pustka in the bow.

Pustka stepped out and climbed the levee and waved down Charles Spivey. "What's the deal?" he asked. Spivey said there wasn't much to it. He thought it was under control. Spivey drove to the end of the levee and followed Moore. Ordinarily, if an inmate was causing trouble, officers would take him back to the "house"—the main building with its cell blocks—and put him in solitary confinement. Then they would write him up for an offense, and give him a date for a disciplinary hearing. That was the proper procedure.

Moore was not driving toward the house. From the top of the levee Pustka could see that Moore was driving across the bridge over Turkey Creek. He stopped about fifty feet across the bridge, a hundred yards from a greenhouse and a garden shed where three inmates were sorting and washing vegetables. Adams got into Spivey's truck and the two drove to the tractor shed a mile away, leaving Moore alone with Brown. Pustka could see the two men in the cab of the truck through the steel mesh on its back window. He walked down to the boat and was about to shove off when Wallace Pack's green Plymouth Fury came down the road from the main building. Pustka waved and Pack waved back. The Fury disappeared from view behind the levee and Pustka shoved the boat off the bank. He and Benny Moore threw out their lines and started fishing again.[1]

Wallace Pack had spent most of the morning at his office and then ate lunch at about 11:30 in the officers' dining room with assistant warden James Williamson and a young guard named Robert DeYoung. About a half hour after noon, Pack told them he was driving out to the garden shed to meet Billy Moore. He guessed Moore had caught a mess of fish he wanted to give him.[2]

Williamson, who had spent twenty-two years in Texas prisons, was sharing weekend duties with DeYoung. Every third weekend he filled in at the warden's office to answer the telephone and answer the questions of visitors.

About fifteen minutes after Pack left the office, the interior phone line in DeYoung's office rang. Interior lines connected only within the prison. The call was from a trusty at the garden shed. The trusty was so alarmed that at first DeYoung couldn't make out what he was saying or where he was. He made him repeat it: He was not at the hog pens; he was at the garden shed. And Major Moore had been shot. DeYoung yelled for Williamson. Williamson ran to the employee parking lot, got in his truck, and sped to the garden shed. DeYoung grabbed the keys to the prison ambulance, summoned an inmate paramedic to ride with him, and followed.

Williamson arrived first. A hundred yards from the garden shed he could see what the trusty was phoning about. Billy Moore lay in the road behind the warden's green Plymouth. Blood was smeared on the trunk. Williamson knelt down to see if Moore had a pulse, but he couldn't find one. But where was Pack? A trusty came out of the garden shed.

"They went down there," he said, pointing to the concrete bridge over Turkey Creek. Williamson started walking south across the bridge. "Be careful," the trusty shouted. "He's got a gun."

Just as Williamson crossed the bridge, he saw Eroy Brown get up from the ditch that drained the sewage ponds into Turkey Creek. He was wet and slimy. His prison whites were gray with mud. His face was bruised and scratched. A handcuff dangled from his left wrist. He had plunged his hand into his right pants pocket. He was walking up the embankment toward Williamson, who was unarmed. Fearful that Brown was reaching for a gun, Williamson took three or four steps forward, threw his arms around him, and toppled him to the ground.

While Williamson was dealing with Brown, DeYoung pulled the ambulance beside Pack's car. DeYoung had barely noticed Williamson. He saw Moore's body and the bullet hole in the back quarter panel of Pack's car and reflexively hit the ground, worried there might be more gunfire. Scared and unarmed, he crawled over to Moore and felt for a pulse. He was going to the ambulance to radio for help when he saw Williamson struggling with Brown on the south side of the bridge. Brown was young and strong, and he was agitated. Williamson was having difficulty controlling him. DeYoung ran toward the pair. Williamson stood Brown up and was trying to cuff Brown's other hand. DeYoung went over and helped, but it was the trusty from the garden shed, James Soloman, who snapped the cuffs shut.

As they marched him across the bridge, Brown declared, "A man has got to do what a man has got to do."

Where is the warden, Williamson asked. Over there, in the ditch, Brown said. Williamson and DeYoung put Brown on his stomach and Williamson left to find Pack. Soloman was ahead of him. They waded across Turkey Creek to the ditch that ran from the sewage settling ponds. The water in the ditch was a couple of feet deep from that morning's rain. They could see the back of Pack's suit jacket floating in the water. Pack's body was so firmly mired in the mud that it took both men to pull him free. Williamson cleaned the mud from Pack's mouth, and Soloman pushed on his chest to revive him, but it was useless. They dragged him across Turkey Creek and up the slope to the top of the bridge.

Where is the gun, Williamson demanded. Down there, Brown said, pointing to Turkey Creek.

DeYoung searched Brown. There was no gun in his front pants pocket, just Wallace Pack's billfold. It held some credit cards, a little cash, and a fifteen-year service pin. DeYoung also found a pair of nail clippers and three padlock keys on an eighteen-inch-long chain fastened to Brown's belt. The keys were for his locker in the tank. Even though Brown was handcuffed and on his stomach, DeYoung said he had trouble keeping him on the ground. Brown got up three or four times, DeYoung recalled. Each time DeYoung would knock his legs back out from under him. Brown was babbling, and he was also complaining. He was barefoot and he had been shot in the left foot.

DeYoung found a hand-rolled cigarette in Brown's shirt pocket and put it in Brown's mouth to calm him down. The other thing that DeYoung remembered distinctly was Brown saying: "You missed the whole play. You know me. I wouldn't hurt anybody." It must have seemed an odd thing for him to say, since two men were dead.

Pustka and Benny Moore had been fishing for a couple of minutes when they heard shots, first one, and after a moment, two more. Another fifteen seconds passed and they heard a fourth and then a fifth. Soon Williamson's brown, free-world pickup came speeding down the road from the prison toward the garden shed and vanished from sight. Two or three minutes later, a TDC ambulance rushed by. Pustka and Moore sat in the boat, listening and watching. A TDC truck roared past, loaded with several uniformed officers. They were armed with shotguns.

Pustka and Benny Moore ran the boat to the spot where Billy Moore's truck was parked. They backed it down the levee, made the U-turn and stopped south of the bridge over Turkey Creek. On the other side of the bridge a cluster of trucks and cars were parked and men were milling about. The back doors of the ambulance were open, and they could see an officer putting someone inside. Before they could get out of the truck, the ambulance turned around and drove past them, heading up the slope to the prison. It was not much of a slope, but enough that inmates and officers sometimes referred to the main building as the "Hill."

As Pustka and Benny Moore got out of the truck, officers and an inmate were carrying a body up the slope that led down to Turkey Creek. It was a hard climb of about ten feet at a steep angle. They laid the body at the corner of the bridge. Pustka and Benny Moore stood there wondering who it could be. The dead man was smeared with mud, but they could see he was wearing a suit and tie. It was Warden Pack.

Then Benny Moore asked a plaintive question: "Where is Billy?" Pustka was looking for Billy Moore too. When he crossed the bridge he saw a body lying at the rear bumper of the warden's car, covered in a green blanket. A pair of white leather sneakers with two broad brown stripes extended from beneath the blanket. "There is Billy right over there," Pustka said.

Benny Moore ran across the bridge and fell to the ground, hugging his brother's body, shouting and crying. Pustka walked over and lifted the blanket from his head. Billy Moore had been shot in the left side of his forehead. Benny Moore clutched his chest in pain and an officer pulled him away. Three days later, when Billy Moore was buried in the Pinecrest Cemetery at the little town of Troupe, two of the pallbearers were Billy Platt, the game warden who had fished with him that morning, and Richard Pustka.

Pack and Moore had died in only a few minutes. It was not yet one in the afternoon. In the history of Texas prisons, they were the highest-ranking officers ever killed on duty.

As with many things in the story of Eroy Brown, there are two versions of what happened next.[3] DeYoung testified that he strapped Brown to the ambulance gurney and drove him to the building. Brown recalled being tossed to the ambulance floor on his stomach. When he reached the gate, DeYoung followed procedures and strip-searched Brown. He couldn't open his handcuffs because mud had been jammed into the mechanism. So he cut off Brown's shirt with a knife. Then he took him to the isolation row. It had only one entry and anyone who came in or out had to sign a logbook. There were two floors with eight cells above and eight below. The guards cleared the bottom floor, but five inmates in the upper row could hear what was happening below.

Brown said he had on two sets of cuffs when a sergeant and a lieutenant put him in the cell. They hung him up by the cuffs on a clothes hook behind his head and began hitting him in the stomach. "Where's the gun, nigger?" they demanded. "I didn't have it!" yelled Brown. "I didn't have it."

When they heard Brown's cries, the inmates on the tier above howled. The beatings occurred three times, Brown said. Brown's foot was swelling, and inmates heard him shouting, "Don't hit my feet, don't hit my feet!" The guards would beat him and then leave, beat him and then leave. Each time the guards left, Brown called up his story to the inmates above. He had accidentally killed Moore when Pack had pulled a gun. "Call my people," he yelled. "Call my people."

One said he heard Brown say over and over again, as he was beaten, "They made me do it." Another said Brown said, "Don't hit me, boss. Why are you doing this, boss?" And more plaintively: "I should never have gotten mixed up with Billy Moore."

Brown's bullet wound was throbbing, bleeding, and muddy. He did the only thing he could do. He waited to die.

Many years later Brown recalled a little black officer who watched helplessly from a chair at the end of the corridor. He said he was new to the job. When the officers left, he told Brown, "They'll kill you." He was sitting there with tears in his eyes, Brown recalled. He said, "I wish I could help you."

About 5 o'clock, Brown was put in another ambulance and taken to the central unit, better known as the "Walls." Every inmate entered and left the prison system through this nineteenth-century, redbrick prison in downtown Huntsville. The Walls also held the death chamber. In 1924 Texas put an end to unseemly public hangings, and installed an electric chair. The state had electrocuted 361 people in the chair, which was affectionately called "Old Sparky." In 1972 the US Supreme Court held most of the states' capital punishment laws to be unconstitutional. The Texas legislature revised its laws to conform to the Constitutional standard. Penniless defendants were to be assigned skilled legal counsel. And if they were to be executed, it would not be in an electric chair, but by lethal injection. No one in Texas had yet been executed under the new laws.

With his foot swelling and throbbing with pain, Brown was taken to the hospital at the Walls. As Brown hobbled in, a correctional officer asked him why he had shot himself. When Brown didn't reply, the officer asked him again. "I didn't shoot myself," Brown said.[4]

Word had already gotten out on the radio that there had been a shooting at the Ellis farm. Brown recalls that the doctor on duty said, "I'm not touching the son-of-a-bitch." An inmate nurse washed the wound, took the bullet out, and dropped the mangled piece of lead in a steel bowl. Brown's right wrist was lacerated by the handcuffs. The cut came, Brown insisted, from being hung by the cuffs at the Ellis isolation cell. After the medical treatment, the sheriff of Walker County swabbed Brown's hands for a test to determine if he had fired a gun. Brown submitted a urine sample as well.

Many years later, Brown recalled that the director of the TDC, W. J. "Jim" Estelle Jr., visited him at the Walls when he first arrived from Ellis. Brown was naked with an IV hooked up to his arm. Brown recalled: "Mr. Estelle said, 'Brown, do you want to talk about this?' and I said, 'Warden, I need a doctor for this foot.'" But Brown wouldn't talk to Estelle. Estelle was accompanied by an assistant warden for the Walls, G. P. Hardy. Hardy told a newspaper reporter the same thing he told Brown, only without the racial epithet that Brown remembered many years later: "Nigger," Hardy said, "you're gonna die by lethal injection and I hope they let me stick it in you."[5]

They put Brown naked into cell CB10, reserved for the medical care of death-row inmates, and placed him on suicide watch. But Eroy Brown wasn't close to committing suicide. Though prison officials denied it, suicide watch was a way of tormenting inmates. For five days Brown was held naked and blanketless.[6] On the sixth day he got a shower. For six weeks the light in his cell never went off. Every fifteen minutes a guard walked by and slammed the heavy steel door at the end of the hallway, waking him just as he was about to doze off. Then the guard would shout down the hall to his commanding officer something that had the ring of doom: "Still alive! Still alive!"

3

ESTELLE'S BITTERNESS

When the director of the Texas Department of Corrections, Jim Estelle, met with reporters the day after the deaths of Pack and Moore, he was angry and defensive. The official story was that Moore had brought Eroy Brown near the bridge at Turkey Creek for smoking marijuana. Somehow Brown got a gun from the glove box of Pack's car, scuffled with the two men, shot Moore, and drowned Pack.[1]

Moore's predecessor as farm manager at Ellis, Buford Smith, said he never carried a weapon inside the prison as Pack had done. "You never saw me with a gun unless one escaped," he said. "They could have taken my truck, but that's it. I had too close of contact with them to carry a gun."

Reporters pressed Estelle about guns in prison. "Our written weapons policy is that they are not allowed inside the security perimeter," Estelle said. He would not comment on an unofficial policy. "Security," he said, "that's nobody's business but the people who need to know."[2]

It was almost as though the prison system was being blamed for the deaths. If inmates and not prison officials had been killed, the public outcry would have been greater, Estelle said. "I guarantee you there aren't going to be any marches on the courthouse," he said, "any wailing or gnashing of teeth, any sackcloth and ashes over this."[3]

The source of Estelle's bitterness was a federal judge with the improbable name of William Wayne Justice. For the last seven years Justice and Estelle had been embroiled in what turned out to be one of the longest-running prison civil rights cases in the history of federal jurisprudence: *Ruiz v. Estelle,* or more simply, *Ruiz.*

David Ruiz was an armed robber who had filed a fifteen-page, handwritten petition in Justice's court charging the TDC with cruel and unusual punishment. In 1974 Justice consolidated Ruiz's petition with several inmate writs, recruited a civil rights attorney from the NAACP, and got the Justice Department involved. Next came a trial before Judge Justice.

The TDC was not used to outside interference. It had long enjoyed a reputation as the best-run prison system in the country: cheap, clean, and orderly, with few escapes and little violence. The state fought the pretrial investigation of *Ruiz* to the Supreme Court and lost. After four years of delays, the trial began in October 1978, with demonstrators picketing outside the courthouse. One of their signs read, "Prisons are concentration camps for the poor." Another said: "W. J. Estelle is a slave master."[4]

Scheduled to last three months, the trial lasted nearly a year as the state, expecting to lose, conducted prolonged cross-examinations of both convict witnesses and prison officials. The core issues were overcrowding, inadequate medical care, lack of safe working conditions, and brutality by TDC officials and their inmate snitches and enforcers, the building tenders.

The case involved 349 witnesses, hundreds of exhibits, and thousands of pages of documents. To demonstrate the problem of overcrowding, the plaintiffs built a replica of a typical Texas prison cell, five feet wide and nine feet deep, and crammed three to five court officials inside.

When Ward James Estelle took the stand, the inmates' attorney, William Bennett Turner, used Estelle's own words against him. For years Estelle had been urging the legislature to reform the maximum-security prisons favored by Texas. He called for community-based halfway houses and other less expensive forms of incarceration that would be more humane and less expensive than locking up every inmate in a prison like Ellis. Turner focused on a 1973 speech in which Estelle told the Joint Legislative Committee on Prison Reform that 40 percent of Texas inmates were nonviolent offenders and didn't belong in maximum-security prisons at all.

In his sweeping history of the Texas prison system, Robert Perkinson writes, "The most captivating moment was Director Estelle's appearance. A handsome, well-spoken man, Estelle tried, against the odds, to strike a convivial tone. . . . Turner tried to keep the exchange respectful. Over the course of the conversation, however, he wove facts around Estelle like a spider wrapping up its prey. In their pre-trial research, the plaintiffs had discovered that the director had regularly highlighted the same deficiencies now being pursued in court. Texas's staff-to-inmate ratio—the lowest in the nation—was 'extremely dangerous,' he had told the legislature in requesting additional funding. The crowding situation was 'severe,' the medical facilities inadequate, the assault rate rising 'dramatically.' In its legal filings, TDC had been steadfastly denying problems in all these areas, but Estelle now had to eat his words, bite by distasteful bite."[5]

Justice took a year to study the record and write his opinion, which he issued in December 1980, a little more than three months before the deaths at Turkey Creek. In more than two hundred pages, Justice described the suspicious deaths and gruesome stories of Texas prison life. In one, a convict whose arms had been cut off in a threshing machine had been left alone to be raped by another inmate. A paralyzed inmate, deprived of his wheelchair by officials, was forced to drag himself on the ground for hours. Officials allowed a building tender to rape and torture an inmate by forcing him to stand in a toilet while they shocked him with wires strung from the ceiling light.

"Nor is the brutality the sole province of a few low-level security officers," Justice wrote. "Many vicious incidents of abuse implicate high-ranking TDC officials."[6]

One newspaper reporter compared Justice's opinion to Dostoyevsky, who had famously written: "The degree of civilization in a society can be judged by entering its prisons."

Justice concluded: "But it is impossible for a written opinion to convey the pernicious conditions and the pain and degradation which ordinary inmates suffer within TDC prison walls—the gruesome experience of youthful first offenders forcibly raped; the cruel and justifiable fears of inmates, wondering when they will be called up to defend the next violent assault; the sheer misery, the discomfort, the wholesale loss of privacy for prisoners housed with one, two, or three others in a forty-five-[square]-foot cell or suffocatingly packed together in a crowded dormitory; the physical suffering and wretched psychological stress which must be endured by those sick or injured who cannot obtain adequate medical care; the sense of abject helplessness felt by inmates arbitrarily sent to solitary confinement or administrative segregation without proper opportunity to defend themselves or to argue their causes; the bitter frustration of inmates prevented from petitioning the courts and other governmental authorities for relief from perceived injustices."[7]

Reporters found Estelle's reaction to Justice's opinion peculiar and quotable. He denounced it for its literary merit. "It read like a cheap dime novel," Estelle said. "I think he overused the adjective aspect of his dictionary. It did not read like a legal opinion and did not even make interesting reading as far as I'm concerned."[8]

One of the state's major defenses during *Ruiz* was that yes, bad things some-times happen in prisons. They were bad places full of bad people. But on the whole, prisons were safe places, with lower rates of murder than the average town. A few bad actions by a few people did not make the prisons unconstitution-al. There was no deliberate pattern here. The state got ready to fight every finding of fact. Estelle was already being briefed for the appeals to the Fifth Circuit. Now Estelle had lost the warden of Ellis prison and his farm manager. It might have seemed to Estelle that the *Ruiz* decision had emboldened Eroy Brown. At least a dozen cases of questionable inmate deaths had been brought up during the trial and three inmate witnesses died during it.[9] For the past three years, the prisons had been restless, with work stoppages and protests. Inmate-against-inmate vio-lence had increased. The state had resolutely defended the prison system, deny-ing every charge brought against it, especially those involving brutality by prison officials. It was time for someone to stand up for them.

"We've had five employees killed in the last nine years and we haven't had an execution since 1964," Estelle told reporters. "If there was ever any reservation in my mind (about the death penalty) the closer it gets to home the less I have. I wouldn't want to be the next person who tried to assault the next warden."[10]

Though he was not from Texas, Jim Estelle fit the TDC tradition perfectly. He backed his men and took no guff from critics. Ward James Estelle Jr. was six feet tall and weighed two hundred pounds. He wore cowboy boots and Western hats, and habitually fattened his lower lip with snuff. He worked in a darkened office decorated with a Lone Star flag and trophy heads of white-tailed deer. The TDC wardens and guards revered him.

When Estelle told a reporter that Wallace Pack reminded him of his father, he probably wasn't exaggerating. Estelle was born into prison work.[11] His father was a guard at California's oldest prison, San Quentin. One of Estelle's earliest memories, at the age of ten, was watching the jute mill where inmates manufac-tured grain sacks burn to the ground. After college at Sacramento State in the early 1950s, he spent eighteen years in the California Department of Correc-tions, working as a guard and a parole officer. At the end of his California career he supervised inmate honors work camps in the forests of northern California. He considered that the best job he ever held in the California system.[12]

In the fall of 1969 Estelle taught a class called "Introduction to Corrections" for the College of the Redwoods in Eureka, California, about 250 miles north of San Francisco. The college offered vocational programs for rural California students, including "correctional science." Several of his lectures were recorded and transcribed and rest in his archive at Texas A&M University.

Estelle was thirty-eight years old when he gave his prison lectures. He was teaching at the heights of the civil rights and anti-war movements, when social change seemed to have an unstoppable momentum. He looked back at the history of prisons and declared that people such as the Quakers, who were once regarded as radicals, had set the standards for future generations.[13]

He told his students there was no doubt in his mind that marijuana would be legalized and sold by Liggett and Myers. He urged them to read James Baldwin, Eldridge Cleaver, and Claude Brown. *Manchild in the Promised Land* wasn't pleasant, but it was real, he said. He held no brief with Eldridge Cleaver, but he thought prison officers should be exposed to his views.

He said he was relieved when as a guard at Folsom prison he was no longer required to carry an ironwood baton. He had an equally good control of inmates without one, and there was always the danger the baton could be taken away and used on him. In the light of what happened to Wallace Pack and Billy Moore, this statement had a prophetic ring.

Estelle predicted that corrections would change and prisons would be replaced with work-furlough systems, seventy-two-hour furloughs, and community correction systems, the same advances that were being called for by prison reformers.

He declared his support of one-man cells. He extolled an "over-and-under" design that prevented prison officials from adding another bunk.

"Of course, legislatures have a way," Estelle told his students, "rather than building safely and housing safely, of making do with what we have. And it's not safe for the people involved directly nor is it safe for the public to have felons housed two or more to a cell. It's a bad practice."

But putting up with the state legislature was what prison directors did. Ten years after Estelle gave his lecture, he wasn't just double-celling inmates in Texas prisons—he was triple-celling them. One man had to sleep on the floor and decide whether he wanted to put his head near the toilet, which was unpleasant but safer, or near the door, where the air was better, but where he was in danger of being "jugged"—kicked or stabbed in the head by anyone who bore a grudge against him.

On the day Eroy Brown was arrested, three thousand inmates were sleeping on the floors of Texas prisons. As for community corrections and work furloughs, Texas had resolutely stuck with building large, maximum-security prisons. Estelle couldn't change the way the TDC was managed without the help of the Texas legislature, and few Texas politicians wanted to be seen as soft on crime.

Not long after he gave his lectures at the College of the Redwoods, Estelle took a job running the tiny Montana prison system. In 1970 Estelle attended the annual meeting of the American Corrections Association (ACA), where he met the man who would bring him to Texas: George Beto. Beto had been elected president of the ACA that year and was at the height of his reputation. Texas was considered a model for prison management. Beto was a commanding presence. He stood six feet four inches tall and held a doctorate in educational administration from the University of Texas. He was addressed as "Dr. Beto," as though he had written the prescription for running Texas prisons. Estelle invited Beto to talk in Montana. He could only pay him his travel expenses, but Beto came for three days in 1971.[14] He liked Estelle, who, like him, was something of an intellectual.

A couple of months before he visited Estelle in Montana, Beto gave notice to the TDC board that he would be resigning in a year to teach penology and criminology at Sam Houston State University. He had served ten years as director of the TDC. Beto had enjoyed the board's unconditional support. In most of its meetings, every motion passed unanimously. The board asked Beto to find and train his successor. Soon Beto offered Estelle a job as associate director. He had ten months to learn the ropes. In August 1972, Beto gave him the keys. Estelle had gone from running one of the smallest prison systems in the nation to one of the largest. At Montana he managed 275 inmates, 20 percent of them Native Americans, and only four of them black. In Texas he had 16,000 inmates, 7,000 of them black, and their numbers were steadily growing.

In his 1970 presidential address to the ACA about the future of corrections, Beto said little about the impact of courts and the prison civil rights movement on the management of prisons. Perhaps he just couldn't see it coming, although there had been plenty of signs that federal courts would be intervening in state institutions, beginning with schools and colleges.

Appointed as judge for the Eastern District of Texas by Lyndon Johnson near the end of his presidency, William Wayne Justice had ordered the integration of Texas schools. He had shaken up the Texas Youth Commission, ruling that its juvenile detention facilities were unconstitutional. Justice had changed Texas political districts to ensure that blacks had fair representation in the state legislature.

By 1975 several Southern prison systems were under federal court orders to reform, including those of Arkansas, Alabama, and Mississippi. South Carolina,

Tennessee, Georgia, Louisiana, and Florida fell under federal court orders during the next twenty years. Prison reform seemed to be a Southern problem.[15] Far from fighting the federal orders, prison administrators in some states cooperated in the suits, and used them to force state legislatures to appropriate funds to improve conditions. For a hundred years, the Supreme Court had followed a "hands off" doctrine with regard to prisons. Now it was hands on.

All over the county inmates responded by filing lawsuits. In the late 1960s the federal courts had been loosening the control prisons could exert over inmates. Inmates had won the right to correspond with judges, attorneys, legislators, and the news media without the interference of the prison mail censors. Black Muslims in Illinois had won the right in federal court to read the Qur'an and hold services. Again because of an inmate lawsuit, a federal court had ordered the TDC to end racial segregation. In 1975 the overcrowded and filthy Harris County jail, while not part of the TDC, had been put under the supervision of federal judge Carl Bue. Every one of these changes had been won in a federal court, and inmates were teaching one another how to file new suits.

With the civil rights movement came a new crop of black politicians who were sensitive to the plight of inmates who were worked in the fields like slaves. A 1965 Supreme Court decision forced Texas to draw up single-member legislative districts that gave urban blacks and Hispanics a chance at fair representation. Redistricting helped Barbara Jordan move from the Texas house to the Texas senate in 1966. She then became the first black female member of the US House of Representatives ever elected from the South. After redistricting, five minority representatives from Houston were elected to the state house in 1972.

They called themselves "The People's Five": Mickey Leland, Anthony Hall, Benny Reyes, Cecil Bush, and Craig Washington, all from Houston. They were joined by Eddie Bernice Johnson of Dallas, who went on to serve in Congress, as did Leland and Washington. Leland had been a civil rights activist at Texas Southern University in the 1960s. He had the help of wealthy Houston philanthropist and art collector Jean de Menil. Washington was a brilliant extemporaneous speaker who could change votes on the floor of the legislature through his oratory, not an easy thing to do in that still-conservative, mostly white body. The new black legislators were tuned in to what was happening to Texas inmates, and a widely publicized beating of inmates gave them an opening for action.[16]

In June 1973 ten inmates at the Retrieve farm in Brazoria County refused to turn out for fieldwork on Father's Day, a Sunday and a heavy visiting day. The warden, Bobby Taylor, sent a squad of eight officers armed with ax handles, baseball bats, and rubber hoses to roust the men out of their cells and send them into the fields. The guards beat several of the men badly and forced them to work barefoot and in their undershorts.

One of them was a civil rights activist from Dallas, Ernest McMillan. McMillan was serving ten years for a demonstration at a supermarket in which more than $200 worth of merchandise was damaged.[17] Taylor gathered the beaten men and urged them to stay quiet about the incident. McMillan got hold of Eddie Bernice Johnson in Dallas and soon she and Mickey Leland were visiting the beaten inmates and announcing a legislative investigation.

The Father's Day Incident, as it was called, created a lot of bad publicity, but Estelle stood firm. He told the press that the beaten inmates were lucky they had Bobby Taylor as their warden and not him. Estelle refused to discipline either the warden or the guards. Estelle asserted that the work stoppage was a form of mutiny and that the inmates had assaulted his officers.[18]

The Father's Day Incident became a rallying cry for prison reformers, among them Charles and Pauline Sullivan, a husband-and-wife team of Catholic activists. In the early 1970s the Sullivans formed a group called CURE (Citizens United for Rehabilitation of Errants). They began their work by arranging cheap bus and van rides for families of inmates from central Texas to the Huntsville area for prison visitation. They learned a lot from the families about prison problems. Mickey Leland and legislator Chet Brooks invited the Sullivans to participate in a twenty-member citizens' advisory committee for the Joint Committee on Prison Reform. The committee hired staff that one of its conservative members considered "the most grotesque collection of radical activists ever put together under one roof east of Berkeley."[19]

The committee delivered its ninety-five-page report to the legislature in December 1974 with a picture depicting seven inmates crowded together flat-weeding a dark patch of ground.

One of the great ironies of prison reform movements is that they almost always have been aimed at giving prison management more resources. The report extolled Estelle's call for more community-based corrections, objecting that Texas always built maximum-security prisons. The reform committee called for an end to building such prisons and wanted the legislature to build a community-based system that used halfway houses and work-furlough programs to help inmates make the transition back into society. The legislative committee called for an end to racial and ethnic segregation in the cell blocks. More racial balance was needed on the prison and parole boards. More Spanish-speaking officers should be hired. More medical services were needed. The committee's chief investigator had witnessed inmate "doctors" with no medical training administering anesthesia and performing surgery.[20]

Most important of all, the committee called for higher salaries for guards, and more of them. More guards would enable Estelle to end the practice of using inmate guards. The reports of violence in the system were frequent and consistent: Texas prison officials ran a taut, fearful system by using inmate guards called "building tenders" as enforcers.

"Technically speaking 'building tenders' no longer exist," the committee wrote. "Inmates are still, however, used to discipline other inmates as forbidden by the law and 'wing floor tender' is one of a number of titles used interchangeably to describe the function of a building tender. During the course of this study, the Committee was told repeatedly that 'BTs' are used to enforce discipline and to carry out physical punishment on other inmates. The staff has seen too many 'incident reports' in which one of the two parties to an altercation turned out to be a building tender to believe that these allegations are unfounded. The continued illegal existence of the building tender system was conceded by several unit officials in staff interviews."[21]

The committee report might have been a perfect opportunity for Estelle to go to the legislature and argue for a change in the course of Texas prison history. But on Wednesday, July 24, 1974, three inmates drove the Father's Day Incident out of the public's memory and ended the momentum for prison reform in the Texas legislature. Estelle was giving a speech at a San Antonio rotary club when he got an urgent call from Huntsville.

Three inmates, each armed with a handgun, had taken over the prison library at the Walls unit. They were holding a dozen guards and civilian employees hostage, as well as another forty or more inmates. They were led by a convicted heroin dealer from San Antonio named Fred Carrasco.

The guns had been smuggled into the prison by inmate "house boys" who worked in the homes of prison officials. The hell of it was, the FBI had warned Estelle that Carrasco was planning an escape, but he had not put him under tighter security. Carrasco tried to get a prison writ writer named David Robles to join him. Robles was at the Walls hospital, about to undergo gall-bladder surgery, but he got out of bed and went inside. He persuaded Carrasco to release most of the inmate hostages, and told him he wanted nothing to do with this madness and went back to the hospital.

The Carrasco siege lasted eleven days and riveted the nation's attention, even though it happened during the resignation of Richard Nixon. Carrasco was a megalomaniac who demanded fancy clothes, good food, and an armored truck.

He and his henchmen improvised some portable armor by fastening law books to rolling blackboards from the prison classroom. When they tried to leave the library down the second-floor concrete ramp, police and prison officials knocked them and the hostages down with high-pressure fire hoses. In a burst of gunfire from both sides, the convicts killed two of the women hostages. One of the three convicts was captured alive.

Whatever public sympathy there might have been for Texas inmates evaporated during the Carrasco siege. In January 1975 Mickey Leland announced that the prison reform effort was over for the session. Opponents would invoke Carrasco every time reform was mentioned, he said, but "they don't realize that inmates are going to revolt, even at the sacrifice of their lives, for prison reform."²²

Leland's words were prophetic. Every issue raised by the Joint Committee on Prison Reform was argued in *Ruiz*. Even though many newspaper writers remained skeptical of the convict witnesses during the trial,²³ *Ruiz* had been a public relations nightmare for Estelle. The prison horror stories had changed public opinion about Texas prisons. Every major story about the deaths at Ellis included a paragraph or two about what Judge Justice had found in *Ruiz*. If a federal judge had found convincing evidence that TDC officials often beat inmates to control and intimidate them, maybe something like that had happened to Brown.

Brown was claiming self-defense, and Estelle retorted that self-defense was the last refuge of a convict when he is out of facts.²⁴

On the Monday after the killings, more than six hundred mourners, most of them prison officials and their families, crammed into the Huntsville Funeral Home Chapel for Wallace Pack's funeral. Another three hundred waited outside. The mood was one of controlled anger. Several burly prison guards wept openly when they walked by the open coffin. Bob Owens, a retired minister from Pack's church, said of Pack, "Like Jesus, in the end he was killed by those he tried to help."²⁵ Later that afternoon, services for Billy Moore were held farther north, near Jacksonville, in the community of White House.

Prison officials were not the only mourners. About a week later, a *Dallas Morning News* editorial writer reported that inmates had contributed $1,000 to a fund for the families of Pack and Moore.²⁶

Estelle made plans to erect a granite memorial under a tree outside the Ellis prison. The words engraved on it read: "In memory of Warden Wallace M. Pack and farm manager Billy M. Moore, slain on the Ellis Unit, April 4, 1981. Their devotion to duty, service to Texas, and courage will always stand as our guide and standard."²⁷

The deaths of Pack and Moore would be remembered and avenged. As for William Wayne Justice's "cheap dime novel," Estelle didn't see any room for compromise. The man who had condemned double-celling to his college corrections class was triple-celling a thousand inmates. The man who thought many of his inmates needed community corrections and other forms of probation and rehabilitation instead of maximum-security prisons kept on building maximum-security prisons. Estelle was a man caught between his ideals and his practice. He was going to fight Judge Justice to the bitter end.

Memorial monument for Wallace Pack and Billy Moore
near the entrance of the Ellis Unit.

4

A CONFUSING SCENE

Eroy Brown had been taken back to the main building by the time the first trained investigator arrived at half past one. Rick Berger, a Walker County sheriff's deputy, was transporting prisoners when he got a call about an escape attempt at Ellis.

Berger lifted the blanket from Pack's body and noticed several abrasions and cuts on his head and neck as well as on both hands. His face was blue from suffocation. Berger didn't notice it at the time, but Pack had also been shot in the elbow. Moore was lying on the ground near the rear bumper of Pack's car. There were abrasions on his face, too. He had been shot in his forehead. Berger took samples of the blood and tissue stuck to the bumper.[1]

The causes of death were evident. The problem was to figure out what happened. Berger got out his camera and notebook and set to work.

On the ground by the driver's door of Pack's car, Berger found Brown's comb and a stainless-steel button that had been torn from Brown's shirt. Probably there had been a struggle there.

On the passenger's side of Pack's car, Berger found more signs of struggle. There was a bullet hole in the right back quarter panel, on the passenger's side. About two and half feet from Moore's head, at the rear passenger side of the car, Berger found a fifty-cent piece on a torn chain that belonged to Brown. The broadcast radio aerial on the rear passenger side of the car had been broken at the base and was hanging by its cable. Berger also found a flattened, blue

Smith-and-Wesson handcuff box, along with Billy Moore's smashed straw cow-boy hat. DeYoung had driven over them when he pulled the ambulance to the scene. The front door on the passenger's side was open. Pack's felt Western hat lay on the bench seat. The glove box was open.

Berger looked under the concrete bridge where Brown and Pack had strug-gled. He found three different bloodstains on the bridge supports and took sam-ples. It looked as though someone had run down the bank, slinging blood on the bridge abutments. He photographed the drops.

Footprints were dug into the steep incline that led down to Turkey Creek. Pack and Brown had either run up or had scuffled down the bank. Berger photo-graphed footprints in the creek mud near the sewage ditch that fed into the creek. It looked like a place where Brown and Pack had struggled.

Using orange chalk, he marked where the car and the truck had been parked, and had them towed to the bus barn, which was where inmates overhauled school buses as part of an industrial training program. There he dusted for fingerprints. He made fourteen lifts from Pack's car.

Investigators' photo re-creation of positions of car and truck relative to garden shed.

Several of the guards waded into the creek to look for the gun, but by four in the afternoon they still hadn't found it. They recruited some convict labor and dammed up two ends of the creek with a couple of truckloads of dirt. Levi Duson, a tractor driver who had been in the garden shed, was sent to get a pump. He backed a tractor down to the bank, hooked up the pump to the power takeoff, and began emptying the creek. It took an hour to drain Turkey Creek of two feet of water.

Walter Pinegar, the chief investigator for the Walker County district attorney's office, arrived. A former parole officer as well as TDC officer, he had been working as the sole investigator for the office for eight years. One of the investigators spotted the gun, stuck barrel-down in the blue-black mud. After taking photographs, Pinegar pulled the pistol from the muck. It was covered in mud and slime.

The four visible chambers of the revolver were empty. Pinegar didn't open it for fear of smudging the fingerprints. He made a note of the serial number and wrote his initials on the inside of the trigger frame. He placed it in a paper bag in a deputy sheriff's trunk to dry, and later stored it in the evidence room at the sheriff's office. Four days later he opened the chamber and extracted five spent shells. On April 13 he sent the gun to the FBI crime lab in Washington.

The gun was a standard-issue TDC revolver, a short-barreled, .38 caliber, five-shot Smith and Wesson called the "Airweight Bodyguard." Its hammer is concealed in a metal casing, giving the gun a humpbacked look. It can be cocked by moving a thumb slide on the top of the casing. Because the frame is made of aluminum, the gun weighs only fifteen ounces empty.

Admirers of the Airweight Bodyguard say it is the ideal concealed handgun. The casing over the hammer prevents it from snagging when pulled from a pocket. The Airweight doesn't have much firepower or many bullets, but it is deadly at close range. During the Tet Offensive in 1968, the South Vietnamese general Nguyen Ngoc Loan used a Smith and Wesson Bodyguard to shoot a Viet Cong guerilla in the head from the distance of a foot. The execution was preserved forever in Eddie Adams's famous photograph.

There was no doubt the gun in the creek was Pack's. Pinegar verified the serial number with Ellis property records. It had been issued to Pack when he started work. Pack's widow told Pinegar her husband's habit was to put the gun in the trunk of his car and check it with the picket guard when he came into the prison. The picket guard on duty that day said Pack did not check any weapon when he arrived at work, and he didn't check out a weapon from the picket when he drove through the gate to meet Billy Moore. The handcuffs that had been cut off Brown's left wrist had also been issued to Pack.

In the early evening Pinegar interviewed three inmates who had been in the garden shed that day. Dale Meyers, a deputy from the sheriff's office, came with him to an assistant warden's office at Ellis. They brought a cassette tape recorder.[2]

They started with James Soloman. Soloman was serving a thirty-year sentence for heroin possession and attempted murder in 1977.

Like Eroy Brown, Soloman and the other trusties, Levi Duson and Henry Kelley, were working on Saturday. They had fried some fish and potatoes on a stove in the garden shed, Soloman said, and were eating lunch when Kelley announced, "Mr. Moore done pull up out there." Soloman walked to the door. He could see someone in the truck with a coat that he was raising and lowering.

"He was looking to see if we were looking that way, and then he pull it back up," Soloman said. "I knowed him to be Eroy Brown."

When Pack arrived in his car, Moore got out of the truck and walked back and the two of them stood talking by the warden's car. Then Brown just opened the door and ran back toward the warden.

Wallace Pack's .38 caliber Smith and Wesson "Airweight" pistol, on display at the Texas Prison Museum in Huntsville.

"Well, you could see the warden when he point his hand like that," Soloman said, "like he was telling him to 'hold him up there.'

"Mr. Moore was coming up with some handcuffs and in the process of this, well, the warden started to the back of his trunk. And when he got to the back of his trunk, he said, 'Get in the car.'

"The inmate ran toward Mr. Moore and hit him; but when he hit Mr. Moore, Mr. Moore hit him back."

Pinegar needed a much more precise description of what happened. As Soloman went over it again, he began talking fast, and jumbling up the sequence. Pinegar slowed him down. Soloman said he saw the warden with a gun in his hand. The warden had a gun, Pinegar asked.

"I wouldn't say a gun," Soloman said. "We'd say a box. He had a box. You could see it was a box."

"That he'd gotten out of the trunk, you think?"

"I don't know whether it was handcuffs or whether it was a gun," Soloman said.

Soloman was feeling his way now. Before Brown shot Moore, Soloman said, "he shot that warden [Pack] first or either he run over and knocked him down getting out of that car. One or the two."

Pinegar asked Soloman to help him draw a diagram so he could understand what happened.

"And the warden goes back here and starts opening his trunk while Brown and Moore are scuffling?" asked Pinegar. "That's right," said Soloman. "You could see the warden. He had stepped back here, and he got a box—looked like a box in his hand, didn't look like a gun to me. It looked like a box."

Soloman became more and more emphatic that he had seen Brown grab Moore and shoot him.

"He just reached up and caught him here and snatched him like that, you know, each time, each time shooting him." Soloman told Pinegar he saw Brown clearly. "I could see him just like I'm looking at you," he said.

Pinegar tried to slow Soloman down. "Mr. Moore is moving back and it looks like Eroy is going to the—into the car?"

"Into the car," said Soloman. When they went over the sequence again, Pinegar said. "He's getting out of the passenger's side—" "Yes, sir," Soloman said.

Pinegar did most of the questioning, but near the end of the interview, the Walker County deputy sheriff, Dale Meyers, gave Soloman another leading question about Brown: "When he bent down here and then he went all the way through the warden's car to come out the other door?"

"Yes, sir," Soloman said. "He had to because he did not come back around here."

The men puzzled over the diagram.

"He shot the man here, correct?" said Meyers.

"Uh huh," said Pinegar.

"He said he shot and Pack fell."

"No, he didn't," Pinegar said. "He lost sight of him."

"Well, I don't know," Meyers said, "but he said he bent down; and he lost sight of him. He was either beside the car or in the car."

"He was in the car," Pinegar concluded. "He had to go—he went all the way across."

Pinegar and Meyers now had the story that Brown got into the back seat of the warden's car, scooted across, and came out the other side with a gun. The warden pulled a box from the trunk, presumably the handcuff box that was found flattened in the road. But if Brown had gone through the back seat of the car, why was the front passenger's door of Pack's car open and not the back door?

Four days later, when Pinegar had a prepared statement for Soloman to sign, it said: "I saw Major Moore backing up as if to let Brown into the car. Brown then ducked as if to get into the car but I don't know if he did or not." By the time of Brown's trial the following spring, "but I don't know if he did or not" had been changed with the handwritten annotation: "and he did get in the back seat of the car." A possibility raised in questioning had become a certainty.

Pinegar ended the interview by reminding Soloman who was in control of his destiny. "We appreciate it," Pinegar told Soloman. "Of course, I know how all this stuff goes, but we'd appreciate it [if] you just keep what you know to yourself."

Soloman knew he wouldn't be living at Ellis prison anymore. He was going to be a protected state's witness. "I'm pretty well situated," he said. "So I don't have no problem with that."

Henry Kelley wasn't helpful. He was fifty-one years old and doing thirty years for murder. He had served sixteen and was two years away from parole. He wanted as little to do with the case as possible. Whatever Soloman said was fine by him. Pinegar took out his drawing and asked Kelley to draw one himself. Kelley said he couldn't draw it. Pinegar pressed him to draw the truck in a diagram. Kelley made a half-hearted effort and then begged off.

"I don't think too clear because I suffer with that high blood," he said. Kelley showed Pinegar his prescription for blood pressure medication. Pinegar gave up on the interview, noting in his report that Kelley was illiterate and had a low IQ.

Pinegar and Meyers moved on to Levi Duson, a heroin addict and burglar from Midland who was serving ten years for burglary.

Duson was not as emphatic as Soloman about how clearly he could see. ". . . [T]he way the car and the truck was parked," he told Pinegar, "we couldn't see that much." This was to be a crucial problem in the trial. The physical evidence that Berger had collected showed that much of the action took place on the passenger's side of Pack's car, out of view from the garden shed.

Duson said he saw the three men talking at the back of Moore's truck, and hinted at something the prosecution wouldn't want to put on: "I don't know if they was passing words or squabbling or what; but I don't know if one of them hit him or what—but anyway, warden told him to get in the car."

Duson couldn't say for sure whether Brown got into the car. "When the warden opened up his trunk of his car and was closing it, that's when I heard the shots."

Duson was maddeningly vague about what happened.

"I don't know if him and Brown had been tussling over the gun or not; but they was close together, you see and when he got shot, he was down." By "he," Duson meant Moore. Brown was standing over Moore when he shot him, Duson said. He didn't know if Brown knocked Moore to the ground or he fell when they were tussling for the gun. But he was certain Moore was on the ground when Brown shot him: "When he shot him, he was standing over him."

Pinegar asked if Brown had got into the warden's car. "Well, I thought he was getting in the car," Duson said. Then Pack went to the trunk and lifted up the lid. "What did he get out?" Pinegar asked. "That we couldn't see," Duson said.

Brown did scuffle with the warden on the passenger's side, Duson said, and fell to the ground. Then the warden ran to the bridge and disappeared, leaving Brown to shoot Moore at the rear of the truck.

Pinegar asked Duson if he heard Moore say anything. "I mean, you didn't hear him say, 'Oh, my God. Don't shoot' or anything like that?"

"He didn't say anything," Duson said.

Meyers pressed Duson about his view of the scene. It was hard to see, Duson explained, because he was looking through the truck glass, "through the back of the truck." When Pack, Moore, and Brown were on the passenger's side of the car and truck, the witnesses could see only their heads and upper bodies. Because of the angle of the garden shed and the placement of the truck to the side and ahead of Pack's car, it would have been difficult for the convicts to see what was going on at the passenger's side of Pack's car.

In the witness statement that Duson signed four days later, the shots begin when Pack closes his trunk and he is shot. He falls down. Brown then goes to the back of the truck and shoots Moore, who was on the ground. Pack runs to the creek with Brown after him. Pinegar noted that Duson "told a similar sequence of events but had people in different places and going different ways than Soloman." Pinegar thought Soloman had seen the most because he was standing in the doorway. Soloman would end up as the lead witness in Brown's first trial.

The day after the deaths, on Sunday morning, Pinegar, Meyers, and assistant district attorney Frank Blazek took a fifty-foot tape measure and returned to the scene along with James Williamson, who had captured Brown. After taking measurements from the markings to the bridge, they moved Moore's truck and Pack's car back to their original positions. Then they took photographs from inside the garden shed through the screened window where Duson had watched, and from the doorway where Soloman had been watching.[3]

Duson had estimated he was fifty to a hundred feet from the cars, but few people are good at judging distances unless they do it often. The tape measure revealed the inmates had been a hundred yards from the vehicles. A hundred yards is a long way to see anything, much less hear something.

Using Soloman's diagram, they tried to reenact what had happened. Blazek took the role of Pack. Two other officers played Moore and Brown.

Pinegar drove the eighty miles or so to Ben Taub Hospital in Houston that afternoon, and picked up the evidence from the autopsy. He had the clothes of the dead men in plastic bags, a series of toothpicks with fingernail scrapings from the hands of both men, and bullet fragments. Pinegar drove home and hung the clothes to dry. Pack's shirt and suit stank of the sewage ditch in which he had drowned.

The next morning, Monday, Pinegar reviewed the evidence with Blazek and Mark Ward, the newly elected district attorney. Blazek had worked for two years in the prison system as staff counsel for inmates. They decided to charge Brown with two counts of capital murder.

Walker County had eyewitnesses to the shooting of Moore. The drowning seemed pretty obvious. Now they needed a motive for Brown. If he was not trying to escape, what caused him to do what he did?

Pinegar talked briefly to the Ellis psychiatrist, Habib Kheribi. He told Pinegar he had talked to Brown and that Brown didn't seem to have any mental disorders. Brown had complained of loss of sleep and the "rigors of confinement."

Why had Brown gone crazy and killed two prison officials? The short answer was drugs. The key witness to the marijuana theory was William Adams Jr., Brown's boss that morning and the man who drove him to see Billy Moore.

Brown was raging about not getting a furlough, Adams wrote in his report, and demanded to see Billy Moore.

"I asked Inmate Brown what he had been drinking and he said nothing but water," Adams wrote in his report. "I told him he had been doing something and he told me he had been smoking weed. I asked him where he got it and he said down at the farm shop and I said where? Inmate Brown said there ain't no more there. I said tell me the truth and he said you know how Scott brings stuff down there in the trash truck and I asked him did Scott give him the weed? He said no, a Mexican gave it to him and I asked him which one and he said the one wore glasses, and I said which one, there is more than one that wears glasses. . . .

"I saw Billy Moore fishing in the lake and I drove over to Mr. Moore. I got out of the pickup and told Mr. Moore the inmate was having problems. Billy Moore and I walked back to [the] pickup and Mr. Moore asked the inmate what was wrong and Inmate Brown said I want a god damn furlough. Moore asked him what he had been doing and he said smoking weed. Mr. Moore said where did you get it and Brown said from Garza. Moore asked how did you get it to the farm shop and Inmate Brown said I brought it out of the dormitory this morning. Mr. Moore asked him how much he smoked and Inmate Brown said what's left of a cigarette.

"Mr. Moore got in the pickup and I got in on the other side and we went to the garden shop. Mr. Moore told me to go with Mr. Spivey and check on the other inmates at the shop. Mr. Moore said I will take the inmate to the building. I went back and checked the shop and could not find any evidence of any marijuana. On Tuesday, April 7, 1981, I questioned each inmate to see if they had seen Inmate Brown smoking marijuana. They said they did not notice anything wrong with Brown except him wanting a furlough."[4]

Several witnesses said Brown was acting strange that morning. But the marijuana rumor seemed impossible to pin down. No inmate wanted to admit having marijuana himself. It was always somebody else he had heard about. It was all hearsay, unusable in court.

But prison officials gave the marijuana story to the newspapers immediately, and the state had a motive. Brown hadn't tried to escape. Rather, he was a drug-crazed inmate who wanted a furlough so he could have sex, and when he couldn't get what he wanted, he flew off the handle and killed two prison officials. It was the oldest stereotype of blacks in Southern history.

The story had a major flaw. Brown had undergone a blood test when he was brought to the hospital, and the results came back negative. Brown did not test positive for either marijuana or alcohol. That didn't stop Adams from posing the theory in his testimony for three trials.

The theory was that Brown, crazed on marijuana and desperate to go on furlough, had gotten into the back seat of the warden's car from the driver's side, reached across the seat, and grabbed Pack's gun from the glove box, come out the back door of the passenger side, closed the door, shot the warden as he was lowering the trunk and coming out with a box of handcuffs, then shot Billy Moore as he lay on the ground. Sometime during this, Brown had been partially handcuffed. Then he chased the warden down to Turkey Creek and drowned him. It seemed a pretty desperate act for a man about to make parole in three months, but it would have to do.

The investigators were so bent on putting their story together that they overlooked a critical piece of evidence. When Berger was dusting the stake-bed truck for fingerprints at the bus barn the Saturday of the deaths, he noticed a pair of worn desert boots sitting on the floor on the passenger's side. When Berger testified later, he couldn't say who picked them up and took them to Warden Pack's office at Ellis. They just didn't seem important.

Three days later, on April 7, Pinegar picked up Brown's shoes from Pack's office at Ellis. They were a beat-up pair of high-topped desert boots with three eyelets, worn rubber soles, and the suede rubbed smooth from wear. Pinegar tied the laces together and stuck a piece of paper in them with the date and the time: 11:23 a.m. He noted that he wasn't sure whether the shoes had been found in Moore's truck or Pack's car. No one had thought to ask the inmates if they had noticed whether Brown was barefoot that day. The shoes would become defendant's exhibit 59. Only Bill Adams and Eroy Brown knew what they meant.

5

THE AURA OF ELLIS

Of the seventeen prisons in the Texas system in 1981, Ellis was easily the most notorious. George Beto had designed it that way. He called it "the end of the road." When Ellis opened in 1963, Beto moved Death Row there, and filled the rest of the prison with repeat offenders serving long sentences and inmates who were considered troublemakers. Beto's plan was to break these inmates with hard field labor and strict discipline, and for many inmates, that worked. Beto was proud of the prison.

It was named for O. B. Ellis, a Tennessee prison manager who was hired in 1948 to reform Texas prisons. After World War II, Texas prisons were among the worst in the nation. Prisoners were mutilating themselves in order to escape the brutal fieldwork. They were crowded into filthy tanks. Solitary confinement wasn't even solitary. Sometimes as many as six men were handcuffed in the "hole," developing deep sores on their wrists from chaffing of the cuffs while they tried to sleep. A legislative committee reported that the eighty-year-old physician who served all the medical needs of four prison farms was the most hated man in the TDC.

The reformers hired O. B. Ellis, the forty-five-year-old manager of the Shelby Prison Farm near Memphis, Tennessee. Ellis had turned a five-thousand-acre prison farm into a profitable operation that made nearly $175,000 in 1947. One of the reformers declared it looked less like a prison farm than a spotless Southern plantation.

Ellis cleaned up the filthy tanks, mechanized the farms, fired the corrupt guards, and raised the salaries of the ones he kept. Within three years Ellis had the inmates producing three-fourths of the cost of their incarceration.[1] By 1960, the state was making $2 million a year growing ten thousand acres of cotton. Ellis added industrial programs as well, so that inmates made not only license plates, but also their own uniforms and mattress covers. They butchered their own hogs and cattle and canned their own vegetables. The prisoners had quit maiming themselves. The inmates, it was said, were too tired at the end of the day to cause much trouble. A prison reformer who had once condemned the Texas system proclaimed it had become one of the best.

The stress of running the prison system cheaply took its toll on Ellis. In March 1961, he wrote a key state senator that his cost in 1959 was $1.23 per man per day while the national average was $3.61. But he was doing it at the expense of the guards.

"I do not want to leave the impression that I am hollering 'wolf,'" he wrote, "but I believe with all sincerity that we cannot continue to work men seventy-two hours a week. The better men we have are just waiting until September to see if relief is forthcoming. Unless additional guards are provided, there is certain to be a down-grading of personnel (if we can find them of any caliber) that is certain to result in trouble."[2]

Ellis couldn't say this outright, but the only way he could run the system so cheaply was to use inmate guards. When he started work, Ellis declared his mission: "To Protect Society from the Criminals and the Criminals from Each Other." He could deliver on the first promise, but not the second.

In November 1961, while attending a dinner the night before a prison board meeting, Ellis collapsed and died of a heart attack. He was fifty-nine. Many of his colleagues believed he had worked himself to death.[3] His successor, George Beto, inherited a prison system with a great reputation, but a dark secret at its core. To be effective, Beto would have to maintain absolute control over the prison system and he couldn't do that with civilian guards alone.[4]

Beto was an astute politician who knew how to drink whiskey with legislators in Austin. He wore a short-brimmed Stetson hat and loved deer hunting. As long as the escapes were few and violence minimal, and he didn't ask for much money from the legislature, Beto could run the prisons without interference. The Texas press loved him.[5]

Eager to maintain his reputation, in 1964 Beto invited a Harvard-trained professor named Bruce Jackson from New York to visit Texas prisons. Beto told Jackson he could go anywhere he wanted in the system and talk to anybody he cared to. Jackson described himself as a scruffy, bearded, long-haired Jew, about the last person George Beto should have allowed into Ellis prison. Ellis held some of the last pockets of black field crews who were still singing the old prison work songs in a rhythm that went back to slavery. Jackson went into the fields with cameras and tape recorders and collected the songs. As more and more young blacks from the cities entered prisons, with their consciousnesses raised by the civil rights movement, they regarded the slave songs with disdain. Jackson was witnessing a relic that was about to disappear.

Jackson brought folksinger Pete Seeger to the Ellis farm. Seeger, too, was eager to get the work songs recorded before they were gone. Seeger insisted on giving two concerts in the prisons while he was in Huntsville, and by Jackson's account, he quickly had guards and inmates singing together. Seeger also brought filming equipment. The resultant thirty-minute film, "Afro-American Work Songs in a Texas Prison," has a staged quality, with black inmates singing the old songs while chopping wood and flat-weeding in unison.[6]

But it also carries a voiceover preface that gives Jackson's take on Ellis prison concisely: "Unlike many prisons in the North where men often spend most of their days sitting around in cells, the inmates work in Texas prisons. In the old days work in the fields sometimes amounted to a death sentence by degree. The guards were brutal, the days lasted from dawn 'til dark, the work pace was vicious. But Texas now has the most progressive of Southern prison systems and those old days have gone."

Jackson went on to do a profile of the Ellis farm for *Texas Monthly* in December 1978 that ended with George Beto's description of Ellis as the end of the road. In describing Ellis, Jackson wrote about how clean it was, about the relentless discipline, how the inmates talked in whispers because loud voices were not allowed, how the food was good, the work was hard, how illiterate inmates were required to learn to read and write. Jackson knew Ellis was a hard place, but that was because it had to be. He wondered why more men at Ellis didn't kill themselves. He hoped for a world in which prisons were no longer necessary. But in a world in which prisons are necessary, he declared that Ellis was as good as a harsh place could be.

When Beto became a professor at Sam Houston State University, he invited Jackson as a visiting scholar and helped him get grants.[7] During *Ruiz*, Jackson went out on a limb by defending the prison system. Jackson had become the TDC's resident intellectual and its apologist.[8] George Beto had dazzled him.

Beto built Ellis prison with convict labor under the strict supervision of a legendary warden named Carl Luther "Beartracks" McAdams. Like Beto,

Beartracks McAdams made a big impression. Over six feet tall and heavily built, he had a reputation for brutality unmatched in prison lore. Inmates claimed he could kick an inmate in the head while he was standing still. His footprint made a mark on a man, the story went.

"Warden C. L. McAdams," Jackson wrote in his book on prison songs, "is the strictest and most highly respected warden in the system; many of the men on his unit were proud of that strictness, proud that they got along with 'Captain Mac.'"[9]

The convicts sang a song called "Grizzly Bear," and Jackson dutifully noted that the song had been around in Texas prison lore long before Beartracks Mc-Adams. But nobody ever called him that. Jackson once asked an inmate about the nickname:

"I seen a guy call him Beartracks and that like to been the end a him. He knows they call him that but nobody ever call him it.

"Because that name rings all over America, I guess. I guess there's people everywhere done heard talk about Track . . .

"He asked me one time on this farm—I was arrested—he said, 'What do they call me?' I said, 'I don't know, sir.'

"He said, 'You lyin'! You know what they call me.'

"I said, 'Some of them say—'

"'What do you mean some of them say?' He made me tell him.

"I told him, I said, 'Somebody called you Beartracks.'

"'Where you hear it?'

"I said, 'Some a them guys what's gone home.'

"'Cause if I told him it was somebody here it might a got somebody in trouble."[10]

"I think the inmates' nicknames for guards are particularly important," Jackson wrote. "There is a certain power people feel when they can *name* something . . . the second name is the one that is used to bring the guard into the convicts' mental economy; the nickname is always hung on a single characteristic, and it limits the kind of worrying done about the person or tags him in a slightly belittling way."[11]

Jackson never revealed the source of the nickname. If the name Beartracks had alluded merely to McAdams's size, big feet, and pugnaciousness, he might have worn it less sensitively. But it pointed to a defect: McAdams had lost most of the thumb on his left hand. The inmate story went that while he was running a prison in Brazoria County south of Houston, he was prone to spying on the inmates and officers through a window at night. One morning after a snowstorm, a freakish occurrence in South Texas, convicts found McAdams's thumbless handprint in the snow on a window ledge. A bear has five digits on its paw, but only four of those digits make an imprint. That was how Captain Mac became Beartracks.

Bruce Jackson was not the only Jewish intellectual to visit Ellis prison in the 1960s. With Jackson's help, Beto gave a New York photographer, Danny Lyon, permission to roam and photograph at will. Unlike Jackson, who testified for the TDC during the *Ruiz* trial, Lyon testified for the inmates.

In his memoir, Lyon tells how an inmate who performed as a rodeo clown in the annual Texas prison rodeo gave him the idea.

"One of the clowns had been inside for twenty years. I thought he was the most pathetic clown I had ever seen. While we chatted, he suddenly said I should come inside the prison to make photographs.

"'What?' I said.

"'You should bring your camera into the prison and take pictures; they'll probably let you.'

"'That's not possible,' I answered. 'Why in the world would they let me? . . .'

"'Oh they probably would,' said the clown. 'They'd like the publicity. They think this is a wonderful place.'"[12]

Lyon secured an interview with Beto and told him that he had been photographing architecture in New York, which was true. He had spent months photographing the sixty blocks of nineteenth-century buildings that were being destroyed to build the World Trade Center.[13] Lyon did not mention that he had worked for the Student Nonviolent Coordinating Committee photographing the civil rights demonstrations throughout the South. He had even gone to jail with Martin Luther King Jr. In Manhattan he had photographed the destruction of a place. At Ellis he photographed the destruction of men.

Lyon cast his proposal to photograph Texas prisons as a work of history, and that seemed to appeal to Beto, who was a student of history too. Beto had told Bruce Jackson that he could never improve prisons without outsiders coming in. Lyon never fell for Beto's line. Years later Beto complained in court that Lyon had promised him that Bruce Jackson would write the text for Lyon's book of photographs and that Beto would get to review the book before it went to press.

"I never remembered that promise," Lyon says, "but I would have said anything to Dr. Beto. My job was to get in there and get photographs. My attitude was that prison systems are public property, they're very expensive and people have a right to know what's going on in there. Their purpose is not only to keep men in, but to keep the rest of the world out."

But there was a huge difference between him and Jackson, he said. "I never saw myself as anything but a spy in an alien world. I thought my job was to pull it all apart. I felt I was a subversive."[14]

Lyon did what he could to look innocent. Before coming to Texas prisons, he took a self-portrait in one of the abandoned buildings he was photographing in lower Manhattan. He was a handsome, brooding, bearded young man with a thick mass of curly hair. For Texas, Lyon shaved the beard and trimmed the hair, making him look like an inquisitive cub reporter.

He may have fooled Beto, but he didn't fool Beartracks McAdams. When Lyon presented himself at Ellis prison in 1967 with a permit from Beto to take pictures anywhere he wanted, McAdams wanted to know why he didn't get a haircut.

"He pulls out a drawer full of home-made knives," Lyon said. "He was trying to show me how tough the inmates were."

It never seemed to occur to prison officials that inmates were making knives not to attack the guards but to protect themselves from each other, especially the building tenders.

"Then he pulls out a photograph of Redwine," Lyon says, "I guess he thought I would be interested in it as a photograph."

Clarence Redwine was a notorious building tender at the Retrieve Unit in Brazoria County who had run a racket in sex and drugs. In December 1948 an inmate named Earnest Jones cut off Redwine's head with a footlong sugar cane knife in the dining hall. Nobody in the mess hall said he saw what happened. Someone—undoubtedly prison officials—photographed Redwine with a smoking cigarette in his hands and his severed head on the mess hall table.[15] The inmate who killed Redwine said it was a preventive murder. Either he killed Redwine or Redwine killed him. Such men were useful. When McAdams left Retrieve to become warden at Ramsey in 1951, he brought Redwine's executioner with him as a trusty and building tender.[16]

"One of the saddest conversations I had at Ellis," Lyon wrote, "was with an older inmate in the garage, who told me what a wonderful warden Mac Adams [sic] was. Mac Adams was, in fact, widely known to be a sadist. . . . He couldn't stop pointing out the fine features of 'Captain Mac.' . . . Whatever had once been inside of this man, making him a functioning human being, had been replaced with something else. Inmates call it 'making one count too many.' Something dies inside the prisoner. He's still walking around and talking but he's gone."[17]

Perhaps Lyon was thinking of this inmate when he titled his book of prison photographs, most taken at Ellis, *Conversations with the Dead*.

Beto got wise to Lyon. In April 1968, Martin Luther King Jr. was assassinated, and Beto's secretary asked him to keep tabs on the inmates for fear of racial unrest. Someone had checked on his background. Near the end of his fourteen months, Lyon rushed into the Ellis fields to photograph a man being carried in after collapsing from heat exhaustion. After that, Beto sent him a note saying he had to keep a certain distance from inmates when photographing them. Instead of talking to them in their cells, he had to go to the visiting room. Lyon packed up and moved on.[18]

Lyon says he never witnessed an act of violence during his time in Texas prisons, but he didn't need to. An inmate told him something that stuck with him for forty years: "There's nothing but a bunch of frightened men in here."

"Here" was Ellis prison. He wrote in the preface to *Conversations with the Dead*:

I had been warned at the outset by Dr. Beto not to let the men con me. I am told by many that I have not seen what these men have done on the outside. That is true. I saw only what was before my eyes. And the material I have collected doesn't approach for a moment the feeling you get standing for two minutes in the corridor of Ellis.[19]

THE WITCH AND THE WRIT WRITERS

Ellis prison and Beartracks McAdams broke many, but not all, of the inmates who came there in the 1960s. Brutality could nourish rebellion. Just as Ellis produced cotton and sugar cane, it also produced writ writers. Writ writers were inmates who filed lawsuits accusing the TDC of violating the Constitution. The lawsuit that embittered Jim Estelle and cast its shadow over the trials of Eroy Brown was born at Ellis prison.

The problem with the control model was that, like slavery, it couldn't brook change, and change was creeping into prisons. It was brought there by people Beto contemptuously called "do-gooders" and "bleeding hearts."[1] The most effective of them was a tiny middle-aged woman named Frances Jalet.

A Radcliffe graduate, Jalet earned her law degree at Columbia University in 1937 and master's degree from Georgetown law school in 1958. After raising six children to adulthood and getting a divorce, in 1967 Jalet took a six-week-long class in poverty law at the University of Pennsylvania and moved to Austin to work for the Legal Aid and Defender Society.[2] She was fifty-seven years old, a slender, delicately featured, gray-haired woman who sometimes wore a miniskirt on her visits to Ellis prison.

Reflecting on Jalet's first appearance at Ellis prison in 1967, Beartracks McAdams declared he thought she looked like a witch.[3] Indeed, she cast a spell on Ellis inmates and antagonized Beto and McAdams to the point that they took her to court and made fools of themselves.

Jalet was not only a bleeding heart and a do-gooder, but also a convict lover. In 1972 she married one of the leading Ellis writ writers, Fred Cruz, a man thirty-one years her junior.

When Jalet arrived in Austin in 1967, a newspaper writer described her as "Portia for the Poor,"[4] a lawyer who helped the helpless. Cruz saw the article and immediately wrote her. Soon she had a dozen or more clients at Ellis, where Beto typically sent writ writers, whom he considered troublemakers. Fred Cruz especially bothered Beto, who feared that his writ writing would give Cruz "unconscionable power" over other inmates. Any crack in the control model was cause for alarm.

Cruz caused trouble by insisting on his legal rights. A Buddhist, he wanted to hold services with like-minded inmates, but that was not allowed, so he sued. Cruz crossed the prison color line and helped Black Muslims who were trying to read the Qur'an file writs. For his efforts he spent a lot of time in solitary, living in complete darkness for fifteen days at time, and subsisting on bread and water with a few beans and vegetables every third day.

Solitary confinement was a form of torture. Many prisoners, including presidential candidate and POW John McCain, report that solitary confinement could be worse than physical punishment. It can destroy men's minds.[5] The harder McAdams pushed Cruz, the more resistant he became. His meditation practice helped him endure the long stretches in isolation.

Within months of her first visit to Ellis, Jalet was writing to the director of the Legal Defense Fund of the NAACP about what she had learned from her clients. She enclosed what she called the "Ellis Report," which gave a sharply different picture of Texas prisons from the one Beto had so skillfully presented to the press.[6]

Jalet described an arbitrary and brutal system in which guards greeted new inmates by beating them. A former inmate named Billy Wayne "Redbird" McCarter recalled the practice at Ellis in the 2007 PBS documentary *Writ Writer* by Susanne Mason.

"When you came to this unit," McCarter recalled, "the first thing that happened is that they had what they called a 'Welcoming Committee.' It was about six bosses. And they'd come out to the back gate, and they had pick handles or axe handles and some of them had baseball bats. Bam! They'd start right on in, beatin' that ass, but they would give you a real good whupping too. There wasn't no doubt in your mind what was gonna happen to you if you done wrong."[7]

In the Ellis Report, Frances Jalet told of a black field squad that protested being whipped with reins and cursed by the mounted guards, or "high riders," when they failed to harvest corn quickly enough in a muddy field.

"Warden McAdams appeared with guards and officers armed with baseball bats, steel pipes, water hoses, and black jacks and they, without warning, attacked the negro prisoners who were waiting where they were told by the building. After a severe beating, they were lined up across the road with a pickup truck behind them and ordered to run towards the field as fast as they could, or get run over by the truck. Two prisoners couldn't make it and were knocked down; they were picked up and spread across the hood of the truck for all the prisoners to see.

"Warden McAdams then said, 'You niggers ain't bucking on me.'"

Jalet also wrote of a group of Mexican prisoners who were transferred from the Harlem units to the Ellis farm. According to one of Jalet's witnesses, "Upon arrival of the buses the prisoners were met by a large security force armed with baseball bats, night sticks, black jacks and axe handles. The men as they emerged had to run the gauntlet as they were hit, kicked and beaten. The medical officer in charge said, 'All right men, you're on Ellis now. This is the end of the road.'"

Disciplinary hearings were arbitrary and capricious, Jalet reported. Inmates often served in solitary for more than the legal limit of fifteen days. Inmates were handcuffed and stomped on, and hung on the bars in straitjackets. They were forced to stand with their noses to the wall for hours at a time. The building tenders beat inmates at the instructions of the officers. Inmates who wrote writs on their own behalf or for others had their law books and papers confiscated and were sent to solitary. Black Muslims were singled out for assault and placed in solitary, and their writs for religious freedom were confiscated.

"Yet the visitor to the Ellis Unit senses none of this," Jalet wrote. "It is hidden—much of it buried in the dungeon—like (all-dark) cells of solitary. As one former prisoner describes it, after drawing a parallel between Auschwitz or Buchenwald and Ellis . . . 'The surface calm fools most people, and the sick activities are well concealed from the public eye by a complex of hypocrisy so phenomenal that Machiavelli would have been awed. It really is not necessary, because so few outside care.'"[8]

Jalet was writing to the NAACP because prisons were becoming the next battleground of the civil rights movement. Lawyers for the NAACP were filing suits under section 1983 of the 1871 Civil Rights Act, which was written to protect blacks from the Ku Klux Klan. Section 1983 provided that federal law would supersede state law when basic rights guaranteed by the Constitution had been violated by the states. The provision had been ignored for decades, but beginning in the early 1960s, the Supreme Court made rulings that enabled federal courts to intervene in state prisons.

In October 1958 Chicago police, pursuing a murder investigation and acting without a warrant, rousted a black couple named Monroe and their six children out of bed and held them naked in their living room while they ransacked the house. The chief of detectives, named Pape, called the husband "nigger" and "boy," and then kept him for several hours in jail before releasing him without charges. The Monroes sued the city under the Civil Rights Act. In *Monroe v. Pape*, the Supreme Court ruled in 1961 that the Monroes had the right to sue the individual police officers, but not the city of Chicago. The case opened the door for inmates to sue their keepers.

In a 1964 case entitled *Cooper v. Pate*, the Supreme Court held that a Black Muslim incarcerated in the Illinois state prison was entitled to the same religious rights as other inmates. The "hands-off" doctrine with regard to state prisons was finished.

By concentrating most of the TDC writ writers at Ellis, Beto had unwittingly provided Jalet a steady stream of clients. Jalet held on to a succession of three tenuously funded poverty law jobs in Austin, Dallas, and Houston. Each time Jalet got a new one, Beto phoned her boss to complain about her activities. In Austin and Dallas she was fired for refusing to give up her inmate clients.[9] In 1971 Beto tried to ban Jalet from seeing clients anywhere in the Texas prison system. The Texas Bar Association protested vehemently, claiming that this amounted to Beto unilaterally telling Jalet she couldn't practice law.[10]

Beto then used section 1983 of the Civil Rights Act against Jalet. Through Beartracks McAdams and other prison officials, Beto encouraged three building tenders to file a civil suit against Jalet, claiming that she had threatened their safety by stirring up violence and revolution through her legal activities.[11] Beto met with federal judge Carl Bue, who saw to it that the building tenders had the free services of three expert trial attorneys from the Baker and Botts law firm in Houston. Bue ruled that Jalet, who was scraping by as a poverty lawyer, would have to pay for her own legal services. The Houston chapter of the American Civil Liberties Union came to her aid.

It must have seemed like a good idea at the time, but *Dreyer v. Jalet* was a terrible mistake on Beto's part. It opened up McAdams, Beto, and the entire building tender system to cross-examination by William Wayne Kilgarlin, a legendary liberal such as only a conservative state like Texas can produce. The trial, held in Houston in the spring of 1972, lasted six weeks and featured approximately sixty witnesses, forty-seven of them inmates or ex-inmates.[12]

The building tender plaintiffs were a disaster. Freddie Dreyer, an Ellis building tender, had never met Jalet and couldn't prove a conspiracy. The second,

Robert Slayman, disappeared two days after he was paroled and never testified. The third, Donald Lock, reversed his testimony and asked that the case against Jalet, who had married Fred Cruz by the time the trial started, be dismissed.

"Mrs. Cruz has done nothing," he said. "She's tried to help me. She's tried to help the entire prison population." Lock contended that prison officials, including McAdams, had pressured him to file the suit. "They didn't come out and tell me to file it," he said, "but you just get used to the way these people talk and you know what they mean. I knew that filing the suit was my only out."[13]

Now he feared for his life. "If given the chance they would kill me," he said. "I think they would do it kind of legal-like . . . put me in a field, shoot me and say I'd been trying to escape."

Federal judge Carl Bue took Lock seriously and sent him to the Galveston county jail for his protection.

When McAdams took the stand, he displayed photographs of the sorry state of Texas prisons after World War II, and contrasted them with the modern, clean facilities that Ellis and Beto had created. This was the party line that newspapers parroted, but it didn't prove Jalet was fomenting rebellion. The real threat she posed was filing lawsuits that exposed the building tender system.

McAdams was a great believer in the use of building tenders, the more violent the better. The prime example was Robert Barber, his building tender when he was warden at the Ramsey Unit. When McAdams moved to Ellis in 1961, Barber came with him. When McAdams went to the Wynne farm in 1969, Barber followed. An Ellis inmate recalled that Barber, a white man, would spend the nights whipping black inmates, and return to his cell in the morning covered with blood.[14]

There was a reason McAdams used building tenders to enforce this kind of discipline. Since 1952 Texas law had forbidden corporal punishment in prison. In theory, a prison official who beat an inmate could be prosecuted, though Judge Bue observed that this had never happened during the twenty years the law had been on the books. Having inmates do the dirty work prevented potential lawsuits. Authorities could just call such incidents an inmate fight.

George Beto was the last witness in the case, and to accommodate his schedule, Bue held the lawyers in the courtroom late into the evening.[15] The building tenders' lawyers walked Beto through an easy line of questions. Beto testified that "prison people who come from other states are astounded at the relaxed atmosphere we have in our prisons." He said he periodically talked to inmates, especially those on their way out, and that they were free to talk or write to him without fear of reprisal.

He described the routine that earned him his nickname, "Walking George." He tried to visit all of the fourteen prisons every two weeks, and he made it to the Ellis and Wynne prisons once a week, any hour of the day or night, without advance warning. Sometimes he would fly in an airplane and land unannounced.

As for building tenders, Beto testified, "I am personally strongly persuaded that the minimum amount of forced homosexuality in our department, the minimum amount of forcing inmates to give up their commissary, the items that they buy at the little canteens, is due to the presence of building tenders."

Building tenders, Beto said, kept prison officials informed of homosexual conduct, but they weren't snitches. "I think generally the inmates regard them as porters, janitors and the like." As for having responsibility for punishing inmates, Beto emphatically said, "None. None."

Beto was asked to read into the record his departmental memo from 1963: "At no time are inmates to be used to perform duties in the area of punishment and discipline. This responsibility rests and must continue to rest solely with custodial officers." Building tenders might occasionally break up a fight between inmates, Beto said, "because they are in a position to which an officer can't immediately come." Occasionally a building tender might get out of hand in breaking up a fight. But they never use weapons, he said, "Just their hands. There are no weapons in these cell blocks."

Beto reiterated the prison policy against weapons. Officers didn't carry them because of the chance that an inmate could get hold of them and use them. Officers in the field carried pistols and rifles while mounted on horseback, but they never allowed inmates to approach them.

As for abuse of inmates, it couldn't be going on, Beto said, because he would know about it. "Then, too," he said, "if abuses of that type were permitted, dischargees, parolees, would be telling kinfolk, telling legislators, telling newspapers of those abuses."

Bill Kilgarlin asked Beto about one of his building tenders, Jesse "Bay City" Montague, who had been a witness for the three building tenders.

"A man with the record like Jesse Montague, who has poured lighter fluid over a guard and set him on fire, who has forced others to submit to homosexual acts, and has taken their commissary from them, these were the exact criteria that you said that building tenders were designed to prevent, the strong preying on the weak and depriving them of the commissary. Now is that the kind of building tender system that you want to have in the Department of Corrections?"

Beto answered, "You are not recognizing that people can change, Mr. Kilgarlin."

Kilgarlin then went after McAdams.

"Doctor," Kilgarlin said, "we have had at least ten witnesses in this case testify as to having observed personal acts of brutality on the part of Warden C. L. McAdams. All of those witnesses may not be telling the truth, because they have all been inmates of the Texas Department of Corrections, but we have had at least ten, and we heard some pretty hair-raising stories and tales. Now, you will concede, will you not, that it's possible that just one or two of those ten could possibly be telling the truth about brutal acts that exist?"

Beto, the prisoner of absolute control, answered, "I'm not willing to concede it."

Beto denied McAdams had a reputation for brutality. "No," Beto said. "On the other hand, I have found inmates that have pointed to kindnesses on his part that are unbelievable." He cited the case of a young inmate who wanted to be at Ellis with Beartracks because McAdams had helped pay for the burial of the inmate's father, who had been in prison and killed in an accident.[16]

Kilgarlin read Beto a passage from Danny Lyon's book, *Conversations with the Dead*, about the aura of Ellis: "Ellis is the hellhole of the system. It is there that the convicts considered the most dangerous are imprisoned. Whether this is true of the inmates there, or even if the aura of this prison is founded on practices no longer in use, it doesn't matter. The presence of Ellis is still the same, for the inmates believe in it and the bosses believe in it. Ellis is a house of damned men."

Kilgarlin wanted to know if Beartracks McAdams, who had started with the prisons in 1938, might be the source of the aura of Ellis.

Beto answered, "I don't think that that aura or that atmosphere prevails at the Ellis Unit. I don't believe that at all."

After eliciting a steady stream of denial from Beto, Kilgarlin ended with a simple question, whether Frances Jalet had ever committed a single illegal activity.

"One that I could prove, no," Beto said.

Judge Bue ruled there was no convincing evidence that Frances Jalet-Cruz had done anything illegal or coached revolution, and he dismissed the case. Bue noted that prison officials took "essentially an absolutist position" about control of prisons. Maybe it was time for that to change, Bue hinted. He proposed that the TDC might benefit from an outside observer or ombudsman. But that would never happen in Texas without more lawsuits.

By the time the building tenders case made it to federal court, Beto had made one more mistake in regard to Jalet's clients. Conceding that Jalet had a right to visit clients, in 1969 he transferred twenty-seven of them to the Wynne Unit, the so-called broke-dick farm for the aged, the crippled, the mentally ill, and the mentally retarded. For the previous thirteen years, Wynne had been run by How-ard Sublett, a man as kind as McAdams was ferocious. Like Beartracks, Sublett had a nickname too, and he didn't care who used it. He was widely known as "Mama" Sublett.[17]

Beto couldn't have a warden named "Mama" assigned to the Ellis writ writ-ers. He needed someone who would torment them, and so he transferred Mc-Adams to Wynne. McAdams brought his chief building tender, Robert Barber, with him. For his building major, McAdams had the man who died fighting Eroy Brown, Wallace Pack.

McAdams organized the writ writers into a field crew called the Eight Hoe squad. Several members of the Eight Hoe squad testified in *Dreyer v. Jalet* that they were told their lives would be easy if they simply fired Jalet as their lawyer. But if they stayed with her, their lives would be miserable. Every time they tried to use the law library, Cruz, David Ruiz, and the others were subjected to rec-tal searches. As the harassment intensified, so did the writ writers' resistance. Concentrated on the third tier of Wynne, they shared ideas and legal strategies. Beto had created a hothouse for writ writers. He inspired them to file what would become the longest-running prison civil rights case in American history.

7

THE QUESTION OF THE GUN

After eight years of practicing law, Bill Habern was almost burned out. He was forty-three years old, he had been divorced twice, and his two daughters were living with their mothers. Habern was ready for a change when he picked up the Sunday paper and read about the deaths of Moore and Pack.

He knew Pack to have been an old-time, ass-kicking warden who had got religion. Most of Habern's clients were prison inmates, and Pack had helped him get cell changes for his clients at Wynne, something hardly any prison official would do. Habern was shocked by the death. He had considered Pack a friend.[1]

Then he wanted to know what happened. He called an official at Wynne and pressed him about the gun. The official couldn't say why there was one at the scene, except that Pack must have had a reason.

Habern had been around prisons long enough to know that you don't carry a gun around an inmate. That was fundamental. If Eroy Brown was pleading self-defense, he might have a case. Practicing law began to look more interesting.

Two days after the deaths, a Huntsville lawyer, Jerry Register, was named as Brown's attorney. Register had been a prosecutor in Houston and an assistant district attorney in Walker County, so he had the right experience for a capital case. As soon as Register was appointed, Habern phoned. Register was delighted to hear from him.

"You're just who I need," Register said. "You know the prisons."

In his first job out of law school Habern had worked for the TDC as an inmate lawyer. He was part of the Prison Public Defenders, a program Beto had helped create, hoping it would quell the inmate writ writers. Habern stayed only fifteen months. There was a central flaw in the arrangement, he thought. Because he was paid by the prison system, he couldn't file for relief for his inmate clients in federal court. He couldn't really advocate for their rights.

Habern launched a practice in post-conviction law, helping inmates with prison and parole problems. Habern's biggest gripe with the TDC was not with the top administrators but with the middle level, the assistant wardens who made his clients work in the fields despite documented medical conditions. It could take weeks for an inmate to get medication or recognition of a medical condition that might keep him from working in the fields.

Habern started a chapter of the ACLU in Huntsville and took on marijuana cases involving long sentences for smoking a joint. He sued the Huntsville school district for tossing a black kid out of school without due process, and he won. He sued and forced the district to overhaul the derelict school it used for kids with disciplinary problems.[2]

Huntsville was as conservative a place as Mississippi, Habern thought, and it was used to running its own affairs without outside interference. Habern could fight these battles because he had little at stake in the town of Huntsville. He didn't aspire to play golf at the country club. He lived in a little house near the Trinity River in the town of Riverside, only a few miles east of Ellis prison.

Law was Habern's second choice for a career. Born in 1938, he was in the last generation that grew up with big band music, and he had a natural calling for it. By the ninth grade he was playing Bob Wills swing at country club dances, writing professional arrangements, and imitating Stan Kenton's style of saxophone. He majored in jazz studies for a while at the University of North Texas in Denton, kicked around in the music business playing for the Ice Capades, and then entered the third law class at the new law school at Texas Tech University in Lubbock.

Habern was interested in prison law because when he was a teenager his father had taken the fall for a failed oil-field deal, and served three years in prison. The TDC broke him. A gregarious, cheerful guy, he left Huntsville a despondent, morose man.

In law school Habern wrote a paper about how the Supreme Court had ended the "hands-off" doctrine. Black Muslims, he discovered, might be anathema to prison officials, but the courts had found that they were model prisoners. They didn't drink or smoke and were highly disciplined. But they demanded the rights to read the Qur'an and have a pork-free diet. They defied the control model. They couldn't be cowed.

Habern had testified in the *Ruiz* trial about inmates' access to lawyers. He told Judge Justice that the only way lawyers could give legal papers to their clients was to hand them to a guard who would examine them for contraband and pass them to the inmate. Often the papers would disappear into a back room to be copied before being given to the inmate. This seemed a gross violation of the attorney–client privilege. Judge Justice ruled that it must be stopped. The TDC had to cut slots at the bottom of the glass partitions in the visiting rooms so attorneys could pass their papers directly to their clients. Some Texas lawyers took to calling the slot the "Habern hole."

That had been the highlight of Habern's career. But the day-to-day life of a sole practitioner didn't agree with him. He whittled down his caseload, and spent most of his time on a job he liked: driving around the state, organizing continuing legal education for the Texas Criminal Defense Lawyers Association. Habern was paid to recruit accomplished lawyers to teach defense techniques. He reserved the hotel rooms and publicized the sessions, then edited and published the papers that resulted. He liked the job. It was like writing musical arrangements and leading a band. He would need those skills in the months to come.

On Tuesday, April 7, Habern met Brown in the visitation room at the Walls to see if he wanted to be on the case. The guard gave them no privacy. In a low voice, Habern told Brown not to talk to him or anyone else about what had happened. They would deal with that later. Brown told him he had acted in self-defense, and he convinced Habern that while he had done a little writ writing on his previous case, he realized he had to let the real lawyers handle this one. Habern knew they could get along.

He phoned Register. He was in. He quit his job with the Texas Criminal Defense Lawyers Association. In 1981 the state of Texas paid court-appointed lawyers of indigent defendants after the trial was over. Habern had several thousand dollars in savings. He owed $300 a month in child support. His lake house cost him a little over $100 a month. This trial wasn't about money. He threw his bills in a shoebox and ignored them. It would be months before he saw a paycheck.

Habern was worried about his new client. Eroy Brown reminded him of a disobedient slave who had been tied up to a tree outside the big house. The guards were pressing all around him. His foot was sore, his face was bruised and scratched, and he had a deep laceration on his wrist where the handcuffs had cut him. Brown looked, he thought, like a man who knew he was damned near dead.

Habern visited as often as possible, almost daily. When he couldn't go, he sent Brown a telegraph with a sentence or two saying there were people outside who cared what happened to him. He filed a motion with Judge Justice asking him

Bill Habern and
Eroy Brown
during the trial in
Galveston. Photo
by Alan Pogue.

to transfer Brown from the TDC to federal custody. He charged that the prison system was tormenting Brown in the strip cell and unnecessarily medicating him with drugs that impaired his ability to communicate with his lawyers. He also charged that Brown was not allowed to meet privately with his lawyers, a violation of Justice's sweeping order of April 20 in *Ruiz*.

In May Justice ruled that Habern had to go to state court with his motion first. But Justice also wrote that if Habern's description of Brown's treatment was true, he would revisit the issue. The strategy worked. On June 8 a state judge ordered that Brown could meet privately with his attorneys and that the TDC was not to bug the room. That afternoon Register and Habern got in to see Brown without a guard present.

Brown was finally allowed to sleep with the lights off. He had a mattress and blankets. Most importantly, he could talk privately to Habern almost daily. Brown told him what had happened at Turkey Creek, and Habern began putting together a plan for Brown's defense. Habern could afford to devote himself to the case, but Jerry Register could not. He had a living to make and payment for defending Brown would not come for a long time. But Register was aggressive in the press about defending Brown's rights, and that didn't sit well in Huntsville. He was hearing grumblings around town.

Habern told Brown that he shouldn't be the lead attorney in the case. They needed a strong first chair, a lawyer who could take the inmate witnesses apart, who could speak eloquently and improvise in a tight situation. His race would matter, too. This was the trial of a black field slave against the white master, with the house slaves testifying against him. The choice was obvious: Craig Washington.

Washington was one of the new crop of black state legislators who had been elected from Houston in 1973. Washington fought the regressive prison laws proposed by Governor Dolph Briscoe. Stopping bad laws from being passed was almost as important as passing good ones. In the summer of 1981 *Texas Monthly* cited him as one of the state's best legislators.

"Washington is that rarest of political animals, an idealist without illusions," the magazine wrote. "He's tough, shrewd, dauntless, but blessed with an uncanny grace of manner, an ability to disguise the seriousness of his work with charm. A spellbinding orator who never pontificates or harangues, he wins admirers even when he loses battles."[3]

One of his best-remembered speeches came in 1979 when he urged the Texas House to raise the support for women with dependent children. He purchased a bag of shoes, t-shirts, and other basic items at a discount store, took it to the floor of the House, and pulled out the items one by one while he talked. He concluded: "What do you have left at the end of the month? Pocket change, members, pocket change." He slammed some coins on the lectern. Some members of the House were weeping at the end of his speech. A wide majority voted to raise the payments.[4]

In 1977 Washington fought a TDC effort to build a massive new prison in West Texas. Prison reformers credited that defeat for preparing the way for more community-based corrections programs.[5] Washington also supported the five-day furlough program for inmates nearing parole. Just such a furlough was at the root of Eroy Brown's problems that terrible Saturday.

Washington served on the House committee that oversaw prisons, chaired by Alan Polunsky of Huntsville. He pushed issues such as conjugal visits and paying inmates wages for their labor, but lost every major committee vote on prison reform by six to five. He opposed the restoration of the death penalty and fought for a sentence of life without parole. His approach was that even if he didn't win, his view would eventually prevail.

Washington was thirty-nine. His father was a labor organizer in the industrial suburb of Galena Park, near the Houston Ship Channel industries. But during his high school summers, Washington worked at a union job in which he refused to pay union dues. Labor withheld its endorsement when he first ran for the House, but he won anyway.[6]

He was a smart but erratic student. He took eight years to graduate from Prairie View A&M, the black college forty-five miles northwest of Houston. He talked his way into the Thurgood Marshall Law School at Texas Southern University in Houston, where he excelled. He loved law school. He said he had learned the art of debate from his father.

Through a string of carefully thought-out questions Washington could lead a member of the House into embarrassing admissions. He could master intricate legal matters, such as credit law, quickly. He could think on his feet and improvise solutions. He could win over juries. He was tall and had a commanding presence. He spoke in a deep, resonant voice.

Habern had worked on a capital case with him, one that they had lost. He vividly remembered Washington's moving closing argument, in which he quoted poetry by Khalil Gibran.

The Texas legislature was in session that spring, so Washington was tied up in Austin until the end of May. Clements called a special session that summer to address several issues, among them Congressional redistricting that would ensure that minority voters could elect representatives in Dallas and South Texas.[7]

State legislators were paid only $400 a month, and they had to struggle to maintain an income and balance their legislative duties. Many were lawyers and on retainer with major companies that had business with the legislature. Washington was a trial lawyer, and had trouble organizing his practice. In 1973 he almost resigned from the legislature because of financial problems, but he regrouped.[8]

It helped that he was a quick study. Habern would have to organize the case. Washington would try it. Habern compared his role to that of a band arranger. He could write the arrangements and hire the musicians. Washington was going to be the lead singer.

Brown's aunt in Houston, Eddie Maryland, had been asking around about lawyers and had been telling him to get Washington.[9] Once Brown had agreed that Register needed to go, Habern picked up the phone. Washington was not surprised to hear from him. "Funny thing," he told Habern. "I was just thinking about calling you."

All they needed was someone who could handle the forensics of the case, another idealist who could wait to be paid at the end of the trial. Habern knew who that would be: Timothy Sloan. Sloan was a rare lawyer who had a scientific background. Tim's mother and father had given her a traditional Scottish name often used for girls. Then they raised her to believe she could do anything she wanted. Habern had known her since they were college students at Midwestern University, in Wichita Falls, and had passed babies over the fence. She had married a musician when she was eighteen. Habern and David Sloan had played in bands together. Tim did her undergraduate and graduate work in biology and was thinking of becoming a paleontologist, but instead entered law school at the University of Texas in 1967. She finished at the University of Missouri, while following her husband to his academic job. She was one of six women among twelve hundred students in the law school. She had a baby in October and finished in the spring. She had been a prosecutor in Missouri for a while and then worked for the best-known trial lawyer in Texas, Warren Burnett. She had five boys by then. Burnett did high-profile defense and plaintiff's work. His pro-bono clients included César Chávez, who was organizing farm workers in the Rio Grande Valley.

Her father was a bit alarmed when he heard about her job. He was G. P. Hardy, and when he retired in 1983 he was the longest-sitting district judge in Texas. He had brought up Tim in Bay City, where she fished and hunted on the Texas coast and was a high school swimmer. Her dad would take her to trials if he thought they were interesting. She didn't have any trouble cutting school because her mother was on the school board.

In the 1950s she went with her father to trials in Angleton and Sugar Land and they would eat lunch in the prisons in Brazoria and Fort Bend counties. The prisons served good country food, soul food, Sloan remembered, and that was where she learned that some of the most trusted prisoners were murderers. She asked a man what he had done and he said he had killed his wife when he found her in bed with another man. Tears came to his eyes when he said it. She learned that murderers were still human beings.

Eroy Brown, she would discover, had a finely tuned sense of morality. He knew when he committed his crimes they were wrong. He fell into crime because of his race and class, she believed. One thing she had learned about crooks is that they don't think they're going to be caught. That's why she didn't believe that harsh punishments are deterrents. Sloan thought that Texas could put a prison in every town in the state and fill them up and it still wouldn't work. People who were nonviolent when they went in would be violent when they come out.

She had learned of the case on the Monday morning after the deaths, when she was driving to work as a prosecutor in Fort Bend County. When she heard Eroy Brown had been shot with the warden's gun in a remote area, her first thought was that Brown had been taken out to be killed. She knew no prison official was ever supposed to take a handgun near an inmate. Good for him, she thought. He killed them before they killed him.[10]

When Habern phoned, Sloan didn't hesitate. She was single and living with her youngest son in Missouri City, a Houston suburb. Her oldest sons were away at college and military service. She had some retirement funds she could draw on, and she figured she could take some other cases and make some money.

"Let me know when you need me," she said, "because I have to give two weeks' notice."

In a little more than two months Habern had put together a major defense team for Eroy Brown. He had a star courtroom performer who could shred a witness with relentless questioning and move a jury to tears in a closing argument. He had a former prosecutor who knew the most experienced forensics experts in Texas, who could take shorthand notes of everything that happened, do first rate legal research, and handwrite motions on the spur of the moment. Habern could consult with every major defense and civil rights lawyer in Texas and he had deep connections among prison inmates. At his back he had the long shadow of public doubt the *Ruiz* case had cast on Texas prisons.

8

THE SHADOW OF *RUIZ*

All the breaking stories about the killing of Pack and Moore mentioned Judge Justice's ruling about the horrific conditions in Texas prisons. This federal judge, it seemed, had made Brown's plea of self-defense plausible. The day after the deaths, an inmate who claimed to have been an Ellis trusty told a reporter that Brown was in fear for his life because instead of being taken to the building, he was being taken to the "bottoms."

"They take you down there to be whipped by the warden or the field major and Billy Moore," the ex-trusty said. "It's what's called a ride to the bottoms and everybody knows what it means."

The bottoms at Ellis was literally a place near the Trinity River, three miles or so from the buildings, behind a flood control levee, out of sight. Inmates would later testify that the bottoms meant any remote place on the farm where an inmate could be punished out of sight.

The ex-trusty said he had been beaten at the bottoms and knew others who had been taken there and beaten, some severely enough to be hospitalized. He said Pack had come into the building wings when he first assumed his new job and had warned inmates about making trouble. There had been strikes and inmate stabbings, and it must stop. Inmates had thrown shoes at him, the former trusty said.[1] It was hard to tell how much of this was true, and how much was an elaboration. Throwing a shoe at a warden didn't seem like something Pack would let inmates get away with. Estelle characterized the story as "one eight-letter word beginning with b."[2]

In the voluminous testimony of the *Ruiz* trial, inmates hadn't talked about a ride to the bottoms, but there was plenty of testimony that high-ranking TDC officials had participated in brutality, and didn't just leave it to the building tenders.

"The defendants have attempted to characterize the staff brutality at TDC as a mere collection of isolated and aberrant acts which are not characteristic of the institutions at large," Justice wrote in his decision. "The record in this case makes it perspicuous that violence by security officers is routine and is not restricted to dangerous situations. Nor is the brutality the sole province of a few low-level security officers; many vicious incidents of abuse implicate high-ranking TDC officials."[3]

Wallace Pack was the highest-ranking TDC official ever killed in the line of duty, and Billy Moore was the second. It didn't take long before a reporter, William Barrett of the *Dallas Times Herald*, wondered if Pack and Moore had been involved in *Ruiz*.[4] He dug through the 42,000 pages of transcripts and turned up some background. An inmate who had been a mental patient at the Wynne Unit, where Pack had long worked, testified that Pack had ordered inmate porters to attack patients who refused to take their medications.

"'Most of them porters would whip them and kick them and strip them buck-naked and take a needle,' the inmate had testified. 'They would be holding him down by the neck choking them to death. . . . Major Pack and other inmate patients would join them because the major told them to do them like that.'"

Barrett described the testimony as rambling and incoherent, enough to make one wonder about it: a mental patient talking about mental patients.

A former TDC guard, James E. Eckles, said that Pack and Beartracks McAdams had gone out of their way to torment the writ writers that George Beto sent to the Wynne farm. Eckles said prison officials told him the writ writers tended to be violent personalities. "We wrote them up for any rule infraction," Eckles testified, "stuff that you would normally let another inmate do and you would kind of impress them on it. . . . He [a writ writer] was arrested for small penny-ante things that other inmates would be turned loose for. He would go to solitary or shell peanuts or do extra duty."

A former building tender named Clarence D. Moore testified that Pack had given him authority over other inmates. "Major Pack told me that he didn't want nothing but the major problems," the former convict said, "and I was supposed to handle everything else, you know. I, you know, could be rather mean."

Two other inmates testified that Pack and McAdams had gone out of their way to threaten and abuse writ writers and inmates who supported the *Ruiz* lawsuit. None of the witnesses built a case that Pack was exceptionally violent. He seemed to be a typical old-school TDC official who intimidated inmates, often with the help of building tenders.

Billy Moore had testified about the death of inmate James Batts at the Eastham farm in 1977. Batts was a schizophrenic who had been hospitalized four times. Instead of sending Batts to the Wynne Unit with other mental cases, the classification department sent him to Eastham, a work farm where mental illness was regarded as a form of malingering.

At Eastham, Batts tried to hang himself twice. The first time, his belt broke. The second time, a building tender interrupted him and brought him to the infirmary. The Eastham psychologist determined that Batts was trying to manipulate the system and get out of a place he didn't like. A prison doctor certified him as fit for work. It was mid-September and hot. Batts regularly took Cogentin, a drug that suppressed muscle tremors produced by the antipsychotic drugs he took. Cogentin also suppresses perspiration. The morning after this second suicide attempt, Batts staggered through his work. The second day he refused to work, and was handcuffed to a wagon wheel and a cotton ladder. By noon he was hyperventilating and taken to the infirmary and given salt tablets, water, and more Cogentin. In fifteen minutes he was dead.

A Walker County medical examiner found he had died of cerebral edema resulting from hanging. Cerebral edema is consistent with a death from heatstroke, not hanging. Batts's relatives raised a fuss about the autopsy. The extensive testimony in *Ruiz* probably led the TDC to settle the case in 1984 for $17,500.[5]

Several inmates testified that guards had beaten Batts while they were riding to the fields in a truck driven by Moore. Moore testified he hadn't seen anything. There was a code of secrecy among officers.[6] Their common answers to a query about violence were: "I wasn't there that day," or "I don't know what you're talking about."[7]

Eroy Brown was indicted for capital murder in May in the court of Walker County's most respected judge, Max Rogers, a close friend of George Beto. The last time an inmate had been tried for killing a prison guard, Rogers was the prosecutor. In 1934, Rogers had won the death penalty for two members of the Clyde Barrow gang. Barrow was little more than a petty car thief when he entered the Eastham farm in 1930 and rebelled at its brutality. The working conditions were so bad that Barrow cut off two of his toes with an ax. A little man, he was beaten and raped by a building tender. Barrow got away with killing his rapist with a pipe because another convict took the credit.[8] Barrow was released from prison early because of overcrowding.

But he came out meaner than a snake, determined to steal enough guns and money to raid Eastham and break out his buddies. When Barrow and Bonnie Parker carried out their plan in January 1934, a much-hated guard named Crowson was shot and killed. Max Rogers won two death penalties in a Huntsville courtroom for the killing, one for Raymond Hamilton and one for Joe Palmer. At his last hearing, Palmer told Rogers what he thought of the chances of getting fair treatment in Walker County.

"You will remember, Mr. Rogers," Palmer said, "that you used one set of witnesses to prove that I killed Crowson and another set to prove that Hamilton killed him. You know the testimony against Hamilton was perjured. I believe that the guards who were instrumental in this case committed perjury, and I believe you solicited it. . . . I killed Major Crowson . . . because of mistreatment to convicts . . . and I am making this statement for the sake of my own conscience."9

Palmer and Hamilton were both executed in the electric chair on May 10, 1935. Frank Hamer, a former Texas Ranger hired by the director of the Texas prison system, had gunned down Barrow a year earlier, making him the first man to be executed for killing the Eastham guard.

It seemed likely Eroy Brown would be executed, too. His trial was shaping up as a big one. The Brown trial would last several weeks and cost a lot of money. Every major daily newspaper in the state would cover it. In June Walker County officials were getting ready to ask the special session of the state legislature for $100,000 to conduct it. Walker County still owed Harris County $33,000 for the second capital trial of Ignacio Cuevas, the surviving inmate of the Carrasco hostage siege of 1974. An open-and-shut case, one in which dozens of police officers witnessed the crime, had been reversed because of questions about jury selection. The newly elected district attorney, Mark Ward, had retried Cuevas in 1979 with the help of the chief prosecutor for Harris County, Bert Graham, and won the death penalty.10 He would need help to try Brown. Habern thought Ward would be easy pickings for a good trial lawyer.

It would be next to impossible to seat a juror in Walker County who did not work for the TDC or have a relative or close friend who did. Corpus Christi had been talked about as a possible site for the trial. If the two sides couldn't agree, then Max Rogers would have to decide. But Mark Ward's parents had a beach house in Galveston. If he had to sit through a six-week-long trial, at least he would have a convenient place to live. He agreed to Galveston. It was only 45 miles down the highway from Houston and 130 miles from Huntsville.

Habern and Washington couldn't have been happier about Galveston. It held a large poor and working-class black population that was likely to be sympathetic to Brown. Craig Washington had political supporters who would show up at the trial every day. A Walker County jury would have convicted Brown with half an hour of deliberation. A Galveston jury might give him a chance.

Shortly after the killings, the governor of Texas, Bill Clements, summoned Jim Estelle to Austin to discuss the case, and said he was satisfied that it was being handled properly. Clements was the first Republican elected governor since Reconstruction, and he was determined to be tough on crime. He had vetoed more paroles than any of his predecessors, arguing that the parole board had gotten softer on crime while convicts had grown meaner. Prison reformers argued that this was not true, but the public's perception of crime seldom depends on data.[11] Clements could have reduced some of the prison overcrowding by easing up on parole instead of tightening it. He was housing roughly 29,000 inmates in a prison system designed for 16,000, and Clements could be blamed for the crowding.[12] In 1979 he had vetoed a bill that provided $30 million to build more prisons.[13]

The Texas attorney general, Mark White, a Democrat, was gearing up to run against Clements for governor and was looking for issues. He chided Clements for the veto. White's office had been responsible for fighting the *Ruiz* case, and after Justice's December 1980 ruling, Clements declared that White needed outside counsel to help with the appeal. White countered that he would decide whether he needed outside help.

If Clements wanted to do something, White said, he should use his contacts in the new Reagan administration to get the Justice Department out of the case. White declared that it was ridiculous for the Justice Department to require Texas to provide "private rooms" for inmates. The expression was political rhetoric on White's part. The language of the lawsuit was always about cells, not rooms.[14]

In response to *Ruiz,* Estelle developed a work-furlough program that would allow older inmates and those who were nonviolent to get out of prison, live at home, and work under supervision. TDC officials found that as many as a third of Texas inmates might qualify for such a program if the legislature would fund the supervisory costs. Clements agreed to push for $18 million to establish a program, but he didn't like the "home" part of work release. He wanted the furloughed inmates to be locked up at night, though where and how was an expensive proposition.

"I am not and will not ever agree to turning those inmates loose on the public and letting them go home to mama," he said. "They can forget about that."[15]

Under Judge Justice's orders, the state was required to hire five hundred more officers. While the state fought *Ruiz* on appeal, Clements had TDC officials move eight hundred inmates at Ellis and five other prisons to six-man wall tents with plywood floors.[16]

"If they are good enough for the Army personnel," Clements said, "if they are good enough for the Marines, if they are good enough for the National Guard, I see no reason that they are not good enough for the inmates in our prisons."[17]

Clements had the National Guard set up tents on the Capitol lawn and invited reporters to give him a better alternative. The tents didn't amount to much as a policy, but they were great political theater. By January 1983 the TDC had four thousand inmates living in tents.[18] Despite his clout with the Reagan administration, Clements couldn't do much about the participation of the Justice Department. The US attorney general wasn't supportive of one man, one cell, but as long as Texas had problems with brutality, understaffing, and medical care, the Reagan administration wasn't going to be much help.

Texas inmates believed that in reaction to the *Ruiz* decision, the TDC might end its use of building tenders as enforcers and do something about overcrowding. But the TDC mindset was not going to soften because of a federal judge. If anything, it was growing harder.

One day in the third week of April while he was trying to talk with Brown at the Walls, Habern was astonished to see an assistant warden walk into the visiting room with a reporter from the *Dallas Morning News* beside him. The reporter, Bill Deener, looked at Habern and Brown and did what any reporter would do—he asked for an interview. Habern was furious and was soon calling Estelle's office.

The assistant warden, G. P. Hardy, continued on a tour of the prison with Deener, who wrote a story about the fear simmering at Ellis prison. Hardy even conceded to Deener that there had probably been beatings at Ellis, though he had not seen them.

But the worst thing that Hardy said, or appeared to have said, for he later sued about the matter, was that inmates shouldn't be so upset about the overcrowding, or so expectant that Judge Justice would get them all in single cells by 1983. Near the end of his story, Deener attributed the following quotation to an unnamed assistant warden, whom most readers would conclude was Hardy: "Hell, these people were brought up in crowded homes. They are used to crowds. These people were raised by whores and slept on the floor."[19]

Three days after the story appeared, more than two thousand Ellis inmates went on a work stoppage. Prison officials blamed the strike on Judge Justice's rulings, but two Ellis guards told a *Houston Chronicle* reporter that while the inmates had been wanting to do a work stoppage for a long time, the comments about the inmates' mothers had set it off. Estelle sent a telegram to the prison units apologizing for the remarks and made it clear that Hardy had been fired. Such unity among inmates was unusual. During the strike, Habern visited some clients at Ellis, who told him they thought the TDC staff was scared to death.[20]

The reality of Texas prisons was that inmates vastly outnumbered guards and could overwhelm them at any time. The irony was that the convicts had sued the state to force it to provide more guards.

Inmates who had testified against the TDC in *Ruiz* were beaten and harassed by building tenders and guards. Three of them had died. Julio Nieto testified in October 1978 that a warden had maced him and denied him his medication. The TDC said Nieto later died of complications from diabetes, but a federal investigator said the death was suspicious.[21] Another inmate witness, Carl Reed, was stabbed to death by an Ellis building tender, who used a knife made of ice cream sticks and razor blades. Reed had asked for a transfer to federal custody along with other *Ruiz* witnesses who felt their lives were in danger. The transfer order came ten days too late. A third inmate, Gus Feist, was scheduled to be a witness but never testified. Feist was in trouble with prison officials for organizing the prison disturbances at the start of the *Ruiz* trial. On October 23, 1979, Feist died of blunt head trauma. TDC officials said he died from a fall to the concrete floor. Inmates said he had been beaten by a gang of building tenders and stomped on the head by a building major. Feist's parents sued. The case threatened to become another exposé of prison conditions, another major replay of *Ruiz*. Estelle eventually settled with the family for $18,000.[22]

The pressure on inmate witnesses was so bad that at the end of the trial Judge Justice transferred eighty inmate witnesses from Texas prisons to federal custody for their protection. One of them, who foolishly requested to come back from federal custody to the TDC, was stabbed to death in October 1981.[23]

Any witness who testified on behalf of Eroy Brown would face the same pressures as the *Ruiz* witnesses. Habern knew that as a lawyer, he wouldn't just be defending an inmate about a crime. He would be explaining a whole world, where one wrong move could destroy a man's life.

WEASEL

Like the TDC wardens "Beartracks" McAdams and J. V. "Wildcat" Anderson, Eroy Brown had a nickname: Weasel. It came from being such a small baby. The name stuck, though by the time of Brown's greatest troubles, he was not under-sized.[1] He was five feet eight inches tall and weighed 150 pounds. He was lithe and strong from lifting weights and tractor tires all day. In 1981 he was thirty years old and had spent much of his adult life in Texas prisons.

Brown grew up in a poor Waco neighborhood called the Southside, a slum full of small wooden houses bordering on the Baylor University campus. Scattered throughout were small taverns and pool halls, such as Tim's Drive In, the Auditorium Club, and the Joy Lounge.

Brown's parents were Eroy Edward Harris and Hattie Lee Brown, also known as "Shorty." The couple lived together for five years. Their first son, Carl, was born in 1949, forcing his mother to drop out of the eleventh grade. Eroy was born two years later, in January 1951. Eroy never got to know his father until after he got out of prison the second time.

Eroy's encounters with the law began when he was nine. He and Carl and another boy admitted to prying the lock off a panel truck and stealing fourteen boxes of cookies worth twenty-one dollars.[2] They promised the juvenile authorities it would not happen again.

Hattie Brown was mentally unstable and had to be hospitalized several times in her life. In 1960 she got into an argument with a woman at a neighborhood bar, the Auditorium Club. She accused the woman of turning her in to the police for shoplifting, and shot and killed a man and wounded the woman. Hattie Brown was convicted of murder and assault in 1961 and spent the next five years in prison.[3]

Eroy was eleven years old when his mother went to prison. He and Carl moved in with their great-grandmother, Alice Green, a tough woman who took in washing and ironing. She had a little wooden house on Burnett Street behind the high school playing fields. The two brothers slept on a living room sofa, while a cousin, Larry, who seemed to Brown more privileged because his mother had a college degree, got a bedroom to himself. Brown resented his great-grandmother.

"Me and Carl was throwaways," Brown says. "We was the black sheep. All she wanted was for us to work. She was old style. She had a big pot where she boiled clothes with lye soap. She had a wood stove. We had to chop the wood. She made me and Carl do all the work and Larry got all the education."[4]

Within a year after his mother went to prison, Eroy got into a fight and stabbed a boy with a broken Coke bottle. The wound was superficial and an officer got the two boys to shake hands. That seems to have been the only violent episode in his boyhood history.

A year later he and Carl got into trouble on the Cotton Palace grounds. The Cotton Palace was once the glory of Waco, a grand, domed exhibition hall built in the Victorian style in 1894 when Waco was the biggest cotton market in Texas. It had burned to the ground and been rebuilt, and then was torn down during the Depression. All that was left were the grounds and a vague whiff of history. Someone was cutting down hackberry trees in the park. A little detective work turned up Eroy and his brother Carl. They had been chopping wood for their great-grandmother's wash pot.

In 1965 Brown and three other boys admitted to burglarizing a junior high school. When he was fourteen, Eroy, along with other boys, was arrested for shoplifting clothes. By this time Brown was well known to juvenile authorities. His great-grandmother was bearing down on him for staying out all night. When juvenile authorities talked to Alice Green, she said she would try to rein him in, but she said Carl and Eroy would not help around the house. She complained that Eroy had a job and made a little money, but he wouldn't share it with the household, and they had no food in the house. The authorities made a note to get the boys into the school lunch program.

In 1966 Eroy attended Moore High School, a black school run by a devoted and strict group of teachers who didn't put up with much nonsense. He played a little football, but that didn't last. When he was fifteen, he was arrested and put on probation for stealing a purse from a car. After school he worked as a dishwasher at a Baylor dining hall but was fired when he was caught stealing a purse from a girl's room. A juvenile officer found him and other boys prowling the Baylor parking lot and ran them out several times. He was caught and charged for another theft from a car in the student parking lot. The haul was pitiful: a straw hat, a white bowl, an electric shaver, a short-sleeve white dress shirt, a flashlight, a lantern, and a pair of shoes. Three Baylor students caught him taking stereo tapes from parked cars.

He was hardly showing up at school. He broke his arm and couldn't play football. The teachers were grinding on him. The school was ready to file charges against his great-grandmother for his truancy. He told the juvenile authorities he had applied for the Job Corps but that went nowhere. In the summer of 1967 he and his best friend were charged with stealing a billfold from a man who worked in a used lumber store. Eroy admitted to being present when the other boy grabbed the billfold from the man's hip pocket and ran. He and his best friend got into an argument with a fifteen-year-old girl at Tim's Drive-In, a neighborhood hangout, and then drove to her house with a friend and ransacked it.

Eroy's great-grandmother kept coming to the police station to talk to detectives. A juvenile judge found him to be a delinquent. Eroy was put on probation and was supposed to report every two weeks.

He was seventeen in February 1968 when he and two friends broke into the old Dr Pepper building, a warehouse by the railroad tracks that belonged to Baylor University. He and Simmie Degrate, his best friend, had been playing pool at the Joy Lounge when a man asked them if they wanted to make some money. They later described him to the police as wearing gray sharkskin slacks and a light shirt. His processed hair was covered in a black do-rag. They said they never got his name. Eroy and two boys climbed over the fence, broke into the warehouse, and had carried seven air conditioners to a shack by the chain-link fence when the police spotted them. Eroy fled, leaving a white leather coat and a Stetson hat hanging in the warehouse. Two days later he was arrested and signed a confession.

Being caught didn't deter him. On March 26, 1968, Brown and two boys broke the padlock off the door to Naylor's Variety Store on Eleventh Street, just around the corner from his great-grandmother's house. In his confession, Eroy said he took seventeen pairs of socks and gave them to a friend. The owner of the store, Henry Naylor, valued the missing inventory at twenty-eight dollars. He pressed charges and Eroy pleaded guilty.

While awaiting sentencing, he worked for a roofing company for two months in the summer of 1968 and came steadily to work. But he abruptly quit without saying anything to his employer.

For the pre-sentencing investigation, a probation officer compiled Eroy's long juvenile record. He described him as a seventeen-year-old Negro male who was "a product of his environment." He had spent most of time growing up with his great-grandmother. He had quit school because he couldn't get along with his teachers. A science teacher told the probation officer, "We at Moore High never did have much hopes for Eroy. He was always going to the little store during school hours and staying out of school a lot. Eroy never could get along with the teachers or the principal. I wish I could help Eroy but he is the victim of a broken home." A barber who had helped Eroy get out of jail and urged him to stay in school said, "Eroy would always rather shoot pool and run around with the wrong kind of cats."

While awaiting the decision of the probation department, Brown enrolled in a work program at Paul Quinn College, where he studied welding. In August, Eroy's brother Carl was sentenced to three years in prison for stealing a four-dollar check from the night deposit box of a finance company.[5] In October 1968, the Waco police arrested Eroy for stealing a car stereo and a couple of eight-track tapes. The caseworker, who had been considering him for leniency, couldn't see any point in probation. A prison sentence had been hanging over Eroy Brown and he was still out stealing.

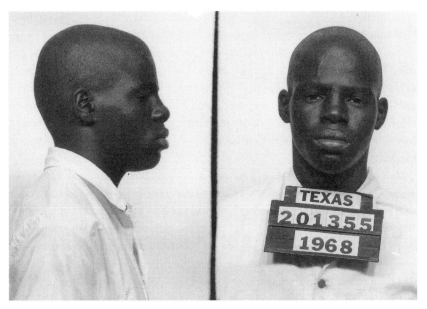

Eroy Brown's mug shot, taken at age seventeen, when he entered the Ferguson Unit.

When he entered prison at the end of the month, the TDC sent his mother a questionnaire about his childhood. She had served her five years and was out of prison, had married, and had a daughter. She was asked when her son first left home and why.

"He never really left," she wrote. "He became of age and like most boys wanted to be his own boss."

He was only seventeen, but he was also the father of a boy named Kevin, born on April 1. The mother was sixteen.

When he entered the TDC diagnostic unit, another parole officer noted that he seemed to be an "immature type individual who has been easily influenced by his associates . . ." Brown said he didn't drink excessively and had never been involved in narcotics. His plan after prison was to live with his mother and stepfather in Waco. The caseworker thought Brown sincerely wanted to reform and that "fear of future incarceration will serve as a deterrent to involvement in further delinquent activities." About that, he was wrong.

Brown was sent to the Ferguson Unit, where he had only a couple of problems. During a shakedown in May 1969, a guard found that he had stashed four aspirin tablets in a Mexana skin-cream box. He was not authorized to have them in his cell. The disciplinary committee sent him to solitary confinement, erased a hundred points of "good time," and busted him back to the hoe squad. Six months later he was caught scuffling with another inmate in the cell block. They both told the guard they were just playing, but he lost "good time" again.

After serving twenty-two months of a three-year sentence, Brown was paroled in August 1970. He was nineteen. He spent three years and eight months in the free world before returning to prison. He worked for seven months as a welder at a factory in Waco, but then quit. The Waco police picked him up in December 1970 for being drunk. He married Kathy Wiley, the mother of his son Kevin. They had a daughter, Tanisha, in July 1973, but by that time Eroy was in trouble again.

In June 1973 he met a couple of men in a Waco bar and rode with them to Temple, about thirty-five miles south of Waco. They pried open the front door of Herring's department store with a crowbar and took several armloads of suits and put them in the trunk of their car. A patrolman spotted them and chased the three down an alley. He captured Brown, but the other men got in the car and sped away. A week later the suits were found in a dumpster. Once again, Brown had been caught stealing something he probably didn't want and that would be difficult to sell.

Two months later, when Brown was out on bond, a woman dropped him off at a Texaco service station on Lake Air Drive in Waco. Noticing that no one was in the station, he took thirty-five dollars from the cash register and left. The attendant and a passerby in a pickup chased him down to a motel parking lot, brought him back to the gas station, and called the police. In his confession, Brown said he was walking by and stopped to get a drink of water. He said he took the money because he was hungry.

Perhaps this was true, but more likely he had another motive. He was a heroin addict now, and his arms were dotted with needle marks. He had spent thirteen months as an outpatient at a mental health center in Waco, and was taking a tranquilizer, Stelazine, but he didn't like the effects of the drug and quit taking it. Medical literature on the drug suggests it can cause a wide range of side effects. It is most commonly prescribed for schizophrenics today, but Brown was never diagnosed as mentally ill.

Brown's addiction was duly noted when he came back to the diagnostic unit at TDC in April 1974. Sentenced to six years for the clothing store burglary, he served another fifteen months at the Darrington Unit in Brazoria County, south of Houston, and was paroled in July 1976. When he got back to Waco, his wife served him with divorce papers. She probably knew that before he had gone into

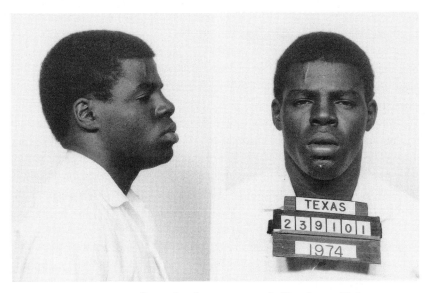

Eroy Brown at age twenty-four, when he was sent to the Darrington Unit.

prison in 1974 he had had a daughter with another woman. His visitation to his children was limited and he was ordered to pay thirty dollars a month in child support.

He had started corresponding with his mother's father when he was in prison, laying plans for a new life away from Waco. After he got out of Darrington, he moved to the south side of Fort Worth and stayed with his grandfather, a retired man of sixty-four who lived with a younger daughter, Brown's age. Brown worked for about a year at a maintenance job for an apartment complex. On August 31, 1977, he and another man held up a Ramada Inn in north Fort Worth. For the first time in his criminal history, Eroy was armed. He pulled a .32 caliber revolver on the night clerk and made him lie down on the floor. He and his accomplice found sixty-seven dollars in cash and fled in a car. He was arrested six weeks later and pled guilty.[6]

His third sentence was twelve years for aggravated robbery with a firearm. He landed in Ellis prison, the place for incorrigibles. In March 1978 Brown was working on a hoe squad at Ellis when he was written up for hitting an inmate with a jelly jar and cutting him behind the ear. Brown complained that his cellmate had fondled him while they were sleeping and that the inmate had confronted him and was spreading stories.

"As to avoid further trouble which might result in to a killing," he explained in a filing, "I requested to be locked up in seg. I'm an outside trusty and my soul [sic] endeavors are to serve my time and return back to society, and at this point this situation had just gotten out of hand . . ." He asked for a transfer, saying he had a good record and could serve his time without difficulty. "My record will clearly show that I've always tried to carry myself in a model prisoners and manly respectful way."

The key word in this statement is "manly." It was a unifying word in prison culture, for both officers and inmates. Brown was being "checked" by the other inmate to see what he was made of. Knocking the other inmate down established his independence. He might be punished for it, but the guards knew why he was in the fight. He didn't get the transfer. He had proven he could take care of himself at Ellis.

In 1980 he made furlough requests, to see his stepmother in Waco, his cousin in Fort Worth, his second wife and daughter in Waco. All three were denied. In January 1981 he filed again to see his grandfather and cousins and a young woman he hoped to marry. That one was denied, too.

He had written his sister, Marva "Candy" Harris, "When you have been doing time as long as I have, you learn real fast how to ride the waves and roll with the punches and above all you can't let it get you down . . ."

"These white folks got me with rocks in my jaws as usual!" he wrote Candy. "Working the shit out of me and steadily keep denying me for furlough, but I ain't going to let it get me down. I'm going to keep on strong. Maybe something will break soon."[7]

On April 14 Habern brought two physicians from Houston in to examine the bullet wound in Eroy's foot. They did not find it infected. They photographed the laceration on his right wrist that the handcuffs had made. On Saturday, April 18, Brown visited with the chaplain, Carroll Pickett, who gave him a couple of envelopes so he could write to his mother and brother. He asked for a Bible, and the next day, Easter Sunday, Pickett brought him one.

By the first week of May Brown had begun to accumulate the basic comforts of convict life: tobacco, lighters, and a cigarette roller, bath soap and hand lotion, a night-light, some ballpoint pens and a notebook, cough drops, Scotch tape, a "stinger" with which to boil water, and a bottle of hot sauce. By May 11 Brown's foot had healed, but he was still under hospital supervision and could not get full commissary like the other prisoners. The hospital administrator told him he would have to take it up with the warden. Eroy wrote asking for newspapers, a radio, and a shaving mirror.

"With your approval, sir, I'd like to be able to purchase the ordinary commissary that's posted on the list, as well as having my shaving mirror that is my

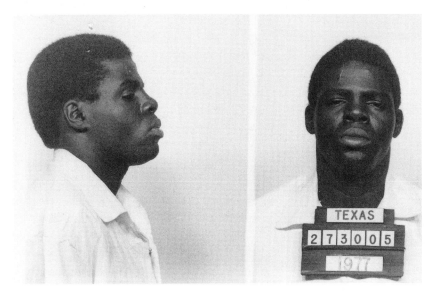

Eroy Brown when he entered the Ellis Unit in 1977, at age twenty-seven.

property, and I assure that I'm not suicidal and have no intentions of creating no disturbance, or for that matter, harming anyone, I'd like to have my mirror to properly shave."

He also requested that the officers quit slamming the outer door to his cell block every thirty minutes, which was making it impossible for him to sleep. He wanted out of the hospital cell block.

"Frankly speaking," he wrote, "I wouldn't mind at all if you'd move me over to the Death Row Area itself with the above privileges." The Death Row area in the Walls was an ominous place. It was where, after being transferred from Ellis when their appeals had ended, men spent their last days waiting for execution.

The TDC kept a log of all of Brown's visitors as well as what officer was on duty at the time. According to the records, the officer was removed from the visiting room on all visits after April 22. Max Rogers had ordered it, but Judge Justice had made it happen. In a letter to the Walls warden, Jack Pursley, Rogers wrote, "This directive is in obedience to the suggestions made by United States District Judge William Wayne Justice."

Early in his stay at Ellis, Brown had used just enough violence to protect himself against another convict. Until Billy Moore took him to the bottoms, he'd scarcely caused a problem. Every time he had gone to prison Eroy Brown had confessed to a crime. For the murders of Pack and Moore he would make no confession, though he would talk about what happened. For the first time in his life, he was going to have a trial.

10

THE DANGERS OF TESTIFYING

By the middle of June, Habern had his client out of TDC custody and safe in the Galveston jail. Eroy Brown was now a defendant like other defendants, presumed to be innocent until proven guilty.

The trial was set in the 122nd District Court of Judge Henry Dalehite. Dalehite had been born and grew up on Galveston Island, went to the University of Texas law school, and passed the bar in 1951. Some defense attorneys considered him a prosecutor's judge, but as the trial progressed, the defense came to see him as a fair man.

Habern filed a motion to obtain copies of Brown's prison and parole records, including his medical files. Both the TDC and the state parole board refused to release them. An attorney from Mark White's office argued that the records were confidential. On September 12, Dalehite ruled that the state should give him the records, and that he would read and withhold any that were irrelevant to the defense. The state appealed, and any hope of a fall trial ended.

In late October Washington and Habern presented their case before the Texas Court of Criminal Appeals in Austin. Habern argued that if Eroy Brown were a free man charged in a capital case, he would be entitled to all of his prison records, including his medical records. To the state's contention that they were on a "fishing expedition," Washington argued that he couldn't be any more specific because he couldn't see the records. It became clear that the state wouldn't win when one of the justices, Sam Houston Clinton,[1] asked the state's lawyer rhetorically, "How come these agencies consider themselves different from a former president of the United States who was told every man must give his evidence?"[2] Clinton was referring to Richard Nixon, who was ordered by the Supreme Court to turn over the Watergate tapes.

In early November, the court ruled that Brown was entitled to most of his medical files. Habern and Washington had to laugh about the comparison of Brown's case to Watergate. It showed that no one, not the president of the United States, or even the Texas prison system, was above the law.

Habern and Washington wanted to educate the judge about the Texas Department of Corrections. They persuaded Dalehite to hold a hearing in Galveston on November 30 to discuss protective custody for the prospective inmate witnesses.

They hired Kent Schaffer to do the investigative work. Schaffer was putting himself through law school at the University of Houston by doing investigative work for defense lawyers, including Richard "Racehorse" Haynes in the Cullen Davis murder trial. His older brother, Randy, was already one of the most respected defense lawyers in Texas. Kent would follow in his footsteps. Habern sent Schaffer out to interview witnesses who could explain the world of the TDC to a jury that had little idea about it. Habern had plenty of leads. One of them was Lawrence Pope, a prolific writ writer and TDC critic who had been the plaintiffs' lead witness in *Ruiz*. Pope wrote Habern from his federal cell in Oklahoma with a long list of suggestions and a check for fifty dollars. He knew Habern would be broke for a long time.

Schaffer found plenty of inmates who would talk to him. Whether they would testify was another matter, and whether their testimony was needed was another matter still. The prison grapevine was extensive and lightning fast. Within hours after the killings, TDC officials had hauled Pack's car and Moore's truck to the Ellis bus barn. After the Walker County investigators took fingerprints, prison officials ordered some trusties to empty the vehicles and steam clean them.

There were rumors that Pack's car had been emptied of liquor bottles, that there were three or more bullet holes in the car that had to be patched up, and that the guards had found a second gun in the creek that had been hushed up. One inmate insisted that Pack had been drunk that Saturday, which was visiting day, and that any number of inmate family members could testify to it. None of these rumors turned out to be true.

Schaffer found five inmates who were in solitary confinement at Ellis the afternoon Brown was put into a ground-floor cell in the segregation wing. They could not see the guards beating Brown, but they could hear his cries of pain, they said. One of them said the guards were stomping on his wounded foot. Another said he saw a guard carrying four "throw-down" knives enter the cell to beat

Brown. If an inmate were killed during the beating, the knife could be thrown down as an excuse. One said he heard Brown say over and over again, as he was beaten, "They made me do it." Another said Brown said, "Don't hit me, boss. Why are you doing this, boss?"[3]

None of the inmates seemed to think Brown was a violent man. If anything, he had a reputation for being passive and maybe a little fearful. One inmate said he was known as the farm manager's "boy." There were a lot of implications in the word "boy," but violence and aggression were not among them.

Habern called four inmate witnesses before Judge Dalehite in the November hearing. He began with Ben Willard Lacy II, who claimed to have been in Pack's office the day he was killed. Lacy was thirty-nine years old and had been in prison eight years. At Ellis, Lacy explained, he was officially assigned to work at the bathhouse, but his real job was to be the "warden's boy," which was another way of saying he was the warden's chief snitch. As proof of Lacy's status, Habern offered a Polaroid picture of Lacy standing by the Teletype machine in Pack's office. The Walker County district attorney, Mark Ward, strenuously objected, but Dalehite allowed the picture into evidence. It was not a hearing before a jury, after all.

Among his duties, Lacy testified, was to find out about anyone, including officers, who was dealing drugs and other contraband in the prison. "Several times there was a bust and transfers came down when an officer was busted," Lacy said.

A rumor had started among the inmates that Lacy and another of the warden's boys had beaten Brown when he was brought through the Ellis building the day of the deaths. A few days later, Lacy testified, three inmates cornered Lacy and beat him up for what they thought he had done to Brown. Once he had held the high status of warden's boy. Now, he told the court, he was an "old thing," a term that would come up in the trial. An old thing, he explained, was a person who doesn't work for the TDC, who tries to stay neutral.

Three weeks after the killings, Lacy was transferred from Ellis to Eastham, where Billy Moore had worked for ten years before coming to Ellis. Lacy said inmates at Eastham told him that he had been sent there to have something done to him. Lacy got some help and was transferred to Ramsey, not an easy prison by any means, but at least one where neither Pack nor Moore had worked.

Prison officials knew which inmates had talked to Schaffer and other defense investigators. Lacy said the Ramsey warden had called him in and asked him how he was going to testify. Lacy said he was going to "do the right thing." Lacy said that guards, turnkeys, and building tenders had threatened him about testifying for Brown. He said a dozen building tenders attacked him and broke his thumb.

He believed they were under orders from the TDC. Habern pointed out that the judge could verify Lacy's story about the beating by checking his medical records.

Ward frequently objected to Lacy's testimony as hearsay, but Dalehite let the convict say enough to give the general picture. Everyone involved in the case lives in fear, Lacy said.

"Well, any way you look at it," he said, "a person in my position loses either way. If I testify against the TDC . . . TDC is down on me. . . . You are always in fear of your life. You have to watch your back constantly. You know there is going to be retaliation. I know this, as a ex–building tender. I have seen retaliation coming in many forms. I have seen knives planted in cells."[4]

". . . Well, TDC if they want you for something minor, they take your good time. That good time is credits earned for good behavior. If they really want you, they will sic a strummer on you, somebody working for them."

A strummer was a building tender who beat up other inmates. The metaphor indicated the impersonality of the beating. It was as impersonal as strumming a guitar. Lacy was thirty-nine years old and had been in prison for eight years without incident, he said. But that was all over.

Ward pushed him about his background.

"And in your capacity as a snitch," he asked, "you would inform on the other inmates to the officials of the Texas Department of Corrections?"

"As well as the officials," Lacy said. "Guards and officials."

Next Habern put on Kenneth Pallend, who claimed Pack had pulled a gun on him at the Wynne unit in 1978. Pallend had written to Jerry Register in April that he had something to offer in Brown's defense. He said TDC officials had warned him off the case, and that at the end of May a guard had caught his arm in a cell door and fractured his wrist. In August, Pallend testified, his cellmate was pulled and replaced by a mentally disturbed man who had cut off his own penis. "He would stay up all night long and breathe heavily into my ear," Pallend testified. "It was just impossible to live with the man."[5]

After Pallend met with the defense investigator in October, he testified that the assistant warden at Wynne told him he "could be a dead motherfucker." He said he had lost his good job in the typing pool at Wynne and was put in a dirty, roach-infested cell in the administrative segregation wing, supposedly for his own protection. He said the assistant warden told him he would get him out of the dirty cell and move him to a good job if he would keep his mouth shut.

"I really didn't understand at first," Pallend testified, "and he told me . . . 'You know what I'm talking about.'"

Pallend also told the court that a month earlier someone had come from behind him at the Wynne infirmary and tried to strangle him with a cord. His eye was blackened and his lip was cut, and he nearly passed out. The medical personnel examined him, he said, and there were cord marks on his neck. But obtaining medical records might be difficult, he said. He had filed a civil suit against the prison because an inmate had administered him the wrong medication, and he said his medical records had disappeared.

When Mark Ward cross-examined Pallend, he asked him if he had ever felt unsafe in prison before the Brown incident, and he said yes. He also asked him if the TDC psychologist had ever questioned him about paranoia. Then he asked him about Pallend's claim that a guard had broken his wrist in a cell door on May 30.

"Isn't it true that that case went before the Grand Jury in Walker County?" Ward asked.

"It sure did," Pallend replied.

"Isn't it true that the case was no-billed by the Grand Jury of Walker County?" Ward asked.

"Isn't that usual for Huntsville?" Pallend retorted.

"I am asking the questions," Ward said.

It all boiled down to safety, Pallend said, and there was no safe place as long as he was in the Texas prison system and testifying for Eroy Brown.

Pallend told the same story that dozens of inmates told in *Ruiz*. He said, "I have witnessed numerous beatings by TDC guards and TDC enforcers, inmates that receive special favors, that are given supervisory situations. All an officer has to do is say that someone has to be beaten or injured and it will be done."

Pallend didn't think he was safe either in the inmate population or locked up in a cell. "If I am left out in the population of TDC," he said, "I have inmate enforcers who will kill somebody and swear it was personal. . . . If I am placed in a segregation cell, like I was, I am at the hands of the inmate enforcers and the guards with keys that will open doors for them. Either way I go, I lose."

Habern pressed his inmate witnesses to compare their safety at other prisons to the safety afforded at the Diagnostic Unit in Huntsville where the TDC was holding the prosecution's witnesses. All inmates went through the Diagnostic Unit when they entered the system. Here they were given medical, psychological, and sociological exams. They were interviewed about their crimes and their family history. Their IQs were measured, and on the basis of the accumulated information, they were assigned to various prisons by the classification committee.

That was one purpose of Diagnostic. But there was another. Diagnostic was where ex-police officers, lawyers, judges, snitches, and other inmates vulnerable to retaliation by resentful inmates were held. Inmates were plenty resentful when they heard about convicts willing to help the prosecution get the death penalty for Eroy Brown.

Within days after the killings the three inmates who been watching from the garden shed were transferred to Diagnostic and given easy jobs in the yard. They had accidentally found a ticket out of the TDC. James Soloman, Levi Duson, and Henry Kelley were going to get paroled. All they had to do was say the right things.

Schaffer and his assistant Leonard Meyer interviewed the three witnesses in September in the eye clinic of the Diagnostic unit. Schaffer asked to see the men one at a time, but they refused to be separated. They had been told that Schaffer represented Brown's defense, and all three said they had nothing to say about the case. Schaffer said he wasn't trying to get them to change their story, but in order to properly defend Brown he had to attempt to interview anyone who had information about the case. Brown's life, after all, was at stake and the three of them could save it.

James Soloman, the most vocal of the three, told Schaffer he couldn't know the kind of pressure they were under. He mentioned that all three had families outside of prison, and that they were worried about their families. Soloman said that none of them had wanted to be transferred to Diagnostic, for that had marked them as TDC snitches for life. If they wanted to change their minds, Schaffer told them to contact him through Craig Washington. Soloman said it didn't matter because none of them wanted to contact him. But, Schaffer observed, Duson looked him in the eye and gestured as if to say he understood what Meyer and Schaffer were trying to do.

Schaffer noted in his report that by the way the men talked and moved, the room in which they were meeting might have been bugged. At the very least, the three men would be debriefed by prison authorities about what they had said. They were in a terrible situation. If they offered evidence that supported Eroy Brown, they might be injured or killed in the TDC. Their paroles could be set off for a long while. If they cooperated, they could be released early.

Of the three, Henry Kelley took the easy way out. Whenever he was asked to testify about what he saw that day, he complained of feeling dizzy. Kelley's performance at the November hearing was typical. Habern asked him a few questions about where the TDC was keeping him and then asked if he had given a statement to the state about the death of Wallace Pack.

"I don't understand what you are saying," Kelley said. "I am sick. I am dizzy."

The judge asked him if he was having trouble hearing the questions, and Kelly said, "I am suffering from high blood pressure. I am dizzy. My head is spinning." He had brought his medication but had not taken it, he said. He was excused and he didn't testify.

Levi Duson did take the stand and under Habern's questioning admitted that he was well taken care of at Diagnostic. He had a good bed, clean sheets, good food, and a job cleaning up around the yard. He felt safe. But he wouldn't want to go back to Ellis, he said, "because there has been a lot of hassle behind this case." A lot of people, he said, thought "we would be wrong about what we saw."

Habern got Duson to admit that an inmate on either side of the case had reason to be afraid for his safety, but Duson began to backpedal when he realized where Habern was taking him. "I don't think it would all come from the TDC officials," Duson said.

Habern's main point was to show that while his inmate witnesses had been beaten up, had lost their job assignments, and had been put in dirty cells, the state's witnesses had been coddled.

Habern's last witness at the hearing was Wendell Dickerson, who had been chief psychologist of the TDC from 1974 to 1978. Habern asked him how seriously inmates took threats, especially threats about a highly visible case such as Eroy Brown's.

People in prison have to be wary of each other constantly, Dickerson said, no matter what color of suit they wear. "It is the nature of the beast," he said. Based on what he knew of the *Ruiz* case, Dickerson testified that a court order could be helpful in protecting inmate witnesses who wanted to testify for Brown.

Ward asked Dickerson whether the fears of inmates weren't exaggerated, more "imagined rather than real." Dickerson acknowledged that some of the fears were unrealistic, but he knew "a good many others where that was not the case." Ward asked Dickerson if inmates didn't try to con him and Dickerson said it happened all the time. If an inmate were willing to testify, as these inmates had testified for the defense that day, didn't that show they weren't afraid?

"Many of us are capable of acting in spite of our fears and in fact, testimony of this sort may . . . be a defense against any reprisals in and of itself," Dickerson said.

Dalehite had heard enough. He was not going to let the defense decide which of its witnesses should be moved to special custody in the TDC or to county jails or federal custody. But he did ask Washington to draw up an order that commanded the TDC to protect the inmate witnesses. If something happened to an inmate witness, the TDC could be held in contempt of court.

The TDC was used to being threatened by courts. A federal judge was holding the entire prison system in contempt of the Constitution, and nothing had changed. A court order from a state district judge was not likely to change the way the TDC did business.

11

OLD THING

In the fall of 1981 Walker County got enough money from the state to try Eroy Brown, but it had another problem. Its district attorney, Mark Ward, had little trial experience and had tried only one capital murder case, that of Ignacio Cuevas, the surviving inmate in the Carrasco hostage case of 1974. His assistant, Frank Blazek, was greener than he was. Wallace Pack's stepson, David Bolton, a Houston real estate developer, was worried about the turns the case could take. He had liked Pack, who had been married to his mother for twenty-seven years. At the end of November he put up $20,000 to hire a special prosecutor.[1]

Bolton settled on Houston attorney Michael J. Hinton. As a Harris County prosecutor, Hinton had won two highly publicized trials against fathers who had committed terrible crimes. In 1975 Hinton prosecuted Kerry Crocker, who chemically castrated his son with radioactive pellets he bought from an oil field supply company. Hinton won the death penalty for Ronald Clark O'Bryan, the notorious "candy man." In 1974 Clark poisoned his seven-year-old son's Halloween candy to collect on a $40,000 life insurance policy.[2] O'Bryan was waiting on Death Row for his appeals to run out. The cases, especially O'Bryan's, had created a national wave of revulsion and fear.

But Pack and Moore hadn't been helpless young boys in the clutches of a fiendish father. They were professional prison officials dealing with hardened criminals. Hinton had to do everything he could to make Eroy Brown look like an angry monster who had gone out of control.

Jury selection began on January 11, 1982.

Habern and Washington wanted Brown tried for the killing of both Pack and Moore in the same trial. The state insisted on two trials, one for drowning Wallace Pack, and a second for shooting Billy Moore. Dalehite ruled in favor of the state.[3]

Habern and Washington had filed several motions for dismissal before the trial started. They argued that Brown had been denied an examining trial with the justice of the peace in Huntsville once the charges had been filed. Washington argued that the law invoking the death penalty for killing police officers created a special class of victims, and that was unconstitutional. Habern argued that Brown's constitutional rights had been violated because the TDC had not allowed him private talks with Brown during the first week after his arrest to identify and photograph his injuries. Washington argued that Galveston's jury selection rules were racially discriminatory because jurors were selected only from voter registration lists. Many brown and black citizens would be excluded because they didn't register to vote as often as whites.

They didn't expect to win a dismissal, but they were laying grounds for appeal in case Brown was convicted. Dalehite turned down all the motions during the thirteen days it took the two teams of lawyers to select a jury.[4]

Seven of the jurors were men, one of them black, one Hispanic. Two of the five women were black. The questioning of the jurors had been lengthy. For the most part they were working-class people. One was a carpenter, and another was a pipe fitter. Tim Sloan was worried about one of them, a white housewife from Galveston named Dorothy Kemp, who had several cats. Sloan didn't trust someone who had a lot of cats. Brown didn't like her, either. He thought she seemed eager to be on the jury.[5] They argued with Washington and Habern about her, but they didn't see Kemp as a problem.

On Tuesday, February 2, 1982, Hinton began his argument. The state had created three scale models of the buildings and terrain where the deaths had occurred. He had a dozen aerial photographs of the prison and the crime scene as well as the photographs investigators had taken on April 4.

In his opening statement, Hinton laid out the order of his witnesses. First up would be the two farm supervisors who took Eroy Brown to see Billy Moore. They would testify that they took Brown to see Moore because he had been smoking pot and was "very agitated and very upset." Two inmates who had seen Brown scream at Moore, shoot him, and chase Pack down the bank of Turkey Creek would follow them. Two Walker County investigators would describe the scene, and four forensics experts would establish the cause of the deaths and that Brown had fired a gun. The case seemed simple: a drug-crazed Negro had gone out of his mind and killed the two men.

William Adams Jr. was a lean, slow-talking crop supervisor from East Texas. He was fifty-three years old, a lifetime TDC employee who expected to retire with the agency. Every fourth weekend he worked at the farm supervising the outside trusties. Besides the inmate witnesses in the garden shed, Adams was the key to the state's case. He had taken Eroy Brown to see Billy Moore for "running his head."[6]

Everything had been quiet that morning, Adams said. Brown had come into the farm shop and asked for a cup of coffee, and Adams had given him one. Later that morning, he had heard Brown raving so loudly that Adams had gone into the shed where the bus was parked to see what was the matter.

". . . I know you are a gentleman," Hinton said, "and this is a court of law you are telling this to, but even though there are ladies here, we need to know what you heard so they understand."

"Well," Adams said, "I heard him out there raving and cussing outside of the office. I went out to see what his problem was and he was just raving that he wanted a furlough. 'I want to fuck a woman like everybody else does.'

". . . I couldn't calm him down. He kept raving about a furlough and about he wanted a God damn furlough like everybody else, and he worked his ass off, and he had a right to one the same as everyone else did . . .

"I asked him whether he had been drinking because there appeared to be something wrong with him. He said he hadn't been drinking anything. I told him there was something wrong with him and he said he had been smoking weed."

It hadn't taken long for the prosecution to establish the Southern stereotype about blacks. Eroy Brown was crazed that day by sex and drugs. Adams said Brown insisted on seeing Billy Moore, who was fishing in the Ellis reservoir near the garden house. Using photographs, Adams traced the route from the farm shop to the reservoir, demonstrating how he drove up the road on top of the dike to a corner of the reservoir and waved Billy Moore in to shore. Moore took over the truck that Adams had been driving, Adams said, and Brown repeated his story that he had been smoking pot.

"He asked him how much he had been smoking," Adams said. "I don't know that much about dope, but he said he smoked a roach, whatever they call it. Mr. Moore asked him how much that was, and he said it was about the same size as a cigarette. Mr. Moore said, 'If you can't smoke no more than that, you better leave the stuff alone.'

". . . [H]e told us two or three stories about the weed. One time he was telling us that they were growing it down there at the farm shop and then it wound up he didn't know where he got it from. For security reasons, that is when Mr. Moore called Warden Pack, and asked him to meet him down there."

Defense exhibit photo of tractor shed, where events started the morning of April 4, 1981. "Pugh" was a trusty working the farm shops. "Adams" was Bill Adams, the farm supervisor who took Eroy Brown to see Billy Moore at the reservoir.

Aerial view of the Ellis Unit. The "building" is marked at the top. The reservoir (numeral 3) is below. To the left of the reservoir are the sewage settling ponds. Numeral 2 indicates where Pack and Moore parked. The "W" indicates the garden shed where the inmate witnesses worked. Numeral 4 indicates the road to the tractor shed where events began.

But Moore didn't tell Pack why he wanted him to meet him, Adams said. Brown had calmed down quite a bit, Adams said, and when Charles Spivey, the livestock supervisor, drove up, Moore sent Adams back with Spivey to supervise the other inmates a mile away at the farm shop. Hinton's last question was whether someone standing in the garden shed could see the bridge over Turkey Creek. Adams said he could.

Craig Washington's first question for Adams was whether inmates knew him as "Boss Adams." It was a question he would frequently ask of inmate witnesses. Adams was Boss Adams, not Mr. Adams and certainly not Bill to the inmates. Washington wanted the jury to understand that the language of prison was the language of the slave plantation.

Only trusties worked on Saturdays out on the farm, Adams said, and Brown worked most Saturdays. About seven or eight trusties were working that day, Adams said. Washington wanted to know if any of them were personal trusties.

"Personal trusties?" Adams said. "I don't know what you mean."

"You are familiar with the expression of 'warden's boy' aren't you?"

Adams did not respond.

Washington pressed him again. "Have you ever heard the expression of a 'warden's boy'?"

"I don't think so."

"How long have you been at TDC?"

"Twenty years."

"You have never heard of the expression 'warden's boy' in twenty years?"

"Not that I paid any mind to."

". . . You have never heard of a 'major's boy'? You have never heard that expression?"

"No."

Attorneys for the inmates at the *Ruiz* trial had put TDC officials on the spot about calling inmates boys and niggers, and they steadfastly denied that they used such language or ever heard it used, except, of course, by the inmates. One hardline officer, Lon Glenn, who had beaten the inmates back to work in the Father's Day Incident of 1972, testified, "No sir, not only have I not used the term, abusive language is not tolerated within the TDC and is not used by officers therein."[7]

But when Washington asked Adams which other inmates were working that day, Adams couldn't help using the prison vernacular: "a Spanish boy by the name of Silva, Aurelio. I think it is Aurelio Silva, he is a Spanish boy." When Silva testified a few days later, the "boy" turned out to be a man with a well-worn face, aged fifty-two.

The trusties were pretty autonomous, Adams said. He didn't need to tell Brown and Silva to clean the bus that morning. "When the bus is in need of cleaning," he said, "nobody doesn't have to tell them."

Soloman, Duson, and Kelley were assigned to water the vegetables in the hothouse. That had to be done every day. Adams took five of the trusties back to the prison to eat lunch at eleven that morning, but Brown and a bookkeeper stayed out in the farm shops. That wasn't unusual, Adams said.

Then Brown started raving about his furlough and wanting to go back to the building, and started walking that direction, a distance of a little more than a mile.

"I left my hat in the office and I walked over there and got my hat and he walked out in front of the pickup and got in," Adams said.

"And you didn't have to force him into the pickup or anything like that?" asked Washington.

"No," Adams said.

"Was he out of his place with you?" Washington asked.

"He sure was," said Adams. He was out of place with "all of the cussing and carrying on . . ." Brown wasn't cussing him personally, Adams said, but he was being disrespectful and calling him Bill, and that was a first. As they were driving toward the building, Brown kept cussing and demanding to see Moore, only part of the time he called him Billy, Adams said. Adams said that Brown told him during the drive that he had been smoking weed. Brown had never been disrespectful to him, but he did have a temper, Adams said.

Washington pushed Adams to develop his story. Smoking marijuana was against the prison rules, wasn't it? Brown had admitted to a major offense, hadn't he? Brown was pulling on his arm, Adams said. Wasn't that a violation of TDC discipline? Washington asked.

"Maybe he was trying to get my attention," Adams said. "Mr. Moore was my supervisor and any time an inmate wanted to see a superior officer, I always let him talk to him."

They both could see Moore's truck parked on top of the levee. When he called Moore over, Adams said he told him that Brown had been smoking weed and "running his head." "Running his head" didn't mean that he was babbling. It meant he was talking dangerously. He was talking in such a way that he was likely to get his business in a wreck.

Then Washington put Adams on the spot. Hadn't Brown said: "All of the things I have done for you and Major Moore, and I can't get a furlough"?

"He probably said that," Adams replied, "But I didn't tell Mr. Moore that, that I remember. . . . I am sure I didn't tell him that."

Washington wanted to know what Moore called Brown.

"Eroy," Adams said.

"Eroy?"

"Yes."

"He never called him 'boy' or 'nigger'?"

"No."

"'Old thing'?"

"Sure didn't."

"He never called him 'old thing'?"

"Sure didn't."

"You never hear any of those expressions used down there; is that right?"

"Right."

Hinton objected and was overruled.

"Have you ever heard the expression, 'old thing,' used down in the penitentiary unit?" Washington asked.

"Old thing?"

"Yes, sir."

"Probably. Years ago. It hasn't been used in several years that I have heard."

"Who was an old thing?"

Hinton objected again and Dalehite overruled him.

"Well, I heard inmates call other inmates old things," Adams said. "I don't know exactly what they were talking about."

"You never heard an employee call an inmate an old thing?"

"Like I say, that stuff has all changed at TDC."

Moore never called Brown anything but his name, Eroy, Adams said.

As for why Moore and Adams didn't drive Brown straight back to the building and put him in a cell, ". . . Eroy had told us that marijuana was growing at the farm shop and Mr. Moore was going down there to see if he could show where it was at."

Washington asked Adams if he or Moore hit Brown. "We sure didn't," Adams said. "He wasn't hit in my presence."

When Washington asked him about Brown's shoes, Adams didn't have an answer.

"I don't know why he would have them off," Adams said.

Washington pressed him: ". . . you never kicked him on the legs and stomped his feet?"

"I sure didn't," Adams said.

"You never did?"

"I sure didn't."

Adams's written statement, made three days after the deaths, said that Moore told him to go on about his work at the farm shop and that Moore would take Brown back to the building. Not to the farm shop to look for marijuana, but back to the building. Adams admitted that was true.

And he didn't find anything back at the farm shop, did he? Washington asked. "You didn't find any growing?" Washington asked. "You didn't find any little roaches or any evidence of marijuana at all?"

"No sir," Adams said. "I wouldn't know what they was if I seen it."

It was an interesting performance: the middle-aged East Texas farm supervisor who wouldn't know a roach if he saw one, but could get an inmate to confess to smoking pot. He was a farm supervisor who never heard the word "nigger" used in the TDC, nor "warden's boy," nor "major's boy," nor "old thing."

Hinton's next witness was Charles Spivey, a livestock manager who had been working at Ellis for two years and in the prison system for five years. By the time of trial he was a bricklayer in Navasota.[8] Spivey had followed Adams and Brown in his pickup from the farm shop to the reservoir. He told Washington he had assumed Adams was taking Brown to the building for running his head.

He hadn't heard Brown's ranting except for one sentence directed at him. Spivey said when he walked up to the truck where Adams and Brown were sitting to ask Adams a question, Brown leaned across the seat and told him "I haven't stole none of your God damn eggs." Spivey had been concerned that inmates had been stealing eggs from the chicken houses and had been hoping to catch someone in the act.

On an aerial view of the prison, Spivey traced the route he and Adams took on the road at the top of a levee to the reservoir where Moore was fishing. He had backed his truck down the dirt track to a pump house where they could turn around and had followed Moore to the garden house.

Adams got in the truck with Spivey and they drove north to the farm shops and left Moore and Pack to their fates. After Brown testified, on February 22, Hinton called Spivey back to the stand to ask him if he could see through the back window of the pickup whether either Adams or Moore were striking Brown as they drove from the reservoir to the garden shed. He didn't. Nor did he think Adams was a dangerous man or had a reputation for hitting inmates.

Eroy Brown had offered a completely different story.

12

EROY AS AGGRESSOR

The two prison officials who last saw Pack and Moore alive said Brown was agitated. Mike Hinton continued that theme with the inmate witnesses from the garden shed. Hinton promised that the inmates would testify that they saw Brown grow extremely angry, that they heard Brown tell Moore "in no uncertain terms . . . he was tired of all this."

"They will tell you that Major Moore and Eroy Brown got in the back seat of Warden Pack's Department of Corrections green Plymouth Fury; that Warden Pack went to the trunk to get handcuffs that he kept in the trunk, and he shut the trunk and as he was walking around the passenger's side the door flew open and knocked him to the ground. Eroy came out, got the gun from the ground, and shot Warden Pack in the arm. Warden Pack fell down. He went back around and confronted Major Moore, and shot him, screamed at him, got him down and shot him in his head and killed him, and that he then became the aggressor again, and chases Warden Pack down into this area right here," Hinton said, pointing to the scale model of the scene.

Of the three witnesses in the garden shed, James Soloman was the leader. He was forty-seven years old and had spent most of the past thirteen years in prison. He was serving a thirty-year sentence for possession of narcotics, assault, and attempted murder. Hinton asked Soloman if he had been promised anything in return for his testimony and he said no.[1]

Soloman identified the garden shed from which he had watched Brown sig-
naling from inside Moore's truck. "He kept pulling his coat up like this right
here," Soloman said, "and then for a moment, then he would take it down and
take it back up and then bring it down. So, we began to watch to see who it was in
the truck."

Soloman watched Moore get out of the truck and then saw Pack pull up. Soloman positioned the model truck and car on the state's model of the scene.

It was only when Brown got out of the truck and ran back to Pack's car that
Soloman recognized him. Moore grabbed Brown and they started to scuffle.
Hinton tried to lead Soloman: "Was there a time in this period when either Mr.
Moore or Warden Pack were able to get one handcuff on inmate Brown?" Wash-
ington objected and was sustained, and Soloman didn't take the hint.

"Tell the jury if he had anything in his hand at the time when he got around to
the front of the car," Hinton said.

"If anything was on his hand," Soloman said, "it had to be his right hand or
left hand. He had both of them free. He was running."

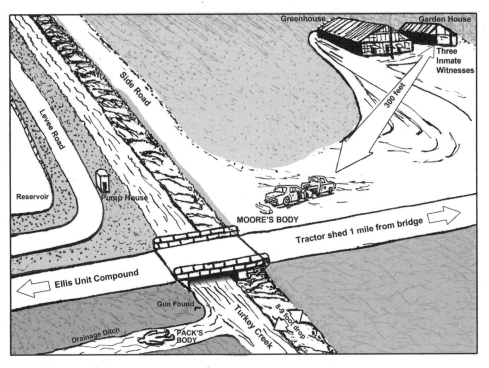

Diagram of crime scene, not to scale.

Hinton brought up the handcuffs later, and all Soloman could say was that they were dangling from Brown's wrist when he got out of the car.

Pack ordered Brown into the car, Soloman said, and he got in and Moore got in with him. Pack was standing by the back door on the passenger side, "and all of a sudden, the door come open on Mr. Pack's side . . . he fell backward, we heard a shot. When we heard a shot, we seen Eroy coming out."

"What happened to Warden Pack, I don't know," Soloman said. "I couldn't see him. He was down when I heard the shot. . . . Then [Brown] stepped out of the car and immediately rushed around the car and wrestled with and grabbed Mr. Moore by the shoulder . . . he grabbed him by the shoulder and took his pistol . . . just like shot the pistol and Mr. Moore fell backward. He grabbed him and pulled him up and said, 'I'm tired of your shit.'"

Hinton asked him again about what Brown said. "I know you don't like to say it in front of the jury."

"He said, 'I'm tired of your shit.'"

"Did he say it one more time?"

"No, he didn't say it no more than one time."

Hinton was hoping for more. He had persuaded Soloman to add the phrase twice to his signed statement.[2]

Hinton asked Soloman what Moore did when the gun was going off.

"He didn't do anything," Soloman said. "In fact when he grabbed hold of him, he came back and shot him again. He fell backward. When he fell backward, Brown, he pulled him up and shot him again. Well, he just dropped him on the ground and Warden Pack got up and started towards the bridge."

Soloman pointed out on the model where Pack ran, with Brown coming after him. The two men tussled and fell down the bank. That's when he ran to the telephone.

". . . I told them, 'This is Soloman. You all get somebody down here right away. There is a killing going on down here. There has been a killing.'"

Soloman described how he helped the assistant warden, James Williamson, handcuff Brown, who was trying to get away. Soloman said that when Brown came up from the creek, he said, "'You missed the whole goddamn show.'"[3]

With the first day's testimony ended, Dalehite instructed the jury to not read the newspaper accounts or watch the television stories that day. The trial was being covered intensively. Texas cities still had competing newspapers at that time. Reporters from the *Dallas Times Herald* and the *Dallas Morning News* were present, along with reporters from the *Houston Post*, the *Houston Chronicle*, the *Fort Worth Star-Telegram*, and half a dozen or more television and radio stations.

The next morning Soloman described finding Pack.

"He was face down," Soloman said, "and you could only just see the back part of him. You couldn't see his side or nothing like that. It was mashed all the way down into the gulley. . . . He was completely wet all over."

It took three men to pull him from the mud, he said.

As for the bottoms, Soloman said, except for a six-month release, he had been in the TDC since 1969 and the bottoms was just a place where the fields were. There was nothing unusual about the bottoms. It meant "no more than work."

Levi Duson followed Soloman. He was thirty-nine years old and serving ten years for burglary. After more than a dozen arrests as a youth in Midland, he had been sent to the Bexar County School for Boys as a truant and a runaway. His father had died when he was young, and he was smoking pot by the time he was sixteen, was addicted to heroin at twenty-six, and was busted for the sale of heroin at thirty-one. He arrived at Ellis in August 1979 after his parole was revoked.

Page 2

door. Warden Pack turned around and went to meet Brown and I heard
Warden Pack say "I told you to get in the car". At this time Brown
turned around and went back the way he had come and I saw Mjr. Moore
backing up as if to let Brown into the car. Brown then ducked as
if to get into the car *and he did get in the back seat of the car.*
~~but I don't know if he did or not.~~ Shortly
thereafter I saw the Warden's head and then shots rang out and I
saw the Warden fall. Brown's head then appeared about where the
Warden had fallen which was on or close to the passenger side rear
tire. Brown then came around the back and met Mjr. Moore on the
driver's side rear of the car. They both grabbed each other and
turned around and then I watched Brown shoot Mjr. Moore with a
throwing motion as if he was throwing the bullets when he fired.
I also heard Inmate Brown say I am tired of you Shit.
After Mjr. Moore fell the Warden got up and came around to the back
and Brown and the Warden started scuffling and they went over the
embankment by the bridge, I think there was another shot fired at
this time. I then ran to the office and called the Ellis Unit and
told him Mjr. Moore had been shot and needed help. I waited until

---

James Soloman's revisions to his signed statement, made in November 1981, two months before the first trial.

Like Soloman, Duson testified that Moore had placed Brown inside the back seat on the driver's side. Brown got out on the passenger's side and shot Pack. He came to the driver's side of the car, where the inmates could see him, and scuffled with Moore. Duson swore he saw Brown shoot Moore while Moore was down on his knees, though he was inconsistent about how many times Brown shot at him. Washington reserved the right to cross-examine Soloman and Duson after the prosecution rested its case.[4]

After Hinton put on his two eyewitnesses, there was not much more to prove. Robert DeYoung was a cocky, twenty-three-year-old guard who had come to Texas from Rockville, Maryland, after graduating from high school. He had gone straight to work for the TDC when he was eighteen. DeYoung had worked at Ellis a year and a half and was in charge of the records of its fixed assets, including the farm equipment. He had issued Pack his handgun. Not long after the deaths of Pack and Moore, DeYoung was promoted from correctional officer to lieutenant, skipping the promotion to sergeant altogether, and sent to the Coffield prison near Palestine.[5]

He was a friend of Billy Moore. He knew Moore's wife, Lola, who worked in the prison mailroom, and his stepson Ricky, who had also worked at Ellis. They were like family to him. He had arrived on the scene in the ambulance and crept to the rear of Pack's car. When he described finding Billy Moore's body, he wept.

"When I got out of the ambulance, I noticed the bullet hole, and I didn't know where they were shooting from. I got real scared and I got down. I got down low and I tried to get to where Billy was. I called to Billy and he didn't respond.

"I got closer to him and I tried to feel a pulse around his neck while I was talking to him. He didn't respond to me. I couldn't find a pulse."[6]

He described Brown as difficult to control, and said that he was constantly trying to get up from the ground, where he lay on his stomach, his hands cuffed behind him. Hinton walked DeYoung through the procedure of shutting down the cell blocks when he took Brown into the prison.

"When I say they cleared the hallways," DeYoung said, "that means that they shut the riot gates. . . . When they shut the riot gates, that immediately stops all inmate movement in the building, the whole building is locked down or secured, and at that time the officers working the cell blocks shake down inmates and send them back into their tanks to clear the hallways.

"The purpose was that there might be a possibility that if perchance an inmate knew what happened, inmate Brown would have been retaliated against."

"Not by guards, but by other inmates?" asked Hinton.

"Yes, sir, other inmates," DeYoung said. "Warden Pack had a very high reputation among the inmates."[7]

Habern grabbed Washington's knee under the defense table and Washington broke into a broad grin. DeYoung had blundered. Hinton had been filing motions to suppress testimony about Pack's reputation, but now his own witness had put the question into evidence. He had even used the word "reputation."

Next came the two Walker County sheriff's department investigators, Rick Berger and Dale Meyers. Berger had taken many of the photographs of the scene, particularly those that had traced the blood trail from Pack's car to the bridge and the creek. Berger testified that the blood spots on the bridge appeared to be human blood, but Washington asked him if it couldn't have been animal blood, and Berger admitted he couldn't tell the difference.

He could say something about blood drops, though, and Washington took him through an explanation. A tear-shaped blood spot could indicate the direction in which a person was walking. A drop with radiating petals like a flower indicated the person was not moving when the drop fell. A bloody palm print had been found on the concrete bridge support, indicating that a person might have been holding onto the structure for support. The trail seemed to indicate that a bleeding man, probably Pack, had gone down the creek bank and paused under the bridge.

Washington walked Berger through the crime scene photos. One detail in particular was important. The radio aerial on the back of Pack's car was broken. It was on the passenger's side, indicating that a scuffle had taken place there. Berger had taken photographs of the scene with all the doors on Pack's car closed and others with the front passenger's door open. The glove box was open. It seemed logical that someone had opened the front door on the passenger's side and gotten something out of the glove box. Was it the gun or the handcuffs? The state's witness, James Williamson, had testified that the usual procedure for a warden with a gun was to leave it with the picket or, if he drove inside the farm, to secure it in his trunk.

The prosecution's story required that Pack had ignored his usual procedure and put his gun in the glove box that morning instead of the trunk, and then ordered Brown inside the car, where he could grab it. Pack then went to the trunk to get his handcuffs, and walked around the car with them. Brown threw open the back door and came out shooting. But how did Pack's cuffs come to be clamped on Brown's left wrist? Neither Soloman nor Duson could say when or how Brown had been handcuffed.

The bodies of Pack and Moore had been sent to Joseph Jachimczyk, who had been the Harris County medical examiner since 1960. Jachimczyk was both a medical doctor and a lawyer, and a legend in Houston. Prosecutors and defense attorneys alike respected his professionalism. After he retired, the Harris County forensic center was named for him.

But Jachimczyk was not immune to making mistakes. In 1979, he declared the death of a wealthy River Oaks woman, Diana Wanstrath, and her husband and son to be a murder-suicide, although no gun was found at the scene. A dogged Houston detective, Johnny Bonds, ignored Jachimczyk's autopsy report and determined that all three were murdered by two gunmen hired by Wanstrath's brother, who stood to gain a considerable inheritance from their deaths.

There weren't any mysteries about what had killed Pack and Moore. Jachimczyk had done the autopsies himself. Pack had been drowned. Jachimczyk observed that Pack suffered from emphysema from chronic smoking, and he had a cancerous tumor on his right kidney. Moore had been shot once in the head. Jachimczyk had extracted the bullet.

Hinton wanted the jury to see every detail of the autopsies and began walking Jachimczyk through two dozen autopsy photographs. Some of them depicted the bruises and abrasions on the two men, indications of the struggles they had been in. Jachimczyk had detected wounds from a bullet that had entered Pack's arm near the elbow and had grazed the webbing between his fingers.

Washington took Jachimczyk on *voir dire* out of the presence of the jury, to argue before the judge whether Hinton needed all the autopsy photographs to show the causes of death. Hinton offered to withdraw a couple but pressed Washington to get on with it.

"Judge," Hinton said, "could we come to a point in time where objections can be made and let this Court rule? We will be here all day long. I wish he would hurry up with his *voir dire*."

"I won't ask him any more questions, then, Judge," Washington said. "Your Honor, I came down here to try a lawsuit and I am doing the best I can. I am not paid by somebody's family to try this lawsuit. If it takes a year to try this lawsuit, I have the responsibility to do the best I can to represent this man. I think I have gotten along with the Court, and I apologize, but Mr. Hinton, when it comes to justice, what is time?

". . . I object to all of them because they are inflammatory," Washington said. "They are not relative to any issue in fact in the case as far as the cause of death. All of these photographs of Mr. Moore, we are not trying his case here today. They are just an attempt to get a verdict of guilty. They are not based upon any evidence because they don't have a case. They don't have a case. All they have is these photographs."

The pictures were indeed inflammatory. In the course of the autopsy, Jachimczyk had to peel the skin back from Moore's face. Hinton wanted the jury to see that photograph.

Washington removed his glasses and approached the bench. He was exhausted and angry. Eroy Brown murmured, "That's all right, Craig."

"I am just trying to do my job, Judge," Washington said, sobbing. "All I want to do is my job. I am just trying to do my job."[8]

Dalehite called a recess. He let in more photos of the autopsies than Washington wanted.

Washington stayed up most of the night mastering the details of wound forensics, and the next day led Jachimczyk through the details of the powder burns, splattering, and stippling that a gun made when it was fired at close range. Soloman and Duson had both said that Moore was shot from a distance of a foot or so. The stippling effects of a gunshot on the body from four feet, three feet, two feet, and contact with the barrel were all different and could be detected by a forensic pathologist.

Jachimczyk declared in his report that there was no stippling or splattering. Stippling occurs when the muzzle of the gun is about two feet away and unburned gunpowder punctures the skin. If the inmate witnesses were right, Moore's wound should have shown stippling.

Washington asked Jachimczyk, "If I were holding a man by the collar and I had a gun out in this fashion, do you think if I shot at him, do you think you would expect to find any stippling?"

"Very definitely," Jachimczyk said.[9]

Jachimczyk had offered a theory to Hinton that Moore's thick hair had absorbed blood and gunpowder residue. Hinton loved asking questions beginning with the phrase "I will."

". . . I will ask you," Hinton said, "whether or not your findings would be consistent with a gun being fired from twelve, fourteen, fourteen to twenty-six inches with someone kneeling on the ground looking up?"

"Yes, sir," Jachimczyk replied.[10]

Brown wasn't being tried for shooting Moore but for drowning Pack, but Hinton wanted Jachimczyk to confirm what the inmates said, that Brown deliberately shot Moore at close range after beating him with the pistol. Jachimczyk identified several abrasions on Moore's body: one on each knee, another two over each eyebrow. He had found bruises on Pack's knees consistent with the theory that he had bumped them against hard objects in a struggle in the creek. Both of the men had been in a struggle the day they died. There would be no argument about that from either side.

Next came the question about whether Brown had fired the gun. The gun had been sent to an FBI fingerprint lab in Washington, but it was so contaminated with mud and water that only eight identifiable prints were found, and none of them belonged to Pack, Moore, or Brown.[11]

A Houston FBI agent had swabbed Brown's hands the day of the deaths and sent the samples to an expert named William D. Kinard from the Alcohol, Tobacco, and Firearms Division of the Treasury Department, who performed a Sirchie test. The test indicated that Brown's hands had been on a gun that was fired. The analysis involved finding trace elements of barium and antinomy on a person's hands, which indicated that he had held a gun when it was fired. Washington bantered with the agent about the nature of atomic absorption tests.

"It is a procedure by which scientifically every atomic substance has certain characteristics and you project a light through a known substance on this end . . . and the unknown light is absorbed by the known light; is that correct?"

"Your theory is roughly correct, sir," Kinard said.

"I have to use very simple terms," Washington said. "I am just a humble Texas lawyer."

"I should object," Hinton said.[12]

Washington threw out a couple of possibilities about the gun. One was that since there is barium in automotive grease, was it possible that barium and antinomy had got on Eroy's hands from working in the farm shop? Kinard didn't think that was likely, because the amounts on his hands were consistent with what is found on the hands of people who fire guns. But the test didn't prove that Eroy had fired the gun himself, only that his hand was on the gun when it was fired. Such a test would have picked up the metals on the hands of Pack and Moore, Kinard admitted, if their hands had been tested.

Washington pressed the FBI agent, Ronald Loftin, who had swabbed Brown's hands for the gunshot residue test.

"Did you do one on Warden Pack's hands?" he asked.

"No, sir."

"Did you do one on Major Moore's hands?"

"No, sir."

"The only person that you did one on was Eroy Brown?"

"Yes, sir."[13]

On Thursday, February 5, the prosecution rested. It had taken Hinton four days and thirteen witnesses to put on his case. Crazed by marijuana and the sexual frustration of living in prison, Brown had tried to break out that day. Hinton planted the theory when he asked Bill Adams one last question: Had Brown said anything about Waco that day?

"Well," Adams said, "he mentioned me and him going to Waco. He was just acting crazy—you know—I didn't pay him that much mind. I knew we weren't going to Waco. I didn't think we was going, at least."

That was the prosecution's story: Eroy Brown was trying to escape. After shooting the farm major and drowning the warden, he was going to drive out of Ellis prison and get back to Waco.

13

THE DEFENSE IS SELF-DEFENSE

The trial was boiling down to whether the jury would believe the state's inmate witnesses. In his opening argument, Hinton had said of Soloman and Duson, "We vouch for these gentlemen's credibility. They are convicts. They were convicts. They will be convicts."

Four days after they were interviewed, Soloman and Duson signed typed statements of what they had seen and heard. In November Hinton met with them to correct their sworn statements. Hinton had tried to head off the issue in his direct examination, but Washington pursued Soloman and Duson about the changes. Duson originally said Brown shot once at Moore and two or three times at Pack. Then he changed it to once at Pack and two or three times at Moore. That conformed with Soloman's account, but Duson couldn't keep his story straight when Washington made him go over it.

Duson testified, "At the time I was confused and under a lot of pressure. I think my memory was better nine months later than it was four days afterward."[1]

Washington asked Duson if he had once said that his testimony was his ticket out of the TDC. Duson said, "Yes, I did." Hinton objected loudly, saying Washington did not ask the question in good faith. Washington declared that he would shove that good faith down Hinton's throat. The judge had to call them to the bench and calm them down.[2]

Soloman, too, testified that he was in a better frame of mind during the trial than when he gave his original statement. He told Washington that he had been extremely upset when he gave his statement on April 4. He suffered a heart condition for which he took medication, but now he was feeling "fair." He admitted that his April 4 statement said that he could not see if Brown got into the car. With Hinton's help, he changed it to say that Brown did get into the car. That conformed with Duson's original statement.

Washington put the pistol in Soloman's hand and asked him to show how Brown had beaten Moore on the head with it and declared, "I'm tired of your shit." Washington wanted to know exactly how close Brown had the gun to Moore when he shot him.

"You take the gun," Washington said.

"No," Soloman said, "I don't want nothing to do with that."

"Would it be like this?" Washington said. "Let me be Brown. Would it be about like this or like that?"

"In a sense yes, in a sense no."

"Tell me how in a sense, yes," Washington insisted, "and how in a sense, no?"

"I will leave it open," Soloman said, and began weeping.

From the defense table Brown burst out: "He is telling the truth. He is telling the truth."

"Mr. Brown, Eroy," Washington said. "Don't say anything. Be quiet."[3]

Perhaps Soloman felt guilty at that moment. He was trying to help the state execute Eroy Brown, and Washington had put him on the spot one time too many. The court recessed for lunch.

After lunch, Washington grilled Soloman about another change in his signed statement. In their original statements, Soloman and Duson both said that Brown had come up from the ditch and told assistant warden Williamson,[4] "I" missed the show, not "you." If Brown said, "You missed the whole God damn show," he meant that they had missed a show that Brown had put on: the wanton killing of two men. But if he said, "I missed the whole God damn show," he meant something radically different. Eroy Brown had missed the show that Pack and Moore were putting on. He had missed being taken to the bottoms and beaten or killed.

The distinctions were lost on Soloman. Washington got him to admit that Brown had said *I* "missed the show," not *you*. Washington wanted to know why he had changed his mind in the months that had passed.

"It is not a question that I have, since I have had time to think about it," Soloman replied. "Just what you say is that I didn't fully understand that right there. Then, it would have been corrected at the time if I had understood that there was a mistake there."[5] It was corrected when Hinton came to talk to him, he said.

Washington asked Soloman whether, like Duson, he had a ticket out of prison, too. Soloman said he did, but it had nothing to do with his testimony. He was eligible for parole; it was just a matter of whether the parole board would let him out.

Eroy Brown and Craig Washington during the trial. Photo by Alan Pogue.

The timing of the cross-examination was perfect. Having created doubt in the jury's mind about the two eyewitnesses, Washington would follow up with the defendant. It would be Soloman's and Duson's stories against Eroy Brown's.

At the end of his opening argument, Hinton had described what his thirteen witnesses would say.

"With that, we will rest," he concluded. "As you know, the defendant doesn't have to testify." Washington objected to that comment and the judge sustained him.

There was something in the way that Hinton taunted the defense that would come back to haunt him. Of all the people at the scene that day, Eroy Brown knew best what had happened.

Five days after the trial started, Washington laid out his theory of the case. It had nothing to do with a violent inmate trying to escape and everything to do with a convict who was being put in his place. Eroy Brown was in fear of being thrown in the river because he had threatened to expose the thefts of "Master Moore," Washington told the jury. "The defense," he said, "is self-defense."[6]

"I think the evidence will show that Moore and Adams were stealing tires," Washington said. "Eroy mounted tires on free-world vehicles."

"Eroy was complaining about his failure to obtain a furlough. He thought he had worked harder than anyone else and he [Moore] wouldn't go to bat for him."

"Adams misconstrued a remark made by Eroy," Washington said, and "he took it as a threat to snitch on them."

Pack's response, Washington said, was threatening: "We'll see if you can talk at the bottom of the Trinity River . . ."[7]

Then Washington put Eroy Brown on the stand.

14

EROY'S STORY

Eroy Brown's testimony is preserved in the record of two trials, in February and November 1982. The story that follows has been drawn exclusively from his testimony. Some minor details, such as how to build a fish trap, appeared in the second trial but not the first, and have been added in the interests of narrative economy.

We caught out the back gate at six-thirty that morning. I drove the trusty bus. There were nine, ten, maybe eleven trusties. I dropped off Kelley, Duson, and Soloman at the garden shed and drove the bus to the farm shop. It was cloudy that morning but it hadn't rained yet. The tractor drivers went out to the fields.

When I was a Class Two trusty, I worked as a tractor driver for sixteen, seventeen months. When I became Class Three trusty I was promoted to the tire man in the tire shop, fixing flats on tractors and state-owned vehicles. I would keep up on the consumption of fuel and anhydrous ammonia and the tubes and tires. I would distribute the anhydrous ammonia to the tractors and the transport tanks. I would keep a day-to-day sheet, a fuel consumption sheet that listed the tractor number and the items used. I would turn it over to the bookkeeper and in turn he would put the actual price to it and charge it to that vehicle in the Ellis front office.

On Saturdays, most of my job would be to catch up on the Caldwell cutters or anything that I couldn't get to during the weekday, an implement that had flats. I would catch up and fix everything up for the next beginning of the week, clean up the office, wash down the slab where the tractor drives in to get the tires changed. If somebody had a flat in the parking lot I would fix it. I would be on call for the dairy-barn tractors. They work seven days a week.

Mr. Moore would have some of his friends come by like the wildlife man and the game warden, and they come over there and when they needed tires and tubes, they would tell me to fix them up. If they wanted a size fifteen-inch tire and a tube, they would tell me to give it to him and write it off on the Caldwell cutter.

The Caldwell cutter is used to mow grass. Some people call them bush hogs. They don't have motors. They turn by the power take-off shaft that is hooked into the tractor. We had four of them at the Ellis Unit. Each one uses four tires at a time. The tires are fourteen- and fifteen-inch tires.

One time I put a tire on a state-owned vehicle. It was a game warden. I did put some on free-world vehicles. I put them on Mr. Moore's vehicle, for his private free-world truck and his car. Christmas morning of '80 I put one on the right rear of his wife's car, a blue Grand Marquis.

I filled butane bottles up. I would give them back to Mr. Moore and sometimes he had people come in and he would just point them or send them to me. Most of them were TDC employees. Some were not. The bottles didn't have TDC numbers. They were free-world bottles.

I would help Mr. Adams get his afternoon money, his drinking money. I put tires and tubes that belonged to TDC in the back of his truck and in the back of his station wagon. I did that many times. I ain't never seen him drink on the job. I did smell alcohol on his breath that day.

The only supervisor that morning was Mr. Adams. He would leave and come back. He isn't the type to sit down and come in. He would go back towards the hill and come back down and check on the tractors in the field. He would leave and come and go.

Around nine-thirty or ten it started raining and the two tractor drivers came in, and they washed the mud down off the tractors and parked them under the shed. After the rain Mr. Adams came into the tractor shed and he told us if we all got our work caught up and ready to go we could go back to the building. I told Mr. Adams I wanted to stay out and cook these two pieces of frozen fish that I had in the refrigerator in the storage room. I had caught them in a fish trap down on the river on Thursday. A fish trap is a screen box. You just bait it, put you a funnel off in there, the fish go in and get trapped in there and can't come out.

Mr. Adams took some of the other inmates in the truck back up the hill. I stayed at the tractor shed with Inmates Pugh and Silva. I fixed some potatoes and cooked my fish. I got potatoes from the garden shed. I had Soloman when he come down through there drop me a half a sack. I cooked it in an electric skillet I found in the dump and rebuilt. I had some hog lard that I got from Soloman that morning, just a little piece in a bucket. I got some corn from the hog barn from Boss Adams. I grind it up and use it on the fish. Inmate Pugh and Inmate Silva and I ate the fish and the french fries.

After lunch there was a lot of trash that needed to be dumped. I made an agreement with Inmate Pugh that if he hooked the tractor up to the cart to take it up to the dump, that I would sweep the bus out and get the shop straightened for Monday morning. Inmate Pugh went to the dump with the cart and I got the bus and pulled it up to the front of my place and opened the doors and let down all of the windows and got the air hose and started in. It was an old International, white with two back doors, and had TDC on the side. I had the air hose blowing the trash out of the bus.

Silva came by from the mechanic's shop and Inmate Silva was jiving and high-signing. That is the way him and I do. Jiving and high-signing means kidding around, playing. Just joking. Me and him were joking at each other.

He said, "Oh, Brown, I see you cleaning up the bus." I would say, "Yeah, I am cleaning out the bus. Man, it don't look like nothing. Everybody else is getting a furlough and me, I am cleaning the bus out. You know, if I ain't going to do it, it will get all over somebody. Somebody will get all over me there."

Silva says, "All right. All right. I don't get no furlough either. I ain't got none, either."

I said, "It's a shame, man, you know, that a man has to be doing all of these three different jobs and putting out this poison and man, this is dangerous, and a man can't get a furlough."

Then I see Mr. Bill, standing on the corner of the entrance door to the mechanic's shop. After I seen him, I kept talking and come out of the bus and he just stood there and looked at me. I was saying that if the place ain't cleaned up, the boss will be swollen mad. Silva, he slacked up talking and dropped his head. I kept on talking.

"Man," I said, "you know how it is. Here is old Brown down here for a long time and he is working on all of this equipment and these tires in this shop."

This time Mr. Bill called me. "Old Brown," he said, "you are doing all this head running. What's that all about?"

"Well, Mr. Bill," I said, "you know how it is."

"Bring your ass here," he said. So I walked up there toward him and when I got up there to him, he said, "What's all this goddamn head running about, Eroy?"

He said that he overheard my conversation between me and Silva.

I said, "I work around here and I can't get a furlough."

He told me, "Well, just shut your mouth up there."

I said, "You know it ain't right, Mr. Bill."

He said, "Well, you and your head running is going to get yourself into a wreck."

I said, "Mr. Bill, you know it ain't right. I had been home three days and it has been a year elapsed, and now, you know, I should get a furlough after all the work I do down here. All I done here for you and Mr. Moore and I can't have no furlough."

Mr. Adams looked at both me and Pugh and then he told me to come into the front side of the shop. Me and him walked through and he said, "What do you mean running your head about what you had done for me and Mr. Moore? What's wrong with you? You've done been into something."

I said, "I ain't been into nothing. All I was talking about was I ain't had no furlough."

He said, "You're going to get up here and see Billy Moore and you just tell Billy Moore what you told me."

I said, "Yes, sir, I am getting in the truck. I didn't mean no harm. I am trying to explain to you. I wanted a furlough."

He said, "Get your ass into that truck."

So I got in the truck.

Mr. Adams asked an inmate did Billy Moore come by here, and he said, "No, he is still up at the fishing pond."

He swung the truck out and got back on the main road. I kept talking to him. We were by the garden field where the onion plants were and I said, "Mr. Bill, I didn't mean no harm. I didn't mean no harm. It just slipped."

He said, "What do you mean slipped? You don't know nothing. Something is wrong with you."

I said, "There ain't nothing wrong with me. Mr. Bill, I just wanted a furlough."

"You done had something," he said. "You shut up."

I said, "I ain't had nothing, Mr. Bill." He backhanded me in the mouth and he said, "Shut up." And I shut up.

We drove on up the blacktop and he seen the truck sitting on top of the levee and we drove on down by the levee and passed that little pump house. I seen Killer and another dude, Spoon, sitting there fishing. And the white dog boy. I seen Mr. Moore out there in a boat. We drove up on the little road on the top of the levee and Mr. Adams hit the horn and stuck out his hand and beckoned for Mr. Moore to come to the bank. Mr. Moore rowed in the boat, and walked up the bank to the back of the truck and talked to Mr. Adams.

I could hear Mr. Bill saying, "Mr. Moore, Nigger Brown down there is running his head. He is down there and he hollered about all what he had done for us. He must have been down there smoking some of that shit."

Mr. Moore come on over to the truck and got in the driver's side and he didn't say nothing then. He just kind of beckoned for the dude in the boat to go back fishing so the man in the boat just went back off the bank and went on, I guess, fishing. Mr. Moore told Mr. Bill to go around and get in on the other side, and that put me in the middle.

So he backed the truck up on the levee and got to the turnaround and Mr. Moore said, "Nigger, what have you done been into down there running your head and talking about what you done for me and what you done for Mr. Adams? What is wrong with you, nigger? Have you gone crazy? You've done been on something. You probably been down there smoking some shit. You don't usually act that way."

I said, "Mr. Moore, I wasn't doing nothing. I was talking to Mr. Silva and Mr. Bill called me over. I didn't know Pugh and them were standing up there. I ain't never tried to tell nothing on nobody."

"Well, you've done been smoking something. I know that shit is in here. The boy that drives that dump truck, him and that Mexican got some of that shit in here. I know."

I said, "Mr. Moore, I ain't done nothing."

He said, "You've been doing something, nigger. You been into something, goddamn it. You tell me before we get back here. You tell me."

I said, "There ain't nothing to tell you. All I wanted was a furlough."

Mr. Moore said, "I know y'all been into something."

Some liquor got stolen at the park. It's about a mile and half back down on the road to the river side on the Ellis farm. The park is for the officers to go fishing and have parties and bring their families and drink. And sometimes the trusties go over and clean up. And somebody had taken some liquor in a dump truck. I told him I didn't know nothing about that.

We had got past the dog boy, who was fishing on the side of the pond and I was saying I didn't mean no harm and Mr. Moore hauled off and hit me. Then he hit me again right across the eye and told me to shut up. I shut up.

So we pulled on out from the levee and turned left on the main road, toward the bottoms. Mr. Moore was just idling, just creeping along and they started hitting me. Mr. Adams was hitting me in the side and stomping all over my foot with his boots. Just before we got to the bridge we come to a stop.

Mr. Moore said "What you done been into?"

I said, "Mr. Moore, I ain't been into nothing. I keep telling you."

"You're lying, nigger. You're lying."

They started hitting me all in the side of my neck and in my back.

Mr. Adams said, "Get your ass off your shoes. Get off your shoes."

I went down. I was going to get off my shoes and Major Moore said, "You're going to tell me, nigger, you're going to tell me."

Mr. Adams said, "I said get off them shoes. I said get off them shoes."

I had on high-top Hush Puppies. I was going to get off my shoes, and Major Moore hit me in the side. Mr. Adams was just stomping on my feet. I was trying to get one shoe off, and he was stomping and kicking me with his boots. I got one of them off. Mr. Adams helped me take the other one off. He got on my foot. He got down there and started kicking on me so the other one just fell off. I didn't have on any socks.

Mr. Moore pulled on down a little further to the bridge, and he asked Mr. Adams, "Where did you say Warden Pack went?" He said, "He went toward the hill." So Mr. Moore got on the microphone and I heard him say, "Tell Warden Pack to meet me at the garden shed. Meet me on the main turn road going past the garden shed."

We got almost to the garden shed and Mr. Adams looked out the window and said, "Here comes Warden Pack, coming down the hill." I could look through the middle mirror and I could see him behind us. So Major Moore pulled over and got out on his side and Mr. Adams got out on his side. I started to get out. I wanted to have a right to tell the warden my side of the story.

Mr. Moore said, "Keep your ass in there. Sit your ass down." I got back in the truck.

Mr. Moore walked to the back end of the truck and threw both hands up like he was telling him to stop and Mr. Pack stopped just across the bridge. I was looking at him there in the rearview mirror. Mr. Bill and Major Moore and Warden Pack were talking in front of the car and I looked. Then Mr. Adams left. I don't know how he left. When Mr. Adams left I started concentrating on something else.

Kelley was standing outside the door at the garden shed, peeping out the screen door looking at the car and the truck. I seen Duson or Soloman, one of them, peeking their head out the door. Kelley was making a gesture. He was waving. He meant, "What's the deal, what's happening?"

Mr. Adams's coat was lying there in the front of the seat. I took the coat and started doing this here, waving it up and down. I was trying to tell Kelley I was in trouble. I could tell he was talking to somebody, kept turning around going back in the door. I could hear voices. I could see shadows going across there. I sat there for a few more minutes. Mr. Moore and Mr. Pack were talking at the back end of the car. I was waving the coat up there. I imagine he seen me. I don't know right to this day if he seen me.

Right after I put the coat down, he called to me, "Bring your ass over here. Bring your ass over here, nigger."

I got out of the truck and started walking back toward that way. I didn't put my shoes on. By the time I got to the hood of Warden Pack's car, Major Moore met me right there. I was trying to talk to Warden Pack over Major Moore's shoulder when I got to the front of the car. I said, "Warden Pack, can I talk to you? Can I talk to you, Warden?" Mr. Pack didn't say nothing.

Major Moore said, "Shut your ass up. Ain't nobody asked you nothing. Shut your ass up."

Mr. Moore grabbed me by the shoulder and took me around the back to the passenger side of the car. I told Warden Pack, "I ain't did nothing. I ain't did nothing wrong."

Warden Pack told me, "Shut up, boy, shut up. Just shut up."

Mr. Moore he pushed me around to the side of the car, and said, "Get your ass up here, nigger. Get your ass up here against this car. You get your nigger ass right up here against this car."

I put my hands on the car spread-eagle like, with my arms on top of the car. Then he kicked me outward. I kept on leaning, looking back toward the trunk of the car.

Warden Pack was going off to the trunk. I said, "Warden, can I talk to you?" He said nothing. "This is a misunderstanding. I ain't did nothing wrong. All I want was a furlough."

Warden Pack said, "You done got your ass in a wreck now."

I had talked almost in a monotone, kind of low. Then I changed my tone of voice. I started talking loud so I could make Kelley and them hear what was going on. "You can't do me any kind of way. People will come down and see about me."

Mr. Moore said, "Nigger, you ain't going to be able to tell a goddamn thing on me. You ain't going to tell shit on me."

I was just trying to get my point over. I said, "My people care something about me. They are going to talk to the Justice Department. You can't do this to me. You all can't jump on me. I have people and they will come and they will check and try to do something. You can't do that to me and get away with it."

Warden Pack was at the back by the trunk. He let the trunk down and he come around and he had this pistol in his hand and he slapped it up. He closed the cylinder up. He said, "Billy, get the handcuffs out of the glove box."

Mr. Moore was keeping me up against the car and he opened the front door and he hit the button on the glove box and he got the handcuffs out of there. He took my left hand and snapped the cuff on.

Mr. Moore said, "Nigger, you ain't going to be able to tell no one what goes on here. We still do away with niggers like you down here."

He backhanded me and he had me leaning up against the car and was pushing me against the car. I started talking loud again. I started telling him that my people would call the Justice Department. There were people who cared about me and I would tell the Justice Department or someone would tell the Justice Department.

Mr. Pack come up to my left side and then he sticks the gun up to my head, right up to my temple. Mr. Moore done got one handcuff on me right there. And he was fixing to get the other one on.

I looked at him and I said, "Well, somebody is going to tell somebody about what is going on here. It ain't nobody going to do away with me."

Then he cocked it. He cocked the gun.

He said, "I told you to shut your ass up, boy. I will splatter your brains all over this street right here."

I was scared. They were talking about taking me down there and drowning me in the bottoms. The bottoms is a place where they take you over the levees and mess you off.

My understanding about the bottoms came back, way back in 1968. It is where they take inmates and jump on them and beat them out of the presence of other inmates where nobody can see. It could be the Ferguson Unit, the Ellis Unit, the Wynne farm. It is any secluded area where guards take inmates and beat them, whip on them, and if they don't take that whipping, then they kill them. Each unit has a bottoms. Every inmate knows what the bottoms mean. They know it is a place where they take inmates and beat them.

I used to clean Major Moore's truck out every day. I would see him take people towards the bottoms. There would be blood on the back of the truck, which he would tell me to clean off.

There has been a couple of times that he told me, "I have been a cold man, a chilly man. In my red-heifer days, I would take one inmate to the bottoms myself. I don't need two or three men with me."

I heard that he took some boy over there to the bottoms and he died. Some people say that he killed him. I think the boy's name was Baxter from the Eastham Unit.

Warden Pack hadn't been there two weeks. I heard he liked to put his handcuffs on people and chain them against the bars and torture them. He liked to torture people. This was on the Wynne farm. I heard that he liked to pull his pistol on people.

If he hadn't cocked the gun I might have thought that he was just trying to scare me, I might not have done anything. I thought he was going to kill me.

I tried to lean back get out of range of the gun. He had the gun sticking in my face. I tried to lean back but Mr. Moore pushed me back up against the car. I turned around and I took my other hand, my right hand, and knocked the gun down and it went off. The bullet went straight down and hit my right foot. All three of us jumped from the impact of the sound of the gun.

Mr. Moore was pulling on this one handcuff and Warden Pack, he was trying to come again with the pistol in his hand. I took my hand and knocked it to the side that time. It went off, still in his hand. Major Moore was behind me. He was trying to put the handcuff on my hand. When the gun went off, he let go of my arm and he just held the handcuff.

Warden Pack was fixing to try to bring the gun back up again and I grabbed hold on it. I finally got hold of the barrel and continued to bend and we both had a hold of it and I twisted it out of his hand and the gun fell to the ground between me and Warden Pack. Then we both grabbed at it. Warden Pack starts grabbing after the gun, reaching with both hands. The major was pulling on the handcuff and he was trying to pull me back. I was batting at Warden Pack's hands. We were reaching for the gun and after two or three minutes I finally got hold of it and I spun around and pointed it toward Major Moore.

I kept backing and I told them, "Don't come at me. You ain't taking me to no bottoms. You ain't going to drown me in no bottom."

I lost my balance and I fell. I scoot down and both of them dived at me. Major Moore had a piece of the handle of the gun, Warden Pack had a hand on the gun, and my hand was on the gun too. They dives at me and I am scooting back and the gun went off, bam, bam.

The gun went off twice and Major Moore fell back this way, which is the way he fell back towards the car. Warden Pack backed off and run towards the fence on the bridge. Then I didn't see him no more. I just sat down. I had the gun sitting on my right-hand side. I pulled my britches leg up and was trying to look at my foot. My foot was hurting and my leg was hurting all up and down my leg where the bullet went into my foot. I tried to stand up and I walked over toward the end of the bridge. I couldn't stand up very good, and hopped around and looked on the side of the bridge. I couldn't see him. I called him and I said, "Warden Pack, Mr. Moore is shot up here. I am shot. Please get us to the building."

He hollered back, "Nigger, you are going to get to the building all right."

I sat back down because my leg was hurting all the way up to my thigh. I sat there for a few minutes and I hollered down there again and he didn't say nothing. I kept sitting there about two or three minutes and I seen him come right up the side of the bridge and when he come up the pistol was laying right on the ground. He reached for it with both hands, and I reached for it and I don't have to go too far to get it and I beat him to it. I turned the pistol in the air, and we started tussling around and I couldn't keep my balance with my right foot and I fell back. When I fell back, me and him started rolling down, tumbling down the hill. While we was tussling, the gun goes off. I took the gun and I tried to throw it. I didn't want to give him the pistol. I wouldn't give him no pistol. He would like to shoot me. He was trying to get hold of it and I flipped it in the creek, trying to keep it away from him.

I dove in where I thought the gun had been. I dove in and he come right after me and landed right on my back. He pushed my head under the water and was standing over me. I get my knees up and turn sideways. I take this arm and I turn over just like that and he falls over. He went down in the water. I held his head down. I did it for about maybe half a minute.

I get up and I walk down a little bit and I lay down on the bank right there. He got up and he come on up and he sat down right up here by me. He's breathing hard. I'm breathing hard, too.

He got out of the water and he started shaking his pockets out. He took his wallet and he pulled it out of his pocket and he shook it. Then he laid it on the ground. I had mud all over my foot. I could see blood coming out of my foot.

I said, "Warden, get us up to the house. I am shot and Mr. Moore is shot. Mr. Moore don't look like he is moving. Get us to the house."

He said, "Nigger, I told you, you are going to the goddamn house."

He reached over and grabbed me and I fell over. I grabbed him and I twisted him. We kept turning over and over and he was trying to get on top of me and I was trying to get on top of him. We rolled over and we ended up in the drainage ditch. I hit the water first. I am face down in the mud. He's on top of me.

I got up on my knees and scooted between his legs. I pulled his leg out and I fell on top. I jumped on him and laid on him. I didn't push his head. I just jumped and had my hands across him. And I just laid on him. I laid down there for a few minutes.

I laid on him and laid on him. I don't know how long I laid on him. He stopped moving.

I was more-or-less resting. I was holding him. I was trying to keep—he kept on. He kept on wanting to fight. He kept on. Man, I begged and I pleaded with him. He just kept on.

(Craig Washington asked: "If he hadn't done those things to you, Eroy, would you have done those things to him?" Brown was weeping when he said the following words and the court took a recess.)

No sir, he just kept on wanting to fight. He just kept on. He just kept on. He just kept on wanting to fight.

After I got up off of Warden Pack, I laid down against the bank by the billfold. It was still laying on the ground. I looked all through it for the handcuff keys. My arm had swollen up. The handcuff had tightened up and it was cutting off the circulation in my left hand. I didn't find the handcuff key. I laid there on the ground and I heard the trucks coming. I heard a bunch of voices, two or three voices, and it sounded like Soloman's voice that I heard. I raised up and I looked, and it was a free-world truck. I picked the wallet up, got up, started up the hill. Warden Williamson was standing right there at the corner of the bridge. I said, "It wasn't my fault, warden," I told him. "I did what I had to do."

I tried to hand the billfold to him. He wouldn't take the billfold. He kept saying, "Where is Warden Pack?" I said, "Down there."

DeYoung, he said, "What's that you got in your hand?" I handed it to him and he opened it up and he said, "This is Warden Pack's billfold."

He asked me my name at the same time that Warden Williamson was asking where Warden Pack was at. I told him my number. He told me that I was a liar. He asked me to recite it again and I repeated it again.

Mr. DeYoung put the other handcuff on me and put me on the ground. Warden Williamson told them to take me away from there. I was trying to get up and look. I was trying to see what they was doing. Each time Mr. DeYoung came back and pushed me back down with his foot. I never did get up. I raised up trying to look around the car. The ambulance came and took me up to the solitary. About four or five hours after, they took me to the Walls.

15

THE PERFECT DEFENDANT

Several times during Eroy Brown's testimony, Judge Dalehite had to quiet the crowd of fifty spectators, many of them from Galveston's black community. The trial was being held in a small upstairs courtroom, and it was packed daily with Brown's supporters and with reporters from across the state. One of them, Cinny Kennard, was a fresh-faced young reporter for KHOU television in Houston. She had just been sent to cover Galveston when Brown's trial was dumped in her lap. She decided to cover it like a beat and was filing stories almost daily. She had been trying hard to be objective about the trial, that is, to stay neutral, but Brown's testimony was a turning point.

Thinking back on the trial more than twenty-five years later, she said, "Eroy was a perfect defendant. He was not a showboat. He was not arrogant. He came across as completely genuine. I sat there trying to be objective as hell, but I found myself saying, 'This guy is really telling the truth.'"

Craig Washington, she said, "had an extraordinary ability to convince people that doing the right thing was most important. There were tears and there was passion. But the biggest point was that when Eroy Brown talked, you knew he was telling the truth. He was a great witness on his own behalf. There were no theatrics and there was no anger in him. He was just an inmate serving time and you knew he felt that his life was at stake."[1]

Although Mike Hinton had much more trial experience, Mark Ward, the Walker County district attorney, reserved the cross-examination of Brown for himself. Ward was confronting a defendant who had told his story in considerable, explicit detail. If he walked Brown through it and failed to shake him, or failed to find inconsistencies, he would end up helping Brown solidify his story in the minds of the jurors. If Ward, a well-educated, white lawyer, seemed to be bullying Brown, a high school dropout who spoke the rural black dialect of Texas prisons, he might build sympathy for him.

Ward chose the bullying approach, though he didn't seem confident about it. He asked his first question in a voice so low that Judge Dalehite asked him to speak up.[2]

His second question was deliberately provocative: "Mr. Brown, I can't go to that door over there and call Billy Moore to the stand because he won't answer me . . ."

Washington immediately objected and was sustained.

Ward then projected photographs of the dead men on the screen and asked Brown if he had seen them in these positions. He said he had seen Moore lying shot at the foot of the car, but he hadn't seen Pack's body pulled up by the side of the bridge.

"When is the last time that you saw him?" Ward asked.

"When he was over in the creek."

"Face down?"

"Yes, sir."

"Was he dead?"

"I imagine. He didn't move."

"He didn't move?"

"No, sir."

"Did you say anything to him at that time?"

"No, sir, I didn't say nothing to him. I backed off and laid on the bank."

Ward took out Brown's "pen packets," the paperwork for each of Brown's three felony convictions, two for burglary and one for aggravated robbery. Washington objected. Brown had admitted to the convictions, Washington said. They had nothing to do with the case at hand, and were inflammatory. Dalehite let Ward continue to question Brown about his convictions, deciding to rule later about whether the pen packets should be admitted as evidence.

Ward wanted to know if Brown called Adams "Mr. Bill" and Brown said that he did. Ward took Brown back over the morning. He had probably said good morning to Mr. Bill. Ward asked him about Aurelio Silva, the inmate he was working with. Brown knew him as Willie.

Was he a friend of yours? Ward asked.

"Well," Brown said, "he is what you call a grinner. We get along. He is a grinner. We never have any problems. He likes to high-sign with me. We are not tight. We are doing time. . . . We just don't never get into each other's way."

Some of the other inmates went to chow but Brown and an inmate named Pugh stayed behind. Ward wanted to know if Adams had given Brown any trouble about that, and Brown said, "No, sir, he didn't give me no trouble. Mr. Bill didn't ever give me no trouble. And, I don't never give him no trouble."[3]

Soon Ward had Brown riding in the pickup with Adams, complaining about not getting a furlough.

"He just hit you in the mouth?"

"Yes, sir."

"Did you draw any blood?"

"No, sir, he just backhanded me. He didn't hit me with his fist. He just backhanded me like that."

"Did you say," Ward asked, "'I want to go back to Waco'?"

"No, sir."

"No?"

"No, sir."

"You didn't mention Waco?"

"No, sir."[4]

On the way to the garden shed, Brown said Adams slowed down at an onion field, and hit him again. Brown said he first saw Moore that morning at the reservoir. He hadn't seen him that morning when the fishermen came in from the rain for coffee at the farm sheds. He denied telling Adams he had insisted on seeing Moore.

Ward took him through his testimony about the tires and tubes and the numerous times he fixed flats for Moore and his friends. When he got to the butane bottles that Brown had filled for Moore, Ward pressed him about their use.

"I done it on numerous occasions," Brown said. "It is the kind of bottle that you would use to hook up something that would—"

"Something that would cook fish, for instance?"

"Yes, sir."

"Are you aware that sometimes they have fish fries at the Ellis Unit for employees?"

"Yes, sir."[5]

Ward asked him what happened when Moore got into the truck and began driving off the levee.

"... He told me, 'Nigger, what you been doing running your head in front of all the rest of them convicts? What you done had?' ... He hit me when we got around the levee.... He hit up side of the face."

"How many times?"

"I don't know."

Ward pressed him about how many times. "Mr. Moore hit some, and Mr. Adams hit some," Brown said. "... Mr. Adams was stomping on my foot."[6]

When Moore stopped the truck before the garden shed, Brown could see shadows moving. He knew Kelley was in there, and as he waited in the truck while Pack and Moore were talking, he tried to signal Kelley.

Brown said he had known Kelley since he came to Ellis.

"Is he a friend?" Ward asked.

"He is a grinner," Brown said.

"He is a grinner?"

"Yes, sir, a grinner."

"Like what? Does he grin?"

"Yes, he is just cool."[7]

Brown estimated he sat in Moore's truck for ten minutes or so while Pack and Moore conferred. He watched them in the rearview mirror.

"And it is your testimony they told you to get out of the truck?" asked Ward.

"They told me to 'bring my ass here,'" Brown said.

"You're fond of saying that, aren't you?" Ward replied. Washington objected to the sidebar comment, and Dalehite sustained. "Mr. Ward," Dalehite said, "just ask questions and please don't make any statements."[8]

When they called him, Brown said, he walked to the driver's side of Pack's car. "I was talking to Warden Pack. Mr. Moore stopped me before I could get a conversation out. He grabbed me."

Brown said he had never met Pack before though he had seen him in the halls of the building. He said he had seen Pack the week before in the farm shop. "He was looking over the area and he was just riding around looking," Brown said.[9]

Ward questioned him about the handcuffing. Was it on the driver's side? No, Brown said, on the opposite side, the passenger's side. This was the side the inmates in the garden shed couldn't see. Moore had taken Brown's hand off of the top of the car and was putting the handcuff on his left hand.

"Warden Pack had the gun up against your head?" Ward asked.

"No, sir," Brown said. "He didn't have it up against my head."

"He had it pointed at your head?"

"Yes, sir."

"... He did cock it?"

"Yes, sir."

"You knocked it out of his hand?"

"Yes, sir."

"... Mr. Moore had ahold of your other hand?"

"Mr. Moore had ahold of my left hand."

Ward asked Brown how big a man Moore was and Brown said he couldn't say.

"He was a fairly good-sized man, wasn't he?"

"Yes, sir."

"Do you consider yourself a fairly tough individual?"

"No, sir."

"And Mr. Moore had ahold of you and you were able to knock the gun out of Warden Pack's hand with one hand?"

"Yes, sir."

"Mr. Moore was just standing there?"

"I grabbed the gun out of Warden Pack's hand and twisted it out. I didn't knock it out, yes, sir."

"It hit the ground? And you picked it up at some point in time?"

"I picked it up."

"You back off, holding them at bay. Is that right? . . . Then, they rushed you with the gun in your hand and they were unarmed. Is that your testimony?"

"Yes, sir."

"And you then shot Mr. Moore in the head. Is that right?"

"I don't know where Mr. Moore was shot at."

"You discharged the gun twice in the general area of Mr. Moore's head, did you not?"

"The gun discharged in my hand, to be correct, sir. Then, me and Warden Pack had our hands on the gun."[10]

Brown said he was on the ground after Moore fell, and was scooting backwards toward the bridge. He sat in the middle of the road near the bridge. Pack had disappeared and was under the bridge.

"And you are sitting up here with the gun still in your hand?"

"No, sir, I laid it down on the ground."

Brown was checking the wound in his foot when Pack reappeared and went after the gun. They tussled and fell into the water.

Ward took him through the gunshot sequences.

"I wasn't counting the shots that were fired, sir . . . to be correct, sir, one shot was fired when I batted the pistol away from him."

"Two shots were fired when you fired in the direction of Mr. Moore's head?"

"I didn't fire in the direction of Mr. Moore's head," Brown said.

"You didn't?"

"Not myself."

"The gun discharged in your hand?"

"The gun discharged when it was in me and Warden Pack's hand."

Then they tussled and fell into the water.

"And he stuck your head under the water and you stuck his head under the water. Is that right?"

"He stuck my head under the water first, and he gets on top of me."

Ward kept trying to get Brown to admit that he was the aggressor, but Brown resisted steadfastly. Pack, he said, had forced his head under water. And Brown retaliated.

"How long did you hold him down?"

"Probably half a minute. Maybe. I don't know. I don't recall the exact time. I wasn't looking at the time, excuse me, how long I held him. I held him and then let him up."[11]

The gun was gone by this time, thrown into the water.

"And, it is your testimony that you and Warden Pack were sitting up here on the bank having a conversation right after you had been in the water, under the water, choking for air, each one of you came up and calmly sit down on the bank. Is that your testimony?"

". . . We were sitting up and Warden Pack pulled his billfold out. He took his billfold out and shook it. He shook it and then he lays it down."

"Then, both of you get your breath and you start tussling again?"

"I hadn't got my breath."

"Your testimony is that he goes for you again?"

"Yes, sir."

"Then you all go into the sewage ditch?"

"Yes, sir."

"And you do the same thing again; is that right? He puts your under first and you put him under second. Is that your testimony?"

"We rolled over into the ditch and I was on the bottom."

"But you did put his head under the water over here in this drainage ditch right under this fence. Is that right?"

Ward was pointing to a photograph, state's exhibit 2.

"That is the ditch that we were in," Brown said.

"And you put his head under the water right here. Is that right?"

"Thereabout, somewhere in that vicinity."

"You stuck it down in the sludge, in the mush, in the sewage. Is that right?"

"After he had me down," Brown said.

"I think he has answered the question," Washington said.

"Yes, sir," said Judge Dalehite. "He has answered the question."

"Is that right, you stuck his head down into the sewage?" Ward said.

"I didn't stick his head in the sewage. I got back up. I got up under his leg and I laid on top of him. I didn't stick his head there. I just laid on top of him. That is all I did."

"You laid on top of him so he couldn't get up?"

"I laid on top of him to keep him from getting up and getting on top of me."[12]

Ward then made a series of accusations designed to imprint the prosecution's theory of the case in the jury's mind. He accused Brown of stealing Pack's billfold after he had drowned him, and Brown denied that.

"Is it also a fact that you had an idea of getting back up here to the car trying to get out of the penitentiary?"

"No, sir."

The ditch where Pack drowned.

Defendant's markup of crime scene, showing signs of struggle on the passenger side of Pack's car, confirming Brown's account. Brown's fifty-cent piece, the handcuff box, the broken radio aerial, and Moore's flattened hat are circled.

"Isn't it also a fact that you cussed and jumped on . . . Mr. Adams at the farm shop and told him you wanted a furlough? You told him you wanted to see Billy Moore. Isn't that a fact?"

"No, sir."

"Isn't it a fact that Mr. Adams, at your direction, went to see Mr. Moore, and Mr. Moore got in the truck and you told Mr. Moore that you were smoking some weed; isn't that a fact?"

"No, sir."

"Isn't it a fact that after you got to the garden shop and Mr. Adams left . . . that you got out of the truck and . . . and got the gun out of Warden Pack's car and shot Billy Moore in the head twice and he was falling back and you turned around to Warden Pack after Warden Pack had been shot in the arm, and ran him down into that ditch, and drowned him?"

"No, sir, that is incorrect."

"Are you saying that the gun never discharged while it was in your hand?"

"It discharged in my hand, but it was in the control of me and Warden Pack."

"Isn't it a fact that you only got rid of that gun because it was out of bullets?"

"I don't have the slightest idea whether it was out of bullets or not."[13]

Washington had a few follow-up questions. He projected a photograph of the scene that showed where Brown's comb, shirt button, and a fifty-cent piece he wore on a chain around his neck were found. The fifty-cent piece was found at the back end of the car on the passenger's side, right where Brown said most of the action took place. The broken antenna was visible as well.

Then Washington asked him about the consequences of admitting to smoking marijuana. Brown was three to four months away from getting his parole. If he had admitted to smoking marijuana, he would have lost his "good time" credits and his status as a trusty, and would almost certainly have lost his chance at parole. The day he was arrested, Brown gave urine and blood samples, but the prosecutors never put on any evidence that he had drugs in his system.[14]

Ward then asked him: "Isn't a fact that you were high on marijuana that day, and that you didn't care who you told about you smoking marijuana?"

"No, sir," said Brown.

"Isn't it a fact that the reason you knew that the gun was out of bullets was because you had probably fired it again?"

"No, sir," Brown said.

"No, sir?" Ward said.

"No, sir," Brown said.

Ward hadn't rattled Brown once.

16

THE TDC ON TRIAL

Eroy Brown had admitted he drowned Wallace Pack. Now the defense had to prove he had the right to do it. Did Brown intend to murder Pack and Moore, or had he been forced to defend himself? The rules against hearsay in criminal trials are complicated and stacked with exceptions. One of the exceptions in a murder trial is the reputation of the deceased. The defense didn't have to prove that Pack was a violent man, only that he had a reputation for being violent, and that Brown and other inmates believed he was capable of violence. DeYoung had helped out by testifying that Pack had a good reputation among inmates.

Washington and Habern lined up forty-one TDC inmates to testify about Wallace Pack and what it meant to be taken on a trip to the bottoms.

The prison grapevine would help jurors sort out what went through Brown's mind that day, Washington said. He used a metaphor that wasn't very complimentary to his client, but it was quotable: "What would it take to make a rat jump on a cat in a cage of cats?"[1]

The day before Brown testified, Hinton and Ward argued strenuously against letting Washington put on a collection of inmates to talk about Pack and the TDC. Hinton sounded like George Beto. These inmates, Hinton said, were nothing but "professional agitators" and troublemakers, and all they could offer was hearsay testimony.[2]

Dalehite let Washington put them on. If the testimony was not relevant, Hinton could object, and Dalehite would sustain or overrule him. The defense was beginning to like this judge.

Washington called the first of his inmate witnesses on Thursday, February 11. Ben Lacy, who had been the warden's boy at Ellis when Pack died, was afraid to testify. Dalehite called the lawyers to the bench for a conference and then dismissed the jury.

During the recess, Lacy's wife, Mary Kay, told reporters that Lacy's life was in danger from both sides. Inmates who supported Brown would get him if he didn't testify, she said, and TDC guards would get him if he did. She also said she had twice received a threatening, anonymous phone call.

"Both times," she said, "the caller told me to tell my husband to keep his mouth shut or else. There's a contract out on his life. He got the word through what the inmates call the grapevine. I'm worried, I'm scared and I'm standing here shaking. It's hard to sleep at night when something like this hanging over your head."[3]

Washington insisted that the inmates should testify and that they should be protected. Hinton was angry. He had taken only four days to put on his case and was hoping for a quick trial and conviction.

"If this is a ploy by the inmates to stall or to be moved to a federal prison," Hinton told the court, "then something like this could work in every case from here on."

Fatigue and frustration overcame Washington and he broke down and cried.

"All I'm trying to do is get to the truth," Washington countered. "There are so many roadblocks with people wanting to stop the truth from coming out. So many people don't want the truth to come out."

Dalehite sent an assistant to search the courthouse for an attorney to help the inmates. A Texas City lawyer named Bruce Fort turned up and was appointed. Fort spent some time with the witnesses and reported back to the press that the inmates were scared, of both TDC officials and other inmates. Fort filed a motion with Dalehite urging him to move the inmates to other state prisons for protective custody. During the weekend Fort interviewed the inmates further and prepared them to protect themselves legally.

On Monday Washington put eight of the inmates on the stand and one after another, each of them said he would answer questions only if he were moved to a federal or another state's prison system. Until that happened, they would not talk about the meaning of the bottoms or the reputation of Pack. Habern and Washington thought it was wonderful. Instead of testimony, they were putting on courtroom theater before the jury that demonstrated Texas inmates were in fear of their lives.

Washington and Habern could count on former inmates who were out of the prison system to testify.

Ray Hill was one of the first on the stand. Hill had not been much of an agitator inside prison, but he was a critic outside. He had started a program on KPFT radio in Houston, called "The Prison Show," to help inmates and their families deal with the TDC. As a source of the prison grapevine, Hill had been invaluable to the defense.

Hill said he had known Pack at the Wynne Unit in the mid-1970s. He described him as a "tush hog." He meant that Pack was a bully, a fighter, a mean character. He said Pack appeared to carry a pistol in his boot. He couldn't claim to have seen the pistol, only the bulge in his boot.[4] Pack's stepdaughter, Peggy Hickson, later testified that because of a foot problem, Pack couldn't wear boots, and indeed, on the day of his death, he was wearing lace-up shoes.[5]

Hinton didn't bother to cross-examine Hill. There was no point in reinforcing his story. He would answer with his own witnesses, presumably more believable than a bunch of convicts who were offering testimony in exchange for transfers out of the TDC.

One of the inmates who did testify and whose testimony was preserved was Aubrey Komurke. Komurke was a big man: six feet, four inches tall and 220 pounds. He was forty-two years old and had obtained a high school diploma and two years of college while in prison.

At Ellis he was caught up with the writ-writing movement. He testified at the *Ruiz* hearing in October 1978, claiming that officers harassed him for his legal activities. He said he was sent to solitary for fifteen days for criticizing the TDC in his diary. Under cross-examination he admitted he subscribed to forty periodicals and had filed more than a hundred grievances against the system.[6] After the *Ruiz* hearing he kept raising hell. In August 1979 he was convicted by a prison disciplinary committee for vulgar language and a disrespectful attitude.

Washington asked Komurke what "the bottoms" meant.[7]

"Well, the bottoms generally means the area away from the building, specifically the river bottom," Komurke said. "The bottoms refers to that area, but it is actually in effect any area away from the building proper."

Washington asked him if there was a double meaning. "On a day when no other work is being done and no other inmates were near there and you were going to be taken to the river bottoms, do you think you would be taken there for a picnic?"

Hinton objected and Washington withdrew the question. He asked what was the connotation of "taking you to the bottoms."

"Yes, sir," Komurke said, "a threatening connotation."

"I renew my objection," Hinton said, "unless this is tied in some way to the dead men in this case, Wallace Pack and Billy Moore. It is an improper question and highly prejudicial and inflammatory."

Dalehite overruled Hinton. Komurke declared that Pack had a reputation among inmates for being violent and dangerous. Hinton objected and was overruled. When Washington asked Komurke about Pack's reputation for carrying a gun inside the prison, Komurke said he had never seen Pack carry a gun, but it was widely rumored that he did.

Washington asked Komurke about an incident he claimed to have seen at the Wynne farm in 1966, when Pack was a lieutenant. Hinton objected that for the act to be relevant, Brown would have to have known about it at the time it occurred. Brown was still in high school in 1966.

Hinton then asked Komurke about his criminal history. Komurke couldn't remember the first offense that sent him to prison. "Could it be fondling children on January 7, 1963?" Hinton asked. "Yes, sir," Komurke said. "Correct."

"Mr. Komurke, were you later convicted of the offense of fondling again and did you receive a twenty-five-year sentence?"

Komurke admitted to that and another twenty-five-year sentence for escaping. His current term was twenty years for sodomy.

Washington wanted Komurke to tell the jury about the Diagnostic Unit and what went on there. Inmates are subjected to IQ tests and psychological evaluations, Komurke said. They are oriented to the farm system and told to behave themselves.

"It is a very intimidating kind of orientation," Komurke said. "Causes fear, at least as I saw it."

Washington asked whether "as a part of the diagnostic orientation that one's head is shaven and one is sprayed with chemicals as a part of the medical program and one is stripped of all outside free-world clothing?"

Komurke had barely got out a "Yes, sir" when Hinton was on his feet, objecting.

"The question is leading," Dalehite said, "but I will overrule the objection. He already answered the question."

Hinton objected again, wondering how this was relevant to Brown and what happened at Ellis.

"I am trying to bring out and to tell the members of the jury about Mr. Komurke's experiences in this line of testimony," Washington said. "Mr. Komurke obviously expresses himself much better than most people could to illustrate to the jury what it is like to be an inmate in the Texas Department of Corrections. He is telling us about his own experiences and they are not any different than

Eroy Brown's. They are all general things and all designed to get to the question of what it is like to stand in his shoes on April the fourth, 1981."

Al Slaton had been an armed robber, and was one of Frances Jalet's clients at Ellis in the early 1970s. He was a free man when he testified for Brown. He was working at a VA hospital in Temple, Texas, and had recently blown the whistle on the cruel treatment of veterans there. Slaton spent the rest of his life taking care of mentally disturbed people, some of them ex-convicts, at a collection of wood-frame houses in Temple called the Rose Garden.[8]

Slaton knew something about reputation in a case of self-defense. After he got out of prison in 1972, Slaton killed Beartracks McAdams's most favored and violent building tender, Robert Barber.[9] While Barber was reaching for his gun, Slaton shot him five times in the head. Slaton turned himself in. A Texas Ranger testified about how dangerous Barber was and a jury acquitted Slaton by reason of self-defense. Tim Sloan's former boss, Warren Burnett, had been his attorney.[10]

Slaton testified that in 1969 Pack had stood by and watched two building tenders use blackjacks to beat an epileptic inmate named Melvin Bunt until blood spurted to the ceiling. Bunt was put in a straitjacket, he said, and hung from the cell bars. He suffered epileptic seizures and died, and there was no autopsy.[11]

Slaton also said that during the same year Pack had hung him up in handcuffs for so long that his wrists were cut. He rolled up his sleeves and showed the jury the scars. When Hinton got him on the stand later, he had Slaton roll up his sleeves further, exposing numerous scars from self-mutilation. Slaton had cut himself in solitary confinement to get medical attention, he said. But he insisted the scars on his wrists came from handcuffs.[12]

Tommy Carlisle, thirty-nine, a car salesman from San Antonio, had served thirteen years in the TDC for murder with malice. He had been a building tender for Beartracks McAdams and then tried to reform. He spent five years at the Wynne prison, from 1969 to 1974. Carlisle testified that he ran afoul of Pack when he cut his Achilles tendon to get out of work. In prison vernacular this is called heel-stringing. First Pack threatened him with a pistol, he said, then kept his foot on his head while he lay on the floor of the ambulance during the ride from Wynne to the Walls hospital.

He said that after his tendon was repaired, Pack had him handcuffed naked to the cell bars and tormented him with a pair of pliers. He pulled his pubic hair, he said, and crushed his nose and his genitals with the pliers. When Hinton objected to his testimony, a young woman stood up in the courtroom and shouted, "Bull!" Dalehite had her ejected from the courtroom.

Carlisle said he was hung up for seven hours by the handcuffs, and like Slaton, stepped from the witness stand to show the jury his scarred wrists.

Carlisle claimed to have briefly been a building tender at Wynne. He said an inmate named Melvin Austin got on Pack's bad side, and Pack told him and another building tender to "knock out the back of the cell with this nigger." He said Austin died of a heart attack from the beating.[13]

TDC spokesman Rick Hartley told reporters that Carlisle and another building tender had been told to place Austin in his cell after he became disruptive, but the medical report showed no signs of violence. Austin had died of a stroke, Hartley said, not a heart attack. Pack was not even a part of ordering Austin's incarceration, Hartley said. But it was an interesting admission on the part of TDC officials that they used building tenders to do disciplinary work such as putting another inmate into a cell. Over and over the TDC admitted that building tenders were much more than floor janitors. They were muscle at the service of prison officials.[14]

Other inmates testified about the bottoms. Henry Giles, a sixty-three-old convicted murderer, said, "Any convict knows about 'the bottoms.' . . . If you go to the bottoms you're going to be in trouble."

Another inmate, Favis Martin, said, "Every prison farm has an area where if they're not happy with your work or if you talk back, they'll take you and beat you or pistol-whip you."[15]

Those were the most sensational charges about Pack. Other witnesses testified about his reputation. One of them was Ernest McMillan, the black civil rights activist from Dallas who had led the protest in the Father's Day Incident of 1972. After serving three years in prison, McMillan went to work for a state representative, Senfronia Thompson, in Houston. He read the inmate mail coming to Thompson's office, and said he had seen plenty of complaints about Pack.

Another major player in Texas prison reform took the stand briefly: Charles Sullivan. Sullivan had been working on prison reform for ten years, and said that Pack had a reputation for being violent and turbulent.

After Carlisle testified, Washington put the director of the prison system, Jim Estelle, on the stand. Washington's main purpose was to pin down Estelle about TDC policy for carrying weapons inside the prison. He also asked Estelle to bring records of violent incidents in the prisons for ten years previous to the deaths of Pack and Moore.

Estelle said that there was a policy against carrying guns inside the compounds, but officials were permitted to carry weapons on the farms and in order to prevent escapes, to quell mutinies, and in self-defense. Estelle kept his voice low and calm.

"Sometimes there are as many as six hundred inmates working in the field," Estelle said, "and they work under the security of armed officers. It has been the history of our discipline over the years, sorry to say, that some prison officials need to carry weapons to control violence. Your neighbors don't send them there for behaving themselves."

Under questioning from Hinton, Estelle said that Wallace Pack "had no reputation for violence. I never received a complaint about him and I have received more than my share of complaints. . . . Pack was a person who would fairly enforce the rules and he was consistent."

Washington put on a physician whom Habern and Register had brought to the prison to examine Brown in April. He noted that the handcuff marks on Brown's wrists, the bruise on his shoulder, and the bullet wound in his foot all matched Brown's story.

One of Washington's last witnesses was a forensic expert from Dallas, Irving Stone. A few days earlier, after the prosecution had entered Pack's clothes into evidence, Tim Sloan had them flown to Dallas for a forensic examination. Stone drew diagrams of Pack's suit jacket, shirt, and necktie, and traced two bullet tracks in his clothing. One track showed a bullet that came through the upper right sleeve and side of the coat and nicked his tie. Another bullet entered the elbow. So two of the shots had evidently been fired in the struggle for the gun. Jurors would later question why the state hadn't examined the clothes itself. It seemed curious that the defense would put on more gunshot evidence than the prosecution.

Washington also called the Walker County investigator, Walter Pinegar, who had taken photographs of the scene indicating the view the inmates had from the garden shed and greenhouse. Moore's pickup almost completely blocked their view of Pack's car. Pinegar testified that Soloman had a better view because he was in the greenhouse for a time, but he had taken no photographs of that view. Nor was it possible. Just as TDC officials had steam-cleaned Pack's car, they had also torn down the greenhouse and garden shed.

17

THE ARC OF THE MORAL UNIVERSE

The prosecutors had a file full of letters from inmates willing to testify about Pack's good character, but they had to be careful about seeming to offer benefits in exchange for testimony.

They put on Robert Freeman, a thirty-four-year-old paroled murderer who worked for a printing company in Jacksonville. Freeman had been at Wynne and said Tommy Carlisle had a bad reputation about not telling the truth, and that Pack did not condone violence. In the process of bolstering Pack's reputation, Freeman did little to bolster that of the TDC. Washington asked him if he remembered that Pack had ordered Carlisle and the notorious Robert Barber to kick to death an inmate named Doyle Cole. Freeman said he couldn't remember the inmate's name, but he had heard about it.

"The man was hit and kicked rather severely," Freeman said. "I heard later he died of heart failure, probably due to the beating he received. Pack was disturbed by the incident. He did not approve of that type of thing. It did happen now and then. Barber was a pet of the higher officials. He was protected by them. Pack was upset with a convict-run penitentiary. He despised that happening. He was disturbed that a convict could get away with something like that, basically got protection from it."[1]

The former TDC director, George Beto, testified about Pack's reputation. The man Jim Estelle once called "the master" had spent the last ten years teaching criminology and penology at Sam Houston State University in Huntsville. Like Estelle, Beto said he had never heard any complaints about Pack.

As an ordained Lutheran minister and former seminary president, Beto could make claims to expertise about Pack's religion. "I could sense from our conversation that he was a deeply religious man," Beto said. "I could tell he had profound religious convictions."

As for the building tenders, Beto testified he was in favor of them. "You'll have them by their own force or the weaker prisoners will allow them to get there," he said. "That's abhorrent. I wanted to pick them. They are hated by the other inmates."[2]

Washington had presented evidence that at least four inmates had died violent deaths at Wynne: Ronald Novak, Melvin Austin, Harold Bunt, and Doyle Cole. Rick Hartley of the TDC said records showed that Novak, Austin, and Cole had all died of heart attacks. When Washington pressed Beto about whether he had heard about these deaths, Beto said, "If there was genuine brutality, the grapevine would get it to me in a hurry."[3]

Washington asked Beto if a prison official should ever put a cocked gun to an inmate's head while the inmate's hands were free. Not under normal circumstances, Beto replied. Anyone who resisted in such a situation, he said, was taking a highly calculated risk.

"Sometimes when defending your life it comes down to taking a highly calculated risk," Washington replied.[4]

Several TDC wardens testified that Pack was not a violent man. One of Pack's defenders was his former Wynne boss, Don Costilow. He denied that Pack had ever ordered any inmate beatings. Costilow was later removed as warden for disregarding many *Ruiz* court orders.[5] Another TDC official testified that Pack had been like a father to him and had helped him and his wife get baptized.

A former inmate named Freeman Sensabaugh said Pack had reprimanded him for threatening in a letter to divorce his wife. He had made him stand with his nose against a wall for four hours, a form of punishment he called "Texas TV." Washington asked him if he was aware that the TDC had recently abolished standing at the wall as a form of punishment. Beto pointed out that it was legal when Sensabaugh was an inmate.

Sensabaugh also said he had seen Pack remove a pistol from the glove box of his car and check it at the guard tower when Pack was working at Wynne. That detail would seem to confirm the state's theory that Brown had seized the pistol from the glove box. But Hinton put on Pack's secretary, Glenda McWhorter, and her husband, Earl McWhorter, a TDC supervisor. They had been Pack's neighbors for ten years, and both said Pack had never had a gun until he was issued one for his new job as warden of Ellis.[6]

On Monday, February 21, Hinton called Evelyn Sullivan, a Waco funeral home attendant who had complained to TDC officials about Eroy Brown's behavior during his furlough. Brown had been rude and profane during the evening of his father's viewing at the home in March 1980. Washington had already been briefed by Brown's half-sister, Diane Harris King, about the matter. She testified that the woman had told Brown she didn't know that his father, Eroy Harris, and mother, Hattie "Shorty" Brown, had married, and that had provoked Brown's outburst. Sullivan denied saying such a thing. The pressure was getting to Brown. He stood up and shouted, "My dad's got nothing to do with it!" and burst out sobbing. Washington had to calm him down.[7]

As the trial neared its end, Washington and Habern wanted to hear the interviews with Soloman and Duson that investigators had tape-recorded. The tape recordings had surfaced when Washington was questioning the Walker County sheriff's deputy, Dale Meyers. Over the objections of Hinton and Ward, Dalehite ordered the state to surrender copies of the tapes.

Washington and Habern were interested in seeing how the story in the typewritten statements that Duson and Soloman had signed had evolved from the inmates' original interviews. The presumption was that the interviews, happening on the day of the deaths, would most accurately reflect what Soloman and Duson had actually seen. Dalehite offered Washington the chance to put the two inmates back on the stand, but Washington decided against it. The differences between the tape recordings and the inmates' testimony was not so significant that he wanted to put the state's key witnesses on the stand again to refresh the jury's memory of the state's case.[8]

Near the end of testimony, Dr. Ralph Gray, a TDC administrator for health services, testified for the state. Gray had reviewed the records of four suspicious deaths involving building tenders at the Wynne prison while Pack had been there. No autopsies had been performed, Gray said, because there was no suspicion of anything but death by natural causes. It sounded a bit like the failure of investigators to test the hands of Pack and Moore for gunpowder residue. There were some things the state didn't want to know.

The last two witnesses for the defense were a former Wynne prison guard and an industrial chaplain from Longview who trained at Wynne for ten months in 1972. The chaplain, Gilbert Thornton, said Pack had a bad reputation for violence among inmates. The former guard, James R. Handy, had worked at Wynne from 1968 to 1971 while going to Sam Houston State. He also said Pack had a reputation among inmates for violence. Handy had left the TDC to become a federal probation officer. Hinton asked him when he had last seen Pack and Handy said he had stopped by to say hello a few years earlier when he was in Huntsville.

"I'm sure he appreciated that," Hinton replied. Washington jumped up and objected. "That's the worst sidebar remark I ever heard," Washington said. "Judge, I think he should be told to try this lawsuit like a lawyer." Dalehite had the comment struck from the record.

Because several TDC officials, including Estelle and Beto, testified that they had never heard complaints against Pack, Washington attempted to introduce several inmate lawsuits that accused Pack of brutality, but Dalehite wouldn't let him put them on.[9]

The trial had lasted almost six weeks, with a month's worth of testimony before the jury. The final arguments were scheduled for Friday, February 26. Dozens of TDC officers arrived in uniform that day, and by 8:30 they had packed the small upstairs courtroom, leaving Brown's supporters to wait in the halls.

D. V. "Red" McKaskle, one of Estelle's top administrators, insisted to reporters that the officers had come on their own time and initiative, and that the TDC administration hadn't orchestrated their appearance. McKaskle had been the state's last witness. Like Beto and Estelle, he said Pack had a good reputation. And he said it was permissible for an officer to carry a pistol in a locked glove compartment.

The arguments did not go on that Friday because the two sides had not agreed on a jury charge. Dalehite postponed the final arguments until Monday. Possibly sensing that their case was in trouble, Hinton and Ward wanted the jury to have the choice of lesser charges such as simple murder or manslaughter. Washington decided to go for broke. It was all or nothing. Eroy Brown would be found either guilty or innocent of capital murder. If convicted, he would get either the death penalty or life in prison. The delay over the charges gave Dalehite the chance to move the trial downstairs to a bigger courtroom. Dalehite apologized to the jury and sent them home for the weekend.

On Monday, March 1, two picketers were walking on the courthouse sidewalk with signs reading "Free Eroy Brown." A courthouse janitor had alerted Washington that Dalehite would reconvene the trial in a large courtroom that held two hundred people. At 7:30 in the morning Brown's supporters packed the courtroom along with approximately twenty-five TDC officers in gray uniforms and another fifteen officials, including several wardens, in civilian clothes. Almost all of the TDC officials were white. About twenty ex-convicts, all of them black, were scattered about the room sitting side-by-side with the guards. The mood was somber. The chatter was minimal.[10]

Dalehite informed the jury that it could not find Brown guilty of a lesser offense. He gave each side three hours for final arguments, but they took only three hours total. The summations did not become part of the trial record, and have been pieced together from newspaper accounts.[11]

Although Brown was being charged with drowning Pack, Hinton reminded the jury that Soloman and Duson had testified they saw Brown deliberately shoot Billy Moore at close range.

"Moore was down on his knees holding his hands up when Eroy Brown snuffed out his life," Hinton said. "It was cold-blooded, calculated, malicious murder."

Hinton deplored the way the defense had sullied Pack's reputation. He called Al Slaton and Tommy Carlisle, two of the former inmates who testified that Pack had tortured them, liars, "people who could care less about the meaning of an oath." Their attempts to tie Pack to inmate deaths at Wynne in 1969 and 1970 were vicious lies designed to slow the trial and detract from Brown's guilt, he said.

"By the grace of God," Hinton said, "we spent days and days and we're able to refute the scurrilous innuendos that Wallace Pack had anything to do with those deaths or even that there was anything improper about those deaths."

"We've seen Wallace Pack dragged through the worst slime," he said. "We have been hearing the trial of Wallace Pack. I have never heard anything so despicable in my entire life. It's ridiculous to drag by these innuendos this good man's death through the courtroom. They picked the wrong man to blaspheme."

To rebut the attacks on Pack's reputation, the state had put on forty-three witnesses. Hinton said he was angry and made a rhetorical apology to the jury: "If I upset anybody because of my own personal anger and ire that Wallace Pack has been drug through worse slime than that in which he ended up dead, then I'm sorry."

Hinton admitted that the prosecution could not account for how Brown came to be handcuffed on his left wrist. Both Soloman and Duson said that Pack was going to the trunk to get the handcuffs while Moore had Brown in the back seat. He couldn't account for why the front door rather than the back door of Pack's car was open when the prison officials drove up to the scene. He couldn't account for how Brown got hold of a gun.

"I don't know how Eroy got hold of that gun," he said. "I know one thing. Eroy Brown got his hands on it."

"It is absolutely incontrovertible that Billy Moore died from a shot in the head by a gun held in the hand of Eroy Brown and his hand alone." Brown was so angry that his hand was jerking off shots in his eagerness to empty the gun, he said.

Hinton doubted Brown's testimony that he and Pack had wrestled into the creek, stopped and rested, then tussled again. "Are you going to believe they chased a while, then stopped and talked, then chased a while and talked?" Hinton asked.

Hinton did say that there was one part of Brown's testimony he did believe, and that was that he had held Pack underwater about a minute. Hinton looked at the jury and then at his watch, and held his silence for a full minute to dramatize the drowning.

The young district attorney, Mark Ward, also spoke. He urged the jury not to let Brown get away with a "perfect crime," though it must have been hard to see how anything that happened that day was even close to perfect.

"Please do not let their deaths go in vain," Ward said. "Only you can write the proper epitaph for them. Tell these TDC officials and all the world we stand on the side of justice. You can make Wallace Pack and Billy Max Moore's lives meaningful."

Bill Habern made a brief opening statement, but he knew well that his role was to let Washington have the spotlight. The heart of Washington's argument was to get the jury to put themselves in Eroy Brown's place, to see the world through the eyes of a convict.

"It was important for you to understand his state of mind," Washington said. "If I have desecrated the memory of anybody, it was for that reason."

Using the defense table to represent Pack's car, Washington walked the jury back through the physical evidence. He pointed out that the one slide the prosecutors had shown of the view from the garden shed showed precious little. Duson and Soloman were a hundred yards away, their view of Pack's car blocked by the truck.

All the action—the handcuffing of Eroy, the scuffle over the gun, and the firing of the shots—happened on the far side of Pack's car, where Soloman and Duson couldn't see it. There was the broken radio aerial on the rear passenger side of the car, the flattened hat, the handcuff box in the dirt on the same side, the fifty-cent piece on its torn chain, the open glove box from which Moore had taken the handcuffs, the bullet hole in the rear quarter panel of the car, also on the passenger's side. Washington walked around the defense table, showing the jurors how impossible it was for Soloman and Duson to see what they said they saw. He insisted that they didn't care what happened to Brown when they told their lies. "Soloman and Duson would try anything to get out of prison," Washington said, "even ride on his life."

Washington questioned why Brown would kill the officials. He was three or four months away from parole. He had a good job as a trusty. Eroy Brown was succeeding in prison in a way that he never had in the free world. He had few problems in prison.

"He's a convict and a criminal," Washington said. "He deserves to be in prison, but he doesn't deserve to have a gun held to his head."

If Brown truly had control of the gun, as Duson and Soloman said he did, and was full of murderous intent, why didn't he just shoot Pack?

"What fool would provoke and be difficult when the other guy has the gun?" Washington asked. "They are playing a game with another man's life."

The true meaning of what happened, Washington said, was that Moore and Pack were worried that Brown had threatened to expose Moore's thefts of prison tires. In another era, the threat by a convict to talk to the outside world would not be likely to worry a warden or a farm major. But in the *Ruiz* era, convicts were being listened to. That was why Pack had pulled a gun on Brown.

"They would have you believe a warden rides around on a prison farm with a gun lying out on the seat," Washington said. "You know that's not true."

Moore and Pack sent Adams and Spivey away from the scene, Washington pointed out.

"You know why they left," Washington said. "They didn't want any witnesses around. . . . They had no business with that gun out there. They had that gun for only one reason: Stop that Old Thing from running his head."

Once Moore had fastened the handcuffs on Brown's left wrist, he was like a bird in a cage, Washington said. As Moore was about to snap the cuffs on Brown's other wrist, Brown had to decide what to do.

"He had to decide whether he was going to live or die," Washington said. "He had fifteen seconds to decide before that second handcuff went on. What do you do? A gun to your head and one handcuff on?"

"His struggle was consistent with human nature," he said. "Everyone wants to live. No one wants to die. It was like being at the end of your rope." The state's version of events was based on lies, Washington said, repeating one phrase again and again in his final argument: "No lie can live forever."

The newspaper reporters didn't pick up on the source of that expression, but it was surely well known to the black spectators who crowded the courtroom in support of Eroy Brown. It came from Martin Luther King Jr.'s speech on the Capitol steps in Montgomery, Alabama, in 1965. King said: "I come to say to you this afternoon, however difficult the moment, however frustrating the hour, it will not be long, because 'truth crushed to earth will rise again.' How long? Not long, because 'no lie can live forever.' How long? Not long, because 'you shall reap what you sow.' How long? Not long, because the arc of the moral universe is long, but it bends toward justice."

18

THE SHOES OF EROY BROWN

The Brown jury consisted of five women and seven men. Eight of them were white, one was Hispanic, and three were black. They came from the city of Galveston and nearby working-class, mainland towns such as La Marque and Texas City. Among them were a carpenter, a pipefitter, a dock attendant, a secretary, and a federal wildlife official.

After the closing arguments on Monday morning, March 1, they went to lunch and then set to work. They selected Joetta Warden, a forty-two-year-old black woman who worked for a Galveston tea company, as foreman. Then they took a vote to see where they stood. It was eight to three for acquittal. After half an hour's discussion, they took another vote. Two jurors had changed their minds. It was eleven to one for acquittal.

The holdout was the cat lady, Dorothy Kemp, a forty-three-year-old secretary from Texas City and mother of seven. It was going to be a long week for everybody. Kemp told the other jurors that they ought to get curtains for the jury room window and a shag rug for the floor, because they were going to be there a while. She said she would hold her view until hell freezes over and the roses bloom.

After an hour, Warden sent a note to the judge asking to see almost all of the 240 trial exhibits, including photographs, autopsy and offense reports, witness statements, and the three scale models of the Ellis prison.[1] Kemp thought Soloman and Duson were telling the truth. She insisted that Warden send a note asking for the transcriptions of the state's tape-recorded interviews with them. The transcripts had been turned over to the defense, but because they had not been entered into evidence, Dalehite rejected the request.

Kemp seemed to believe that the defense didn't want the jury to read the transcriptions. The next morning Warden sent a note asking Dalehite which side had moved that the tape-recorded interviews of Soloman and Duson be withheld from evidence. The judge instructed them that the court had determined what was admitted, and that they should not concern themselves with who objected or whether any objections were made.

Then they asked to hear the transcribed testimony of Aurelio Silva, who had said that Brown provoked his problem by talking loud and complaining about not getting a furlough. This was as close to a motive as the prosecution had. They came back into the jury box and spent the morning listening to the court reporter, Paul Porter, read the testimony from his shorthand tapes. The lawyers sat and studied their faces.

Kemp was basically running the jury now. That afternoon they spent three more hours listening to Porter read the testimony of Soloman and Duson. Duson had testified that Brown fired three shots at Moore, but Washington had reminded the jury that that wasn't possible, since four bullets in the five-shot gun were accounted for: one in Brown's foot, one that hit Pack, one that hit Moore, and a fourth that punched a hole in the rear quarter panel of Pack's car.[2]

Both Hinton and Washington told reporters they were encouraged to know that the jury was going over the testimony of the two inmates.[3]

Hearing the testimony changed no one's mind, and tempers were running short. At ten o'clock on the third morning of deliberations, Warden wrote the judge: "We cannot come to a decision. We have been like this since the first day. We thought that reading of the testimony would help, it hasn't, we are hopelessly deadlocked. We await your instructions."

Dalehite told them to keep deliberating.

Most of the jurors did not believe the testimony of Duson and Soloman. They felt that their view was obstructed and that they could not have clearly seen what went on from a hundred yards away. The physical evidence simply didn't match up with their testimony.

As for Brown, one juror later said, "He knew he was in trouble. That guy was scared. I believe he was provoked."[4]

No matter how hard they tried, they couldn't change Kemp's mind. Kemp didn't believe Brown for a second when he said that if he had let Pack up Pack would have killed him. She believed Brown could have retreated. She believed he was the aggressor.[5]

"It was hell," Kemp later said. "The other jurors really made it rough on me. They pounded the table and screamed, and there was a lot of cursing. But I wouldn't budge."[6]

A huge amount of energy had gone into the trial. The jurors had heard a month's worth of testimony from nearly a hundred witnesses. The state alone had spent more than $200,000. The total cost of the trial was in the neighborhood of $500,000.

The jurors made one more attempt and they wrangled for fifteen minutes more before Warden sent out another note: "To the court, with all due respect. It is beyond our ability to come to a conclusion as you wish. We have been in this situation throughout our deliberations. Every piece of evidence and testimony that we have requested has been done in the spirit of reaching a verdict. We implore the court's understanding in this unfortunate situation."

Dalehite pressed them to continue. Read the court's charge, he wrote, and continue to discuss the evidence.

At 12:40 Warden wrote in large cursive letters, "We want to go out to lunch." After they came back, at 1:55, she wrote another note, saying they were unable to reach a decision. "Still 11-1," she wrote, without saying which way the verdict leaned. "No amount of evidence or testimony read back is going to change the opinion of the one juror." A half-hour later she sent another note: "hopelessly deadlocked," and asked if she could speak to the judge privately, but that, of course, could not be done. An hour later she sent another note saying the holdout was unshakeable, as were the other jurors. At 4:40 she sent a note that they were still deadlocked eleven to one. "We wish to retire early," she wrote. "(Now.)"

Washington had already anticipated a mistrial and had objected to it. He was convinced, he told a reporter, that the jury favored acquittal, because four members had looked him directly in the eye when they came back to the courtroom to report on their deliberations.[7] "I think it's our panel," he said. Hinton said he had a strong feeling that the jury was leaning for conviction.

Washington, Sloan, and Habern consulted with Brown, and they all agreed. They would go for a so-called dynamite charge. The legal term was an "Allen charge," named for a case from the late nineteenth century. The lawyers scrambled into the library looking for more recent examples of such a charge, and found one in a case in Dallas. In exchange for having the judge give instructions to the holdout juror, the defense would agree not to object that an unfavorable verdict had come through improper coercion of the jury. Dynamite charges were usually encouraged by prosecutors, not defendants, but nothing was usual about this case.

Dalehite crafted an argument to encourage the holdout to reconsider. "No juror should go to the jury room with a blind determination that the verdict should represent his opinion of the case at the moment," he wrote, "or that he should close his ears to the arguments of other jurors who are equally honest and intelligent as himself . . .

"You should listen to each other's arguments with a disposition to be convinced. If a much larger number favors one side or the others, a dissenting juror should consider whether, in the light of opinions that are expressed by the other jurors in the jury room, he is not in error in his views."[8]

Kemp could not be moved. The jurors deliberated for half an hour and then returned to their motel for the night. That night Kemp dreamed that they had acquitted Brown, and as soon as the verdict was announced, Brown got up, addressed them with an obscenity, and said, "I fooled you all!" At breakfast, she told the other jurors about the dream.

On the fourth morning, March 3, one of the jurors tried to shift the balance by changing his vote to guilty. At mid-morning, Warden sent out a note. They were now at ten to two. At eleven, Dalehite called the jurors into chambers and asked Warden if she thought they could reach a verdict. Warden said she thought they could. The lawyers were astounded. They were expecting a mistrial.

The juror who changed his vote hoped this would be a way for Kemp to save face. He planned to change his vote back to acquittal, hoping Kemp would go along. But the plan backfired when Warden said she thought they could get a unanimous verdict. Kemp was indignant. Within minutes, Warden sent back another note: "I was misinformed about reaching a verdict. We are still deadlocked. I'm sorry. I didn't understand."[9]

Dalehite called them in again. Dalehite said, "You did make some changes this morning to 10-2 instead of 11-1. Do you feel that you will reach a final decision in this case?" Warden said they could deliberate some more. But it was useless. Her last note to the judge ended with the word "futile."

Eroy Brown kept silent and expressionless when Dalehite called them back and declared a mistrial.

The jury foreman, Joetta Warden, wept.

"It was very emotional and very upsetting," she said. "It was a letdown. We could have deliberated until next year and still not reached a verdict. Everyone is entitled to their opinion, though."

All the jurors but Kemp adjourned to the Victorian cottage kitty-corner from the courthouse where Washington had stayed during the trial. It was a party of sorts in which they discussed what had worked in the trial. But nearly winning was not the same as winning. Washington would have to defend Brown all over again.

Kemp consulted with the prosecutors, giving them tips on what went wrong from the jury's point of view. She posed for *Life* magazine that summer: a pretty, slim, middle-aged woman with dark shoulder-length hair, looking over her shoulder while holding one of her cats. A kitten on the foreground desk gazed up at them.[10] Kemp said her biggest fear was that she would be regarded as a racist because she was a white woman who refused to acquit a black man. She pointed out that she had believed Soloman and Duson and they were black.

Pack's stepson, a Houston real estate developer who had put up the money to hire Hinton, was disappointed, but counted a mistrial better than an acquittal. But he hated to see his mother put through another trial. The day the mistrial was declared would have been the twenty-seventh wedding anniversary of Pack and Faye.

Faye Pack said, "There will be another time, another place, another jury, and another judge. I have not lost confidence yet. The defense is so ridiculous. It doesn't lend any credence. We will win."[11]

Eroy Brown's aunt, Eddie Mae Maryland, and his sister, Diane King, were equally convinced that the next trial would lead to acquittal.

There wasn't any question that the state would prosecute Eroy Brown again. Hinton said he thought a different judge might not allow the defense to put on all the inmate witnesses to testify about Pack's reputation. But one juror, Al Chandler of La Marque, said that the reputations of Pack and Moore were not important.

"We had to eliminate the last two weeks of testimony altogether," Chandler said. "I don't think Warden Pack was on trial and I don't think Billy Moore was on trial."[12]

Several jurors were persuaded that something was amiss that day. If Moore had driven Eroy Brown straight back to the building and put him in solitary, nothing would have happened. Some of the jurors wondered why the warden was called out for what seemed like a minor infraction, a convict mouthing off, maybe smoking pot.

"I feel sorry for those men," Chandler said, ". . . but if they had done what was right, this wouldn't have happened."[13]

Shortly after the trial, *Houston Post* reporter Richard Vara interviewed the sole Hispanic juror, and probably the only one with a college education, Carlos H. Mendoza. Mendoza was a young staff biologist for US Fish and Wildlife in League City.

He said the stress was so great in the jury room that he had started smoking again during the last two days of the trial. With his scientific background he was surprised that the prosecution didn't examine Pack's clothes or test the dead men's hands for gunpowder residue. Like the other jurors, he didn't believe Soloman and Duson. Like Chandler, he wondered why, if Brown was causing problems, Moore drove Brown away from the prison building instead of taking him back to the building.

"That decision resulted in the needless loss of two lives," Mendoza said.[14]

Many years later, Dalehite talked about the trial.[15] He was in his mid-eighties and his memory of the case had dimmed but he still remembered how ably Brown's lawyers had fought for him. What he remembered most were the shoes of Eroy Brown, the shoes Washington had urged the jurors to put themselves in. The shoes had been found on the floorboard of the cab of the truck that Moore had driven that day, right where Brown said he had put them. The shoes were not just metaphorical. They were a pair of worn suede desert boots that Brown had worn without socks: defendant's exhibit 57.

Defendant's exhibit 57, the shoes of Eroy Brown. Photo by author.

19

POLITICS AND PRISONS

After the mistrial, reporters wanted to interview inmates and guards at Ellis for their reactions, but Jim Estelle refused to give them access. Estelle and other prison officials worried that the verdict would create more problems in the prison system, and their problems were already considerable. Appeals by reporters to the governor and to Louis Austin, the chairman of the Texas Board of Corrections, failed to help. Austin said he didn't like the decision but had to agree with TDC officials.

"I guess I'm too close to the prison system sometimes," he said, "but that whole thing down there is more volatile than I think Judge Justice realizes, the monitor or anyone else."[1]

By "monitor," Austin meant the special master Justice had appointed to monitor Texas prisons. The appointment came at the end of April 1981, only three weeks after the deadly events at Turkey Creek. Justice was following precedent in other federal prison cases. The special master could not run the TDC, but he was supposed to have unlimited access to records and know what went on inside. To prison officials, who had been running the TDC with unquestioned authority and a rubber-stamp board, the world had been turned upside down.

The TDC had recommended two insiders for the special master's job, one of them a sociology professor with little prison experience and the other an associate of Estelle. Instead, Justice appointed Vincent Nathan, a native Texan who had become a college professor, attorney, and court master in Ohio. The TDC resented Nathan mightily and did everything it could to buck his authority and have him thrown off the case.[2]

In June 1981 the TDC board and Mark White hired the Houston firm of Fulbright & Jaworski to appeal the *Ruiz* rulings to the Supreme Court. During the next three years the TDC ran up $2 million in legal bills with the firm.

Two authorities on the *Ruiz* case called the brief the "$600,000 appeal." It consisted mainly of denying the factual conclusions that Justice had reached after his yearlong hearing. Any problems in the prisons, the brief stated, were exceptional and didn't require the systematic relief that Justice had prescribed.[3]

While the state was preparing its denial, Vincent Nathan appointed four monitors to gather information. One of them, David Arnold, collected information about the building tenders. For three months in late summer and fall of 1981, Arnold toured thirteen prisons and studied thousands of documents. Not surprisingly, he reported that inmates were terrified of cooperating with him for fear of retaliation. Arnold concluded that some building tenders wielded more power than the uniformed guards. The building tenders themselves told Arnold they had security keys, chose their cells, ran inmate stores, and carried weapons.

A week after the mistrial, Eroy Brown's older brother, Carl, filed a handwritten federal civil rights suit complaining that he had been harassed by homosexual inmate guards, administrative snitches, and building tenders at the Darrington Unit in Brazoria County. His troubles had begun, he said, the week his brother was arrested at Ellis.[4]

But the TDC officials persuaded their lawyers, including the Texas attorney general, Mark White, and the Fulbright & Jaworski lawyers who were arguing the *Ruiz* appeal, that the building tenders had no special powers or privileges.[5]

Arnold filed his report with Nathan in mid-October 1981 and immediately released it to the press, creating a slew of news stories and resentment from TDC officials, who had not had a chance to read it. They assigned Steve Martin, a new agency lawyer who had been on the job for a month, to examine Arnold's report and find ways to rebut it for the *Ruiz* appeal. It was not Martin's first job at the TDC. Ten years earlier he had worked his way through college as a guard at Ellis Unit. He knew from experience that building tenders had extraordinary powers that far exceeded what the TDC officials admitted in court. Building tenders, for example, had trained him in his duties as a guard at Ellis.

Martin checked in with a building tender he had known at Ellis, who said that they were still taking care of business but they were taking heat from the special master's office. Martin found the same practices that Justice had confirmed: an inmate nurse sewing up a patient without pain control, a building tender with the key to a box of riot batons. Martin uncovered instance after instance of building tender practices that confirmed the special master's report.[6]

Other problems were showing up. A New York physician named Robert Cohen found serious shortcomings in prison medical care, and that was reported widely in the press. In November 1981 Ellis inmates engaged in a major work stoppage. Then five hundred inmates rioted at the Darrington Unit. Prisoners at the Eastham prison set fire to their tents and broke cell block windows. Guards used tear gas to break it up. As Eroy Brown was preparing for his first trial, all hell was breaking loose in Texas prisons.

Nathan met with TDC attorneys to issue a statement condemning the violence. With his eye on the governorship, in January 1982 Mark White filed a brief with Judge Justice accusing Nathan and his staff of causing inmate disturbances. White was particularly aggrieved that the monitors refused to identify inmates who were armed with homemade knives and clubs unless the inmates were granted immunity from punishment.[7] Governor Clements joined in, saying Nathan had encouraged the disturbances. Nathan and the court-appointed attorney for the inmates, William Bennett Turner, countered that the refusal of the TDC to follow federal court orders had fostered the unrest.

In December 1981 Clements, White, and most of the TDC board had met with Estelle to discuss the building tenders. The civil rights division of the Justice Department had indicated it might withdraw from the *Ruiz* suit if it could be satisfied about that issue.

TDC board member Harry Whittington had heard from a Fulbright & Jaworski attorney that the special master's allegations about building tenders might be true. He asked Estelle pointblank if inmates put handcuffs on other inmates.

"Are those things that actually happen, Jim?" Whittington asked. "I can see how that's authority, putting handcuffs on a man."

"If an inmate had put handcuffs on another inmate," Estelle replied, "I number one don't know about it and number two it's an exception to the rule, practice and policy."[8]

Clements wondered if White shouldn't establish an investigative office for the TDC, but White insisted that he believed his clients.

In 1987 Steve Martin published a vivid history of the *Ruiz* case with University of Texas sociologist Sheldon Ekland-Olson; it included a preface by Whittington. In *Texas Prisons: The Walls Came Tumbling Down*, Martin and Ekland-Olson wrote:

Whittington began his own independent investigation of the issue through interviews with prison employees and inmates. Ultimately Whittington was successful in persuading key state officials that the building tender system did exist in Texas prisons, that it was wrong for the state to continue to support prison officials who engaged in such practices, and that it appeared to him that prison officials, including Estelle, had knowingly deceived the governor, the attorney general, the prison board, and their own attorneys about the existence of such an illegal system.[9]

Whittington also concluded that the prison officials who had denied the existence of the building tender system under oath had perjured themselves. Shortly before the March hearing, Martin and Whittington met with Mark White and explained to him that the special master's report was right. The building tenders were armed enforcers. White, Martin wrote, was "dumbfounded." Estelle had been lying to him for three years.[10]

The bills for the state's resistance were adding up. The same week that Brown was nearly acquitted, Texas reporters were writing about the $1 million the state owed Fulbright & Jaworski for its yearlong effort to fight Justice's orders. Texas owed another $1 million to William Bennett Turner, the California attorney who had represented the Texas inmates in *Ruiz* for nine years. Mark White defended the Fulbright & Jaworski bills, but insisted Turner's fees were too high, and refused to pay.[11]

Ray Farabee, a state senator and lawyer from Wichita Falls, called a halt. A centrist Democrat who sat on the Senate Committee on Criminal Justice, Farabee had developed an expertise on prisons. Farabee was so well liked in his district that he ran for seven terms without opposition. Unlike White and Clements, he didn't need to play politics with prisons. He wrote Estelle that the TDC was spending money on Fulbright & Jaworski that the legislature had intended to be used for compliance with Judge Justice's orders. The all-out fight against *Ruiz* was shaping into an expensive campaign that Texas was likely to lose. The March hearing in which the TDC was going to challenge Justice to abolish the office of special master was expected to take two months with 180 witnesses, and run up Fulbright & Jaworski's bills even higher.

On March 15, inmates produced by the special master's office began testifying about the use of weapons by building tenders. One former building tender testified that he had won a knife in a dice game with a correctional officer. The TDC was getting bloodied in the news. Fulbright & Jaworski was charging $100,000 a month, and it didn't look as though the state could come close to getting Justice to shut down the special master's office. Farabee and Whittington huddled, and the following week Estelle and Nathan worked out an agreement to reduce the expense of the special master's office and end the TDC's opposition to its existence.[12]

During the weeklong hearing, an inmate testified that Butch Ainsworth, whose brutal rape of another inmate had been cited in Justice's finding of facts in December 1980, was still working as a building tender. The TDC removed him from the post and agreed to a detailed settlement.

Next up was the issue of staff brutality, a problem that, along with the building tender system, Estelle had steadfastly denied existed. White had become less certain about the TDC. He assigned Rick Gray, a lawyer in his office, to determine how the issue of staff brutality might play out. What, for example, would happen in the prisons when the building tenders were abolished? Justice warned that since the Fifth Circuit had overturned some of his remedies and placed the responsibility with the TDC, it should prepare itself for a power vacuum.

As in the Brown case, the inmates' lawyer, William Bennett Turner, had obtained an order prohibiting the TDC from abusing inmates who had been witnesses in the building tender hearings in March. But getting the TDC to obey a court order about how it treated its prisoners was nearly impossible. In June, eleven inmates who had been witnesses in the March building tender hearing staged a hunger strike to protest the narrowing of Justice's reforms by the Fifth Circuit Court of Appeals. One of the strikers had also been a witness in the Eroy Brown trial.[13]

In the last months of 1982, as Eroy Brown was being tried a second time, the TDC's lawyer, Steve Martin, and the assistant attorney general, Rick Gray, were investigating the abuse of inmate witnesses, which seemed to be deliberate and systematic. Gray was becoming more and more aware that he couldn't trust his client, the TDC, to speak the truth.

In the spring of 1982, the prison population hit an all-time high of 33,000 inmates, and was becoming dangerously overcrowded. In May Estelle and the TDC board were asking for a special appropriation of $85 million, with $48 million to go toward a new prison that would hold two thousand inmates.[14] Even with those funds, inmates would be living in tents for years to come.

Clements's refusal to grant paroles had kept the prisons full. To comply with the federal limits on the inmate population, Estelle threatened to refuse new inmates from the county jails. Clements was furious, but he relented on paroles,

and Estelle quickly released six hundred inmates.[15] Estelle said he could safely release nine thousand inmates on parole if he were allowed to pick them.

In June 1982 the Fifth Circuit overturned some of Judge Justice's rulings, such
as restructuring the management of the prisons and the single-celling of inmates,
an expensive proposition estimated to cost $300 million at the time.[16] But all of
Justice's legal opinions were upheld, including the unconstitutionality of the system and the use of the special master to correct it. Bill Turner regarded the ruling
as half a loaf for each side.

Ignoring the fact that Texas prisons were still under Judge Justice's authority,
Mark White declared victory. In 1979 Clements had vetoed a $30 million appro-
priation for new prison construction, and all summer White hammered him for
bungling the prison crisis.[17] Both men argued about who had done the most to
settle *Ruiz* issues in negotiating with Ronald Reagan's assistant attorney general
for civil rights, William Bradford Reynolds.[18]

White hadn't made any secret of his gubernatorial ambitions while serving as
attorney general under Clements. In December 1981, he gave a *New York Times*
reporter his standard defense of the Texas prison system, describing it jokingly
as the opening statement of his campaign against Clements: "We believe first of
all that prison is a place of punishment and that punishment is a loss of freedom.
The Texas prison system houses some of the most violent men on earth, the most
antisocial, but they are less likely to be assaulted there than is a citizen walking
the streets of Houston, Texas."[19] It was one of those ludicrous assertions that
prison authorities made throughout the *Ruiz* trial and have continued to make,
using statistics about assaults per thousand people.

Clements and White had argued about Texas prisons, but other forces swung
the election. The economic recession helped the Democrats, who organized an
extraordinary campaign to turn out the vote. Clements had made a belittling
comment about women when White promised to appoint a housewife to the
Public Utilities Commission. When White was elected governor in November,
the headlines were not about prisons but about the new appointment.

But at least the Texas legislature was addressing the overcrowding by building two new prisons in Grimes County, near Navasota. In June Estelle asked
the TDC board to name them for a man whose career was "marked unmistak-
ably with integrity, courage and sensitivity," a man "respected by both staff and
inmates for his consistent fairness." The new prisons were named for Wallace
Pack.[20]

20

THE STATE TRIES AGAIN

After the hung jury, Habern and Washington pressed for a speedy trial, to begin as early as June 1982. In April the thirty-four-year-old Walker County district attorney, Mark Ward, crashed his car into a tree and had to be pried from the wreck with heavy machinery.[1] He suffered a serious head injury and abandoned his plans to run for another term as district attorney. His assistant, Frank Blazek, took over.

Blazek tried to move the trial out of Galveston, arguing that the case had generated so much positive news coverage for Brown that the state did not stand a chance. Dorothy Kemp, the holdout juror, testified that Galveston County jurors would be afraid to convict Brown because his supporters had picketed the courthouse during the trial. But she did say the news accounts had been fair.

Washington argued that the state was not entitled to a change unless conditions in Galveston were so lawless that the lives of the defendants or witnesses were in danger. Galveston County district attorney James Hury testified that he thought a fair jury could be picked under the right circumstances. Blazek's motion was denied. Brown would be tried in Galveston again.[2]

The Galveston district judges picked Wallace "Pete" Moore of the 184th District Court in Houston to retry Brown. Walker County won a grant of $113,000 through the Texas Prosecutors Coordinating Council. Blazek promptly put down $16,000 to hire a special prosecutor from Houston, Mack Arnold. Arnold had prosecuted many cases in Moore's courtroom and Moore was helping him run for judge. Washington didn't like that relationship one bit.

Arnold had just left his job as a Harris County prosecutor to run as a Republican against the only black state district judge in Texas, Democrat Thomas Routt. Arnold made Routt's tender treatment of a former state district judge, Garth Bates, his campaign issue. After Bates served four months of an eight-year sentence for accepting bribes, Routt gave him "shock probation." Harris County prosecutors argued that Routt had elevated a former judge above the law. Defense lawyers and members of the black community in Houston defended Routt, pointing out that Bates was sixty-four, in poor health, and not likely to commit such a crime again. Governor Clements piled on, saying the Bates case showed that the state's shock probation law needed to be toughened.

That summer TDC supporters raised money to supplement Arnold's fee. At the end of July, the Texas Department of Corrections Women's Association held a barbecue to add to the Wallace Pack–Billy Moore Fund.[3] At an Elks Club function that summer Arnold urged people to donate, to see that Brown was properly "grilled."[4]

The trial had taken its toll on Eroy Brown. Three days after the mistrial was declared, he was transferred from the Galveston county jail to the TDC wing of John Sealy Hospital in Galveston and treated for tuberculosis and hepatitis, two common prison diseases. After six days he was returned to jail. In July Galveston county jail doctors wanted him transferred back to John Sealy Hospital. Brown had tuberculosis of the liver, but he was in no physical pain, and he refused to leave his cell. He didn't want to do anything that would delay his trial. Washington urged him to get medical care.[5] He was in no hurry to begin the trial.

With Republicans beating their chests about how tough they were on crime, Washington announced that he was going to do everything necessary to delay the trial in order to mess up Mack Arnold's campaign for judge. Washington, who was running for the Texas senate that summer without opposition, declared that the appointment of Arnold as special prosecutor stank politically. It was designed to get Arnold a big fee and a lot of publicity as a crime fighter while the trial was being held in the weeks leading up to the November election. Arnold insisted the appointment was intended to help him pay his bills until the election was over. "If there's anyone who understands politics," Arnold told a *Houston Chronicle* political reporter, "it ought to be Craig. I want politics out of it. All I want to do is try Eroy Brown."[6]

On August 2, Moore held a hearing in which Washington threatened to withdraw from the case if the trial wasn't postponed. The transcripts of the first trial had only been partially completed, Washington said, and he could not properly defend Brown without studying them all. "I can't legitimately call myself a lawyer when I'm not ready," Washington told Moore. "This man is on trial for his life," he said. "I'm not ready to go to trial without the record."

Moore was reluctant to postpone. "The issues are the same and you've had the facts at your fingertips," Moore told Washington. Habern and Sloan were tied up in other trials and did not appear with Washington that day. Brown told the judge he didn't want any other lawyer than Washington. Moore was dismayed at Washington's threat to withdraw.

"I think it's a terrible sin, Craig, because you're a damn good lawyer," he said. "I hate to see you do this to yourself."

"I hate to see you do this to yourself," Washington replied.

"I don't know what you mean," Moore said. "What do you mean?"

Washington said he didn't want to discuss it in the courtroom, but Moore pressed him. Was it about Mack Arnold?

"No," Washington said, "it doesn't have anything to do with Mack Arnold. Do you remember Leroy Green?"

Green was a client of Washington who was convicted in Moore's court in 1980. Washington had filed an ethics complaint against Moore about Green, charging that Moore had signed a dismissal order for a charge on which his client was then convicted. Moore said that the dismissal order involved a different charge.

Whether the ethics complaint was valid or not, it could cloud Brown's trial. There was every possibility that the State Judicial Ethics Commission would be holding an inquiry about Washington's complaint against Moore at the same time that Moore was trying Brown. Moore delayed the trial until the end of August, but a week later he withdrew. He thought Washington's tactics were low. "It's a Catch-22," Moore said. "If he wants to lower himself to that level of practicing law, I can't help it."

The Walker County administrative judge, Max Rogers, found a new judge, Darrell H. Hester, to take the case. Hester was fifty-seven and had been a Cameron County prosecutor before becoming a well-respected judge. The county later named a Brownsville juvenile detention center in his honor. Washington declared he was happy with Hester's appointment.[7]

Governor Bill Clements unexpectedly delayed the trial by calling a special session of the legislature for September 7. As a member of the Texas house, Washington was entitled by law to a thirty-day continuance while the session went on. Judge Hester, Blazek, Arnold, and Washington held a conference call, and the trial was moved to October 18, right in the middle of the campaign. The special session lasted only three days, giving Washington time to prepare. The statewide Democratic sweep ended Mack Arnold's judicial aspirations. Routt was re-elected when Arnold was in the thick of a trial against an opponent who would do everything he could to win.

It took only a week to seat the entire jury. A lot of the drama had disappeared from the newspaper coverage. Eroy Brown's story had already been told. The question was whether it would be believed again.

Mack Arnold had his work cut out for him. If Dorothy Kemp, the most stalwart believer in Brown's guilt, didn't believe a jury would convict him, how could he win this case? He had a list of more than fifty points that had been gleaned from Kemp. The jurors believed Eroy's version of events and not the prosecution's. They wondered about his shoes being off. They did not believe Brown was raving and talking loudly. They believed Moore was stealing and that he and Pack were going to beat Brown. If Brown was a problem, why didn't Moore take him straight to the building? They didn't believe Brown was smoking pot. His urine test was clean. They thought Soloman and Duson were lying to get out on parole. If Duson was truthful and Moore was shot at a range of a foot or less, why was there no gunpowder residue around the wound? The medical examiner's testimony that Moore's thick hair had absorbed all the stippling seemed phony. They thought if Brown had intended to kill Pack, he could have shot him when he had the gun. They believed Brown about the two men resting on the bank, exhausted from their struggle, because the autopsy had shown Pack had emphysema. They wished they could have visited the prison and seen the scene of the crime and checked out Soloman's view from the steps of the greenhouse. They figured the prosecution had a photo of that view but had withheld it. They figured there were discrepancies between the testimony of Soloman and Duson on the tape recordings the state had withheld from evidence. They thought Robert DeYoung, the young lieutenant who had wept on the stand, was a phony.

Some of the jurors had relatives who had been shoved around by police and prison officials. They thought Pack had to try to kill Brown because his gun had been taken away, and he had a macho image to protect.

No wonder Dorothy Kemp didn't think the prosecution had a chance. There didn't seem to be a single strong element in the prosecution's case. Given that Washington had the transcripts of the first trial, it would be difficult for the prosecution to enter much that was new. But Arnold and Blazek tried.

Their first witness was Richard Pustka, the assistant prison warden from Coffield prison who had been fishing with Moore that morning. He heard the shots and saw the ambulance rushing from the building to the bridge at Turkey Creek. Pustka could establish the scene: the quiet morning, the approach of Adams in the pickup truck with Brown in the front seat. But he couldn't offer much of anything about the deaths. The stories that Adams, Williamson, and DeYoung told were much the same. They had to be. Washington had their testimony under oath from the first trial.

The prosecution testimony started on Thursday, October 29, and on Friday Arnold put his inmate witnesses on the stand. Both Soloman and Duson were out of prison on parole, and had been brought to a Galveston hotel to go over their testimony and prepare for trial. Of the two, Soloman was the better spoken and more of a leader. But he was also the witness who had declared in the first trial that he had a ticket in his hip pocket to get out of prison. Duson had been less sure in his testimony, and more suggestible. Arnold didn't have any good choices. He decided to keep Soloman off the stand and rely on Duson.

Duson testified again that Brown had been put in the back seat of Pack's car and came out shooting. Brown had looked back at the garden shed and then chased Pack down the bank of Turkey Creek and disappeared from view, when Duson heard another shot. Then he described the capture of Eroy Brown.

Duson was to have been followed by Henry Kelley, the third inmate in the garden shed that day. As Walter Pinegar was bringing Kelley in to testify, Kelley collapsed in the hallway. Washington insisted that if Duson was to identify Kelley as one of the witnesses in the garden shed, he had to do it in front of the jury. Kelley was brought in weeping, and then was taken to John Sealy Hospital.[8] It would be hard to say whether or not Kelley was faking, but it is clear that whatever he had seen and heard that day, he was terrified to talk about it.

Arnold took only three days to put on his case. He wanted to portray Brown as the aggressor who emptied the gun at Pack and Moore and kept pulling the trigger after the bullets were gone. But the spent cartridges that remained in the chamber seemed to bear only one imprint of the firing pin. A light-weight, well-worn handgun such as Pack's would have "yoke shake," and was unlikely to strike a cartridge twice in exactly the same spot. Arnold's ballistics expert testified that it was possible for the firing pin to strike a cartridge twice in exactly the same place, but the argument was technical and hard to prove, and Washington showed how unlikely it was. It was about as likely as the medical examiner's theory that Billy Moore's thick hair had absorbed all the gun-powder stippling from a gun fired a few inches away. Arnold's best hope was his cross-examination of Eroy Brown. If he could somehow rattle him or get him to contradict himself, maybe he could convict Brown.

Brown calmly and deliberately told the same story he did in the first trial. Habern and Washington helped him reenact the positions of the three men, with Washington portraying Brown, Habern as Pack, and Brown acting as Moore. The difference was that Brown didn't cry this time.

Arnold kept Brown on the stand for three hours. Brown was cooperative, but he held his ground. Arnold reenacted the moment when Moore had one handcuff on Brown and was trying to pull him away from the gun. Arnold put the cuff on Brown's left wrist, pulled hard, and drew Brown near him.

"A 223-pound man could not pull you off that gun?" Arnold asked.

"He did not do that," Brown said.[9]

At one point Brown lay on the ground playing the role of Pack, while Arnold lay on top of him, trying to demonstrate how long Brown had held Pack underwater.[10]

Arnold pressed him about why he had drowned Pack. "I let him up once and he wanted to keep fighting," Brown said. "What was I supposed to do?"

"My intention was to keep him off of me," Brown testified. As for how long he had held him under water, Brown said, "I was acting out of passion. I wasn't keeping up with the time. . . . I just laid on him to keep him from putting me back up under there. I laid on him. I did not count the minutes."[11]

Brown stood up well to Arnold's pressure. Arnold couldn't rattle him.

21

A CAT BATTERS A MOUSE

In the second trial, Washington conducted a devastating cross-examination of Levi Duson, leaving him angry and confused. To question him, Washington used four documents: the transcripts of two tape-recorded interviews made on the day of the deaths, the statement officials wrote for him that he signed four days later, and his testimony in the first trial. To prepare, Tim Sloan had brought an eight-foot-long piece of brown butcher's paper and pinned it to the wall. The lawyers took turns listening to the tapes and mapped every inconsistency on the paper. Washington had absorbed them all and caught Duson in contradiction after contradiction. It was like watching a cat batter a mouse.

Washington's theme was simple: Duson was uncertain about what he saw that day and said so to the investigators, but as the first trial grew nearer, the prosecution helped him resolve his uncertainties. Washington came as close as a lawyer could come to accusing the state of suborning perjury.

Duson had gotten parole after testifying against Brown in the first trial and was living in Midland. He and Washington got into a dispute about when Duson got his parole. Duson accused Washington of trying to confuse him.

Duson was cleaning fresh fish that the dog boy had given him. When Pack pulled up, he moved to the window and sat on a table to watch. Something was up and the inmates weren't going to miss it. Pack and Moore were talking at the back of the truck when Brown got out of the truck to say something. Duson could hear Pack tell Brown to get back in the truck.

"Warden Pack went to the trunk of the car," Duson said. "Mr. Moore and him passed a few licks."

By "him," Duson meant Brown. Brown hit Moore in the chest with his fist, Duson said, and Moore hit Brown back with his fist. From the distance at which he was standing, Duson said, he couldn't tell where the blows were landing, but there was a scuffle.

"A few licks was passed," Duson said. "By this time, the warden had taken out a black box or a green box. It looked like a little black box."

Duson was soft-spoken when he testified and had to be reminded to speak up.

"A little black box or a little red box?" asked Washington.

"You said you was going to quit guessing," Duson replied.

"I think I hear you—I have to ask the question in an answer form," said Washington.

"I didn't say red at all," Duson replied. "I said green."

"A little green box or a little black box," Washington said. "I'm sorry. I just don't hear well. So then the warden got the little box out from the trunk of the car while they were scuffling?"

"You are guessing again," said Duson. "Not letting me explain."

"Okay," Washington said. "I'm going to have to ask it that way, Mr. Duson."

"But I'm not going to get mad," Duson said. "So you might as well quit trying to confuse me. I will tell you the best way I saw it. I'm going to tell the truth about it."

"Did these lawyers tell you I was going to try to make you mad and confuse you?" asked Washington.

"The lawyers don't have to explain that to me," Duson said. "I swore I will tell what I saw."

Nevertheless, Washington said, he had to ask him questions. "Did you say that you saw a box that the warden brought out of the trunk, but you are not sure whether it was green or blue?"

". . . It was a dark box," Duson said. "I didn't say blue. I said black."

Washington had given Duson an easy chance to confirm the prosecution's theory, that Pack had gone to the trunk for handcuffs; the handcuff box found on the ground was blue.[1]

By the time of the shooting, Duson said, he was standing under the shed by a tractor. Once the scuffle began, all of the convicts had moved there to get a better view.

Washington asked Duson how far it was from the garden shed to the shooting scene, and Duson said fifty feet. When Washington pointed out that the state's scale model showed the distance was a hundred yards, Arnold objected and Duson said the model was incorrect.

"You are saying that the scale on this that has been vouched for and admitted into evidence is incorrect?" Washington asked.

"The model itself is not right," Duson said. He stuck with fifty feet.[2]

When Moore and Brown met at the back of the truck, three shots were fired, but Duson said he could only see the gun in Brown's hand when the third shot was fired. This was the fatal one that Brown was supposed to have fired when Moore was on his knees.

Duson said he got a good view of the gun in Brown's hand. Washington got Duson to take the gun and point it at him from the right distance. It was "six to seven inches," Duson said.[3]

Washington walked Duson through the three changes Hinton had urged him to make to his statement.

"You were going over it with him," said Washington. "You are telling us he convinced you that there were not two or three shots when the warden was at the trunk but one?"

"Yes," Duson replied. ". . . But we were under a lot of pressure. We were afraid for our lives at that time. That would make a lot of difference."[4]

"All right," Washington said. "I realize that you were under a lot of pressure and stuff. Are you now saying that they didn't tell him to get out of the truck?"

"That's what I'm saying," Duson answered. "It's been some time since that happened." Even though Duson was wearing a microphone, Washington had to remind him to keep his voice up.

"And a lot of things that I said that I probably said on that tape. . . . I'm saying that if you listen to it, you can tell I was under a lot of pressure and I was nervous."

Washington pointed out that Duson, Soloman, and Kelley had been living at Diagnostic since a few days after the incident. He asked, "Have you-all had an opportunity to talk about what you-all saw out there on April 4, 1981?"

"When I was in the joint, I didn't talk about it."

Washington was incredulous. "Your testimony is to this jury that from the date that you saw what you saw out on Turkey Creek on April 4, 1981, to this day, you have never talked about it with either Soloman or Kelley?"

"No, I haven't," Duson said.

Duson had testified that Brown got in the back seat of the car on the driver's side, slid across to the passenger side, opened the door, and knocked Pack down. There was nothing in his tape-recorded accounts that supported his later testimony. Washington relentlessly prodded Duson about the contradictions.

"Did you say on the tape Brown went around behind the warden's car?" he asked.

"Yes, I did."

"And that . . . [isn't] what you are testifying to now, right?"

"No, it's not."

". . . And you never saw Brown go around behind the warden's car?"

"On the passenger side?"

"To get to the passenger side."

"No."

"The way he got to the passenger side was to go through the car?"

"Right."

"To the other side?"

"Yes."

"Is that what you saw?"

"Yes."[5]

Washington pressed Duson about why he had made these changes.

"After Mr. Hinton took the case," Duson said, "and we talked about it and things became more clear, that's when the changes were made . . ."

"After you and Mr. Hinton talked about it, things become more clear to you?"

"Yes."

The more Duson talked, the deeper the hole he dug for himself.

Washington played a long passage with Walter Pinegar and Dale Meyers going over what Duson saw and planting seeds for a more dramatic testimony at trial.

Did Brown run after Pack to the creek? Pinegar asked.

"He just walked," Duson said.

"Did Moore say anything before he was shot, say when he was on the ground, did you hear Moore say anything? . . . I mean, you didn't hear him say, 'Oh my God. Don't shoot.' Or anything like that?"

"He didn't say anything."

"He didn't say anything that you know of," Pinegar said. "Did Brown say anything when he was over him with the gun? Before he shot him, did he say anything?"

"No," Duson said.[6]

That was another contradiction. Duson had testified that when he shot Moore, Brown said, "I'm tired of this mess." Soloman testified Brown said, "I'm tired of your shit," words that Hinton added to his statement. A week after the deaths, Pinegar told a newspaper reporter that the inmate witnesses had heard Brown say, "I'm tired of your shit."[7]

Washington cast doubt on what Duson could see. Duson had said on tape that it was hard to say what happened because they were looking through the truck glass. "So, from your viewpoint," Meyers said on the tape, "you were looking through the truck glass at the three persons' top part of their bodies?"

"Yeah," Duson said.

"And that's all you could see?"

"See," Duson said, "that's what I say—usually, whenever there's something like that, well, they always put handcuffs when they're bringing him in."

"Right."

"So that's why I couldn't figure out why there was no handcuffs."

And a bit later, Duson said, "See, at first, we didn't know who was shooting. . . . We didn't know if it was him or the warden or Mr. Moore or who."

After replaying that, Washington closed in. "The reason you thought Brown shot the warden was because you saw the warden fall?"

"Right," Duson said.

"You don't know who had the gun at that time, do you?"

"No."

"The warden could have had it and fallen down with it and a shot could have been fired, right?"

"Right."[8]

At that moment Duson confirmed Eroy Brown's story.

Washington then played Duson's interview with the Texas Ranger, Wesley Styles.

"So," Washington said, "based upon what you saw . . . did Eroy get into the Warden's car?"

Duson's answer was not very convincing: "I believe that he did."[9]

Washington walked him through the prosecution's story. Brown got into the back seat alone and came out the other side.

"Where did Eroy get the gun from?"

"I don't know."

"How did Eroy get a handcuff on his arm?"

"I don't know that either."

". . . And you don't know what Warden Pack got out of the trunk?"

"No."[10]

". . . Neither Warden Pack or Major Moore ever got in the car to put any handcuffs on Eroy?"

"I didn't see it."

"Are you now satisfied as to what it was that Warden Pack got out of the trunk of the car?"

"No."

"You still don't know?"

"No, I don't."

"Could you see anything in the warden's hand?"

"From where he was standing, no."

"When you said a black box or a green box, you were just guessing, right?"

"Yes."

"You were going by something you saw later on?"

"Yes."

"Which was a handcuff box on the ground?"

"Right."

"But you didn't actually see the warden with anything in his hand when he opened the trunk and closed it, did you?"

"No."[11]

Then Washington went after the testimony from the first trial in which Duson said that after putting Brown in the back seat, Moore got into the back seat too.

"Is that right?" asked Washington.

"That's wrong," Duson said.

"That's what it says, though, right?"

Defendant's exhibit 159, showing the positions of Pack and Brown while Brown was being handcuffed.

"Yes."

"When you made that statement at the prior trial, the statement was untrue when it was made, was it not?"

"It was."

"Sir?"

"Yes, it was."

"And it was untrue and made under oath?"

"Yes."[12]

Now Duson was admitting to perjury in the first trial.

Washington pushed him about TDC procedures. Prison officials were not typically armed, Duson said. Washington asked him about how guards subdue inmates if they get belligerent, and Duson took it upon himself to make an objection.

"Before we go any further," he said, "I refuse to answer the question that you just asked me, because it doesn't have anything to do with what you have me for as a witness. I can't speak on that."

"The way it works," Washington replied, "is if Mr. Arnold thinks it doesn't have anything to do with it, he'll make an objection. . . . So unless he stands up and makes an objection, and unless the judge tells me I can't ask it, then I'm going to ask and I think you will answer."

Washington walked him through a fact of prison life that every inmate knew, that when a high rider got off his horse, he handed his gun to someone else on a horse. A guard never took a gun close to inmates. Then he got Duson to describe the typical procedure for handcuffing someone, having him spread-eagled on a car.

Duson described what Brown said happened. The handcuffs are put on one at a time. It would be unnatural, Duson admitted, to put someone in the back of a car with only one handcuff.[13]

Duson saw some of the action through the rear window of the pickup, and Washington tried to pin that down. Duson had been watching from three different places. He was looking through the screened window of the garden shed and the back window of the pickup truck during the scuffle, but he also saw over the back of the flatbed pickup. When he heard the first shot he went to the door. Defendant's exhibit 103 showed the view from the shed and through the back window of the pickup.[14]

The truck is quite small in those images, yet Duson said that he saw Moore put Brown into the back seat on the driver's side, and that he saw Brown and Pack on the passenger's side when he heard the first shot. Washington made Duson swear one more time to a story that no one on the second jury believed. Then he passed the witness.

Arnold began with how Duson came to know police procedure about hand-cuffs. It was from being arrested. And wouldn't every inmate on the Ellis Unit know the procedure as well? Duson agreed with that. Arnold put on a pair of handcuffs on his left wrist, moved to the back of the room, and demonstrated that the cuffs might have been difficult to see.[15]

Then there was the question of lighting and focus in the photographs. Photographs were not necessarily representative of what the human eye can see, and as the sun moved and shadows moved, the view changed. Arnold got the jury up to see the slides projected as Duson was seeing them. Arnold fussed with pictures and elevations. Duson had been standing on a slab, so he had a little better view.

Arnold asked a string of questions that established all the more clearly that the truck was blocking Duson's view. Duson admitted that all he could see on the far side of the car were the heads of Pack and Brown. Duson heard a shot and Pack's head went down. "And the next thing," Arnold said, ". . . there is a scuffle,

Investigator's photo showing the inmates' view of truck from the garden shed.

boom, or boom, boom, or boom, boom, boom, whichever it is." Duson agreed. The point seemed to be that it didn't matter if Duson couldn't be precise about the sequence of shots.[16]

Billy Moore was five feet, ten inches tall, but his straw cowboy hat made him taller and easier to see, Arnold pointed out. "If you had seen Warden Pack and Billy Moore on the passenger side of the car, would you have told Ranger Styles if you had seen them over there?" Duson said yes. As for being under pressure, Arnold pointed out that a lot of "bosses" had descended on the scene to question the three inmates who saw what happened. It was enough to make Duson nervous.[17]

"What do you mean by 'under pressure?'" Arnold asked. "Did somebody stick a gun to your head and make you give this tape?" Considering Eroy Brown's version of events, the question was a bit tactless.

Washington took Duson back through the physical evidence one more time, going over whether the front door or the back door of Pack's car was open and the location of Billy Moore's mashed straw hat and whether he could actually see Moore on the far side of the car.

If Duson was feeling a little secure at this point, he shouldn't have. Washington read from his transcribed description that he had said he thought Eroy had got out of the front passenger's seat, not the rear. Which was it?

"The rear," Duson said.

"So you may have been confused at the time," Washington said, "but now your memory is refreshed?"

"Yes."[18]

He had done his work. Duson admitted that he never saw Brown shoot Pack, just inferred it, and he wasn't so sure about Brown getting into the car. He couldn't see if Pack got a gun or handcuffs out of the trunk. The testimony of the state's chief witness had been destroyed.

22

In defending Brown for drowning Pack, Washington emphasized the TDC's policy about weapons. It was Pack who had brought the gun into the farm and into close proximity to an inmate.

Washington wanted Arnold Pontessa, a federal prison administrator for twenty-nine years, to testify. As a witness in the *Ruiz* trial, Pontessa had strongly criticized the TDC. He had also testified in Brown's first trial about prison policy on carrying guns. Arnold argued that Pontessa's knowledge had no direct bearing on the case, and Hester excluded it. It didn't matter much. Washington had cross-examined James Williamson, the assistant warden who captured Brown, about the TDC's no-guns policy. He'd even gotten Duson to verify it.

Larry Fletcher, a firearms expert from Dallas, testified that the trigger pull on Pack's pistol was so light from wear that it could easily have gone off in a scuffle if two men were grappling for the trigger. Arnold's expert insisted that the gun wouldn't have gone off by being bumped or kicked. Another defense expert explained that Pack's clothing revealed two different bullet tracks, confirming Eroy's account of the shot sequence. Trying to support Duson's account, Joseph Jachimczyk contended that one bullet could have accounted for the nicks in Pack's clothing.

On Friday morning Washington put on a former Midland policeman who had known Duson for eighteen years and doubted his truthfulness. Arnold pressed him for a specific example of a lie that Duson had told, but the man couldn't come up with one. Charles Sullivan of the prison reform group CURE again testified that Pack had a bad reputation for violence among inmates and their families. James Handy, a former guard turned federal probation officer, again said that Pack had a reputation for violence among inmates, but a good reputation among TDC employees.

Washington had been staying up every night until two or three in the morning and the stress finally caught up with him Friday afternoon. He felt dizzy and asked Tim Sloan if she would get him an aspirin. Then he lay down on the bench behind the defense table, and had to be taken to John Sealy Hospital for a couple of hours. A physician told him the tension and fatigue had made him hyperventilate. He was exhausted but he was physically fine. Judge Hester sent everyone home for the weekend.[1]

On Monday, November 9, inmate witnesses were supposed to testify. At the last trial, the former building tender, Tommy Carlisle, had been out of prison when he testified that Pack had hung him up with handcuffs and tortured him with a pair of pliers. Now he was in the Bexar county jail, accused of shooting his twenty-year-old wife. Another paroled inmate, the Rev. Joe Burgum, who had testified that Pack had a bad reputation for violence, was also in trouble. He had been investigated by the Brazoria County district attorney's office for assaulting a juvenile who was staying in a home for runaways Burgum had established in the coastal town of Quintana. The charges were dropped, but Burgum wasn't going to be called.

A federal judge in Houston had ordered the TDC to protect the inmate witnesses, but federal court orders were of little help. By the end of August, eighteen of the twenty-one witnesses said their lives had been threatened in prison, usually by building tenders and their associates. Robert Reed claimed that two inmates had thrown a pillowcase over his head, held him down, and carved the name PACK into his torso. The TDC said the wounds were superficial and self-inflicted. Joe Bailey Peacock claimed to have been stabbed, but TDC officials stated he had suffered three superficial puncture wounds that were also self-inflicted.

If an inmate chose to remain among the general population, where he could hold a job, recreate, and use the law library, he was vulnerable to the building tenders. If he asked for protective custody, he couldn't go to the mess hall, hold a job, or attend classes and other rehabilitative programs which would help him make parole. Protective custody, the inmates maintained, was a form of punishment.

The defense brought fifteen inmates to Galveston. Five of them were put on the stand and refused to testify, even after Judge Hester ordered them to.

The first was Aubrey Komurke, the sex offender who had testified in the first trial. Washington wanted him as a witness because he was well spoken. Shortly after the first trial, Komurke's son, who was also in prison, was assaulted by another inmate with a hammer. Once Komurke was sworn in and Washington asked him about Pack's reputation for violence, Komurke said, "If I may say so, sir, I testified in the first trial. When I returned, my son was almost killed—"

Arnold stopped him in mid-sentence, but the damage was done. The jurors might not hear any testimony from Komurke, but they were treated to the spectacle of an inmate too frightened to testify. Expecting more of the same, Judge Hester cleared the jury from courtroom. Four more inmates—Charlie Lopez, Dale Hart, Dale Lee Tedrick, and Joe Bailey Peacock—took the stand and refused to testify because they feared retribution.

One of the inmates who felt most threatened was Robert James Franks, a black inmate from Houston serving life for aggravated robbery. Franks was forty-seven years old and had been in and out of Texas and federal prisons. He had a record of being disruptive in prison. Franks asked for protective custody after TDC officials housed him with an inmate who threatened him with a knife he kept in his pillow. Franks said the TDC guards knew the inmate had a knife but would do nothing about it.

Franks testified that he had been in the Wynne Unit from 1966 to 1968. He said he was examined by the prison psychiatrist, who found that there was nothing wrong with him. Franks said that when he asked Pack, who was the building major at Wynne, to be transferred to another prison, Pack and a lieutenant beat him on the face so severely he had to be hospitalized and received several stitches. Pack, he said, was a "very violent man."[2]

The second trial lacked some of the spectacle of the first. Neither George Beto nor Jim Estelle was called.

On Tuesday morning, November 9, the two sides made their closing arguments. Arnold said that lying was at the center of the case, and Brown was "a liar by necessity."

"He needs to save his life. He cold-bloodedly assassinated Billy Moore and when there were no more bullets, he killed Warden Pack with his bare hands."

All the elements of capital murder were in place, Arnold told the jury. "The only question is," he said, "is it self-defense?"

Then he took a gambit that did not serve him well. Rather than putting on a parade of TDC witnesses to defend Pack's reputation, Arnold told the jurors that prisoners at Ellis ought to have been frightened of Pack. Pack had to be tough.

As though invoking the *Ruiz* case, Arnold observed that there were very few guards at the prison, as few as one for every hundred inmates. This was an exaggeration. According to the *Ruiz* data, the TDC averaged one guard for every twelve inmates. But at times, on the night shift, for instance, Arnold was probably right.

Ellis was the toughest prison in the system, Arnold said.

"When you get to be warden of that, you better walk tall," he said. "People better be afraid of you or you're not going to survive. It's the nature of the system . . .

"Those people were afraid of Warden Pack, isn't that the nature of the prison system? It's to keep those 35,000 people away from the 15 million of us for what they have done."

Bill Habern began the summation for the defense. He argued that Pack and Moore had only one reason for keeping Brown out on the farm and that was to punish him for threatening to expose Billy Moore.

"If they were really searching for marijuana," Habern said, "marijuana isn't going anywhere—they can take him and put him in the building and go back there and look for the marijuana."[3]

Washington closed the argument. He called Duson a pathological liar who would say whatever prosecutors wanted him to say. He couldn't possibly have seen clearly what he said he saw, Washington said. He was a hundred yards away with the car and truck blocking his views.

Brown couldn't retreat, Washington said, because "they would have said he was escaping and shot him down like a dog."[4]

The jurors withdrew that afternoon to deliberate. They included an electronics technician, a plant instrument foreman, a pipe fitter, an insurance company clerk, and a bank-teller trainer. There were eight men, four of them black, three whites, and one Hispanic. Three of the four women were white and one was Hispanic.

After two hours and twenty minutes, they returned with a verdict. The quick verdict gave Mack Arnold hope for conviction. But soon he was holding his head in his hands.

The first vote was nine to three for acquittal, but two of the jurors said they voted for conviction for discussion purposes. Soon they were unanimous. None of them believed Duson. Washington's cross-examination had been devastating.

"I think Duson was the state's burden," one of them said. "His testimony wasn't credible. . . . It's just like a two-year-old trying to build a story up. He was steadily stretching it out, stretching it out."[5]

They believed "90 percent" of what Brown said. Unlike the first set of jurors, who said they discarded the testimony about Pack's reputation, the refusal of the inmates to testify and Franks's testimony that Pack was a violent man also weighed heavily.

Washington burst into tears. The team of Washington, Habern, Sloan, and Schaffer embraced their client.

Eroy Brown wept, too. His aunt, Eddie Mae Maryland, reached across the railing and hugged him. Maryland had stood by Brown's side since the day he was arrested at Ellis. As a boy, he had often spent summers with her in Houston.

"I just knew the Lord was going to do the right thing today," she told reporters. "This is a wonderful feeling. All of our prayers have really paid off."

Brown wept, but he did not jump and shout. "I realize the public has a right to know how I feel," he told a reporter, "but I have to be careful because my case is still under litigation. I feel like the truth was brought out. I don't consider it a victory. I didn't win or lose. I consider it justice being done."[6]

Brown couldn't go with his defense team to the party afterward, of course. But when Washington met with him in the county jail, he wept.

It wasn't over yet. The state had promised to try Brown for shooting Billy Moore. Tim Sloan said they would argue that a trial for the shooting of Moore would amount to double jeopardy.

Arnold told the press that the jury's verdict was contrary to the evidence. He thought it was a fair trial, but he speculated that the jury might have hesitated to contradict its predecessor. The director of the TDC, Jim Estelle, refused to comment on the acquittal. His press spokesman, Rick Hartley, denounced Washington's use of inmate testimony.

"It's clear to me," he said, "that Mr. Washington did a good job of confusing the jury in regards to the facts."

Moore's brother Benny, who had been fishing with him that last morning, said he wasn't sure whether he wanted another trial. "In a way I do and in a way I don't," he said. "We can't bring Billy back, and I hate to see all of us have to go through this again. I do know that Eroy Brown killed my brother and a lot more happened than what Eroy admitted."

Moore's widow, Lola, said through tears, "I'm just surprised. But we still have a chance on my husband. If he's guilty I want him found guilty."

"They lost this case on the physical evidence and the testimony," Washington said. "I don't know how trying another death will change it. At some point this has to stop."[7]

"There are now twenty-three jurors who voted for acquittal and one for conviction," one of the jurors said. "I think that tells the story."[8]

23

STILL NOT PROTECTED

Three weeks after the first trial, one of Brown's inmate witnesses wrote to the new warden of Ellis, Oscar Savage, saying that he now wanted to help the prosecution.[1] He claimed that a "solidarity" committee of inmates had pressured him to help Eroy Brown. When he arrived at Ellis about a month after Brown was arrested, inmates who had seen scars on his back in the shower asked him if he would testify to save a man's life. The four thick scars, twelve to eighteen inches long, impressed the defense investigators. The inmate said that during the early 1970s, an Ellis warden had beaten him with a bullwhip after he had failed to pick enough cotton. He said that Beartracks McAdams, then the warden, told him if he ever complained about what had happened, he would have the building tenders kill him.

It was a plausible story. The inmate had taken off his shirt in Judge Dalehite's chambers in the November 30, 1981, hearing when Habern was arguing they needed protection. Habern says that when Dalehite saw the scars, his eyes widened.[2] There was nothing that the defense would have liked more than to get the inmate on the stand and have him take off his shirt before the jury. But it never happened. The inmate refused to testify.

Now he had a change of heart.

"So you see, sir, the whole thing, all the inmates here on the Ellis," he wrote, "it's all just one big lie, and now I am free of it.

"And in return I ask only one thing of you, if it is released to the press, or to anyone else that I wrote this letter, the minute my name is out, no place here on

Ellis will my life be worth ten cents. . . . There are 3000 convicts here who would kill me if they knew, so please keep my name as close to you as possible."

He was playing a dangerous game. A week after Brown was acquitted, the inmate wrote a five-page complaint to the Walker County district attorney's office.

"The jail staff were not concerned about state witness for the prosecution, they merely came to the bars and shouted out the question: 'Are there any prosecution witnesses in here?'

"At that time [an inmate][3] went forward and told that officer, a sergeant, that there were two state witnesses in the tank, and named himself and called my name as the other. Every inmate there . . . turned to look at me, and I just laughed and tried to play it off."

He wrote that a jailer advised him to keep calm, refuse to testify for the defense, and then testify for the prosecution as a rebuttal witness. He refused to testify for the defense, and was never called by the prosecution.

Two days after Brown was acquitted, he wrote, on Friday night, November 11, several of the inmates took turns beating and raping the prosecution's potential witness with a wooden stick. The letterwriter said he had a fight with a couple of the inmates and stayed out of it. The abuse went on all night, he wrote.

"After the fight I minded my own business and [the raped man] went completely insane, he still is, God help him.

"I feel that [he] and I were crossed out, used and discarded by you and your office, and that you never had any intentions of helping us, or having us moved and placed in a place of safety.

"One way or the other," he wrote, "if [he] and I are not moved to the Walls lockup, protective custody soon, and [he] is not given proper psychiatrist [sic] treatment, I promise you this: everyone in Texas, and *Life* magazine, and the USA will know what happened.

"And you should remember, too, you are going to re-try Brown on the murder of Major Moore, I know for a fact that I will be at that trial, and short of killing me and my whole family, I will tell it, the whole thing, over the radio, newspaper and anywhere else people will listen."

After these threats, he ended with a supplication:

"I am not trying to be a smart ass. . . . Please help us, you can, you promised protection, hell just keep your end of the bargain [sic]."

The letter displayed the inmate psychology well. Trapped in prison, he becomes a prisoner of his narcissistic fantasies. Someone somehow will rescue him. He is at once threatening and pleading. Because he is powerless, his threats mean little. Because he has changed sides, his suffering means little.

According to Aubrey Komurke, the writ writer who had testified in Brown's first trial, the inmate who was raped arrived in Galveston already insane, driven crazy by eight months of abuse in the prison system. That's why he was ready to turn state's evidence.

Two days after Brown was acquitted, Komurke typed a single-spaced, four-page letter to his son at the Darrington Unit about what had happened at the trial. He had just bought an electric typewriter with money from the sale of his paintings at the prison rodeo. The mail censor photocopied the letter and sent it to Walter Pinegar.

Komurke anticipated that Brown's inmate witnesses would get a new federal hearing to protect them.

"I saw some of the guys who were claiming of being cut or stabbed and beaten," Komurke wrote. "There is little doubt. I saw one medical report: the three wounds went 6¾, 6½, and 4½ inches deep. Cinny Kennard of Channel 11 saw a kid [from the first trial] and the first thing she said when she saw him was, 'My God, what happened to him? He wasn't like this the last time.' She was virtually in tears when she heard what did happen to him: he was kept in isolation, beaten, subjected to harassment and verbal abuse, beaten some more, and on and on for eight months! They're not playing games.... This is serious shit. You should have seen how that kid acted: he was really messed up and went in and out of real sensibility. Man, every time I saw that kid I could see you in his place. PLEASE put in for a transfer ... TDC people even threatened Washington's life after the trial, according to him.

"When I took the stand and Washington asked me questions about the joint, I addressed the judge to say that I had enormous respect for the court, but that although I testified in the first trial I could not do so at this one—and this was before the jury! I went on to say that less than a month after my return, you were nearly killed by an inmate guard in two separate attacks and that while I could make the decision about whether to jeopardize my own safety, I could not as a parent ... morally take a position that may jeopardize yours as well ...

"As I walked out I saw the woman juror near the end of the box which we walk by with tears in her eyes. I made it a point to look at each of the jurors as I explained and as I walked out. I saw no hostile expression."

He also told the story of decent treatment in the Galveston jail.

"... You wouldn't believe the way Galveston treated us. It was even more sensitive and relaxed than the last time. They had a new jail major, captain and lieutenant, and we were uptight that they might be redneck. But when they sent up for a spokesman for the tank, the guys chose me to go out to talk for them. And it was

STILL NOT PROTECTED ||| 179

unreal; we sat in his office and the major and I talked on a real eyeball level. None of the bullshit role playing, and it was plenty OK. Nearly all the regular jail cops were absolutely unbelievable, too: even better than the really decent guards here. As we left the jail last evening, the major came by the door and I called him over to tell him that we weren't accustomed to be treated like that and that I spoke for all of us in expressing our appreciation for the way we were handled. He said he was new to this kind of work, but that he felt men should be treated like men, and he found that it seems to work. . . . I ribbed him that if his 'new wave' works and word gets around, he'd have every redneck sheriff in Texas on his ass for stirring up humane treatment of prisoners. Hell, he let Cinny Kennard and her cameraman come right to the tank and to film and talk with us. And *she* is something else."

The Galveston sheriff, Joe Max Taylor, had even gone so far as to put a phone in the witness's tank and let them call Ray Hill's radio program. *The Prison Show* normally ran two hours, but when Hill realized all the inmate witnesses from the Eroy Brown trial were available and ready to talk, the show that Sunday ran three and a half hours. Komurke organized the inmates. Lawrence Pope, who had recently been released from federal prison, was at the studio to add his thoughts. The jurors might not have heard their stories, but the public could.[4]

Komurke had high hopes that the public would become more and more aware of Texas prison problems.

"I got hot at the whole team of attorneys the first couple of visits, just like I said on *The Prison Show* . . . in case you heard it. I demanded for all of us to know why they had made practically no effort to enforce the protective orders during those eight months between the trials, that when they needed us, they called us, exposed us and our loved ones to jeopardy and then didn't follow up. I got on Fort's and Habern's asses for not having your name added to the witness protection orders and asked what they intended to do about it."

But there was little Habern or Fort could do about how the TDC ran the prisons, even with court orders. In a 1977 ruling about the protection of *Ruiz* witnesses, the Fifth Circuit Court of Appeals had observed: "The record discloses that in response to their participation in this litigation, these inmates have been subjected during its pendency to threats, intimidation, coercion, punishment and discrimination, all in the face of protective orders to the contrary by the district court and our long-standing rule that the right of a prisoner to have access to the courts to complain of conditions of his confinement shall not be abridged."[5]

The only relief Komurke and the other inmates could hope for was that the federal courts would remove them to federal prison. In the meanwhile, they had to put up with whatever happened in Texas prisons.

Komurke hoped that the reporting by Cinny Kennard, Ray Hill, and others could help them get more coverage. He was thinking big: "Donahue, Merv Griffin, Frost, Carson, 20-20, 60 Minutes and the like . . ." That weekend had to have been one of the highlights of Komurke's life. A television reporter had told him that he talked like a Southern lawyer. A man who was one of society's despised criminals, a man who sexually molested children, had managed to be heard, in a small way, about Texas prisons.

The TDC was not happy at all. When Brown's acquittal was announced, someone in the courtroom reported to the court that he had heard a man in gray threaten Washington's life.[6] A few days after the trial, Craig Washington drove Habern to Habern's little house in Riverside, about five miles from Ellis prison. The picture window and the front door of the little place had been riddled with .22 caliber bullets.[7]

A little after midnight on December 7, 1982, as Eroy Brown sat in the relative safety of the Galveston county jail, the TDC took a black inmate named Charlie Brooks to the state's new execution chamber. Brooks and his best friend had been convicted of kidnapping and shooting to death a Fort Worth mechanic. Neither man admitted pulling the trigger, but because of a problem with jury selection, Brooks's friend managed to plea-bargain for forty years.

For the same crime, Brooks got the death penalty. He was given a last meal, strapped to a gurney, and as he prayed to Allah, he was injected with a trio of drugs that killed him. Charles Colson, the Nixon White House insider who went to prison and became an advocate for reform, wrote that the execution was not without pain. A picture of Brooks's body, taken at a Huntsville funeral home, was published in the *Huntsville Item* and picked up by *Newsweek*.[8] It was the first execution in Texas in ten years. Although Eroy Brown had been acquitted for drowning Wallace Pack, he still faced a needle for shooting Billy Moore.

24

PAYING FOR JUSTICE

Walker County and the Texas Department of Corrections were separate enti-
ties of one mind: No matter what twenty-three jurors had found, Eroy Brown
had to be tried for shooting Billy Max Moore. The judge of the Walker County
commissioners court said he thought the nineteen hundred TDC employees
in Walker County needed to be protected. The acting district attorney, Frank
Blazek, said he felt that same way.

"The only pressure," he said, "is the pressure that I feel in my own conscience,
that if an inmate can kill a guard or kill a prison employee, and then turn around
and so no other guard or no other employee witnessed it—and only other inmates witness it, and you can't believe them—and then claim self-defense and get
off, it makes it very, very difficult for every employee at TDC."

Blazek didn't add that it would also be very difficult for him to get elected
district attorney without the support of the TDC employees of Walker County.
Months after his April automobile accident, Mark Ward was still in the hospital
and wasn't running for re-election.

For the TDC's defenders, the Eroy Brown case had become like *Ruiz*. In *Ruiz*,
there was nothing wrong with the facts—there was something wrong with the
judge. In Brown's case, there was something wrong with the juries. Blazek needed a better jury. Less that two weeks after Brown's acquittal, Blazek applied to
Judge Hester for a change of venue, arguing that the news coverage would preju-
dice a third Galveston jury.

A third trial, Washington argued, amounted to double jeopardy. "The jury already heard all the evidence in Moore's case when they heard Pack's case," he said. "It is the same evidence."[1]

That argument didn't go anywhere. Who was going to criticize Hester for trying a penniless black convict a third time?

In early December Hester held a hearing on the change of venue. A former prosecutor from Galveston County, Jack Brock, said three-fourths of his circle of fifty friends in Galveston believed Brown was innocent. The Galveston county clerk, V. V. Beninati Jr., said he thought the trial got no more publicity than any other capital case, and that a fair jury could be found. Washington argued that the case could be moved to Houston, if necessary. He produced a Rice University graduate student and a data-processing executive from Houston who testified that despite the news coverage, neither of them had heard of the case. Washington had commissioned a public opinion survey that supported his argument. Two Galveston County district judges both said they didn't think the trial was of vital importance to county residents. Washington observed that ninety-six thousand people were registered to vote in Galveston County. It shouldn't be difficult to find a jury that wasn't familiar with the case.[2]

But the arguments didn't work. Judge Darrell Hester had been tougher than Dalehite. A former district attorney, Hester had a reputation for law and order in the Rio Grande Valley, where he was nicknamed "Hang 'em High Hester" for his belief in punishment as a deterrent to crime.[3]

If Hester kept the trial in Galveston or Houston, Walker County and the TDC could blame Hester for stacking the deck against them and back out on a third trial. Hester granted the state a change of venue. By Christmas, both sides were still wrangling about where the next trial would be. If they couldn't agree, Hester would decide.

Texas prosecutors had long used peremptory challenges to keep blacks off juries. No one was better at this than Henry Wade, who served as district attorney for Dallas County from 1951 to 1986. In 1986 the Supreme Court overturned the murder conviction of Thomas Miller-El because of Wade's jury selection policies. Wade's prosecutors believed that members of minority groups almost always empathized with the accused. One of his prosecutors recommended against permitting "Jews, Negroes, Dagos and Mexicans or a member of any minority race on a jury, no matter how rich or how well educated."[4]

Blazek wanted a small rural county with a conservative Anglo population and few blacks. If they couldn't get Houston or Austin, Washington and Habern wanted Corpus Christi or San Antonio.

Washington wanted the third trial to come soon—in February 1983, if possible—while the case was still fresh in his mind.

But there wouldn't be a third trial if Walker County didn't have the money, and that depended on the state legislature. The state had already spent $500,000 in attorneys' fees and other trial expenses, and Walker County was broke.

Walker County applied for a state grant of $150,000 from the funding commission of the Criminal Justice Division. The commission consisted of the governor, Mark White; the lieutenant governor, Bill Hobby; and the comptroller, Bob Bullock. Hobby and Bullock declared that the legislature had made it clear that it didn't want to spend any more money on trying Brown. In August Hobby and Bullock voted against funding a third trial. Bullock's press spokesman, John Moore, said, "We figured the state had gone far enough. We figured if they [Walker County officials] wanted to go farther, they could pay for it."[5]

Walker County commissioner Wayne Hooks insisted that the state should pay for another trial. Walker County was already stuck with bills from the Brown trial and for that of Ignacio Cuevas, the survivor of the Carrasco episode in 1974. Cuevas had been tried and convicted three times for capital murder, but the Texas Court of Criminal Appeals had reversed the decisions because of errors in jury selection.

Seeing that Hobby and Bullock opposed the grant, Walker County withdrew the request. That summer the legislature redrew the membership of the panel, allowing Mark White and the speaker of the House, Gib Lewis, each to appoint four of the eleven members of the board. Lewis and White were sympathetic to a third trial. Walker County went back for more money. Hobby and Bullock were out of the way.

In July the *Huntsville Item* ran an article critical of Bill Hobby for not supporting the trial. Frank Blazek had told Hobby's aide, Steve Dial, that he had new ballistics evidence that would turn the third trial around, but that hadn't changed Hobby's mind.

The more Blazek explained his evidence the less likely it seemed to have any significance. Blazek said the prosecution actually had the "new" evidence available in the second trial, but held it back until after Brown testified. The plan was to call a ballistics expert to prove that Brown was lying about how many times he had fired the gun.

"We wanted to get his [Brown's] explanation of the physical evidence before introducing the [new ballistics] evidence," Blazek said. "As it turned out, his testimony was a total failure for the defense, and so we didn't think there was any need to call a rebuttal witness."[6]

This was an astounding statement, considering how persuasive Brown had been on the stand. If Blazek had convincing ballistics evidence that showed Brown was lying about how many times the gun had fired, it would seem logical to put it on. But Blazek went further, saying that his problem was getting a change of venue. Galveston was the problem.

"In a location where the state of Texas can get a fair forum," Blazek said, "I believe Brown would get convicted whether or not the new evidence existed." So maybe the new evidence didn't matter.

Washington doubted the new evidence existed. He had written Hobby that summer that he should turn down the grant. The legislature had failed to fund inmate trials that session. The whole system of paying lawyers for indigent inmates was in turmoil. Washington, Habern, and Sloan had been paid after the hung jury, but as the weeks went by, the state wouldn't pay Washington and Habern for the acquittal. There was a price for success. By July Washington and his team were owed $220,000, including attorneys' fees, the costs of investigations, and payments to expert witnesses.

Alarmed by Brown's acquittal, White proposed creating a statewide prosecution team to try TDC inmates for crimes. Washington said he would support such a bill.[7]

Mark White seemed surprised when he was told that while he was working to fund a third trial for Brown, Washington and Habern hadn't been paid for the second trial.[8] White had his deputy at the Criminal Justice Division ask Walker County commissioners to lower the costs for a third trial by seeking a lesser penalty. Capital trials were expensive.

In October Frank Blazek decided to reduce the charge of capital murder to murder, which carried a sentence of from five years to life. Brown no longer faced execution. The trial would take only two weeks and cost the state about $45,000. Mark White happily approved the grant.

Habern said reducing the charge didn't mean a thing if the state expected some sort of plea bargain. "They can reduce it to driving while intoxicated and a five-hundred dollar fine," he said, "and we wouldn't talk to them."[9]

On October 27, Washington sued Mark White and the Governor's Criminal Justice Office in an Austin federal court for $1.35 million in actual and punitive damages, charging they were denying Brown the right to a fair trial. He also asked the judge to stop Texas from giving Frank Blazek $45,000 for the next trial until the defense had been compensated.

The suit charged: "The actions of the defendants are another chapter in a long history of open, blatant, willful and utter malicious trampling of individual civil rights by the governing authorities and administration of the state of Texas."

White invited Washington to meet with him privately to discuss the matter, but Washington refused, saying he would meet with White's lawyer, the attorney general of Texas.[10]

In early November Washington and Habern argued in federal court in Austin about being paid. For three days Washington tried to subpoena Mark White to appear at the hearing, but was unsuccessful. A trio of well-known defense lawyers—Roy Minton, Will Gray, and Vincent Perini—testified that it would be difficult for Brown to have a fair trial a third time if his lawyers hadn't been paid for the earlier trial. Near the end of the hearing, an assistant attorney general, Paul Rich, offered the defense a $45,000 grant to match the one given to Walker County. Washington declared the offer an insult. The federal judge blocked the state grant to Walker County for ten days to give Washington time to study the issues. But he told Washington that Judge Darrel Hester in Brownsville was the court where he should seek relief.[11]

Soon Washington was threatening to put Bob Bullock, the state comptroller, in jail for contempt of court. Bullock, the brilliant, manic, alcoholic Texas comptroller since 1974, knew something about strong-arm tactics. He had made a name for himself by padlocking businesses that had not paid state sales taxes, seizing their assets, and selling them. Bullock was thinking about running for governor against Mark White in the next Democratic primary. Bullock retorted that Washington knew that as comptroller he couldn't pay a bill from a fund in which there was no money. He told reporters that Washington must have forgotten who controlled the money. Mark White, he said, could solve the problem with "his number two pencil." All he had to do was pay Washington and Habern from the Criminal Justice Planning Fund, which had a balance of $12 million.

"He wouldn't even have to write his name," Bullock said. "I would honor his X on a voucher to pay this claim if it were properly witnessed."

The reporters hurried to White's office to get his response. "Did he say that?" White asked. "I'm appalled." White insisted there was no money to pay for the case.[12]

At a pretrial hearing in early December, Judge Darrell Hester ruled that the state had to come up with $50,000 for the defense or he would dismiss Walker County's case for the shooting of Billy Moore. But that didn't solve the problem of payment for the second trial. The money for paying for the trials of indigent defendants hadn't been appropriated. Assistant attorney general Dave Richards testified that the criminal justice fund was overcommitted by $19 million, and nothing short of a special session of the legislature could ensure that the funds would be available.

Hester could see that it would take months to sort it out. He set a trial date for April 16 and ordered the state to pay the defense $50,000 for the trial, matching what Walker County had been given.

Saying it was in his client's interests to be tried a third time, Washington accepted the deal.

Washington said Eroy Brown wanted to be vindicated. "He wants to go to the well three times and have thirty-five out of thirty-six jurors find him innocent. Then he won't have to live listening over his shoulder to whispers that he would have been found guilty if he had been tried. Eroy Brown's good name is important to him."[13]

When the hearing was over, Washington addressed Brown in the courtroom so reporters could hear. He declared he would represent him no matter what, even though he hadn't been paid for the earlier trial.

"My obligation is to you," he told Brown. "I don't give a damn if I never get a dime."[14]

25

THE END OF AN ERA

Frank Klimko had been covering cops and the courthouse in Port Arthur and Beaumont when he landed a job as the Huntsville writer for the *Houston Chronicle*. He began work in February 1982, just as Brown's first trial ended with a hung jury. He was a skinny guy, only twenty-five years old, who had grown up in New York state. Klimko wanted to be an investigative reporter, but he was green. He had the good sense not to tell people in Huntsville that he was from New York. When they asked where he was from, he said he grew up "all over," as though he had been a military kid. He hadn't had much luck finding local sources. He went to a barber favored by TDC officials, but all he got, he recalled, was a crappy haircut.

He was getting nowhere with the TDC, the expected topic of most of his stories, and his editor was on him for getting beaten by other newspapers and even *Texas Monthly*. He ran into Habern one day at the Walker County courthouse and asked him some naïve questions about the TDC.

"Boy," said Habern, "have you ever read the *Ruiz* case?"

Klimko realized he hadn't done his homework. He pulled the clips of the *Chronicle*'s Zarko Franks and compared their cynical take to the other coverage. Then he read Justice's decision. He was shocked. He hadn't realized how much official violence had been done in the prisons by the building tenders. Klimko had visited Ellis and had seen the building tenders and the warden's boys at work.

"An inmate was in the front of the warden's office," he said, "accessing inmate files and typing updates on inmate stuff to the warden. Later during the tour, it was inmates, not the guards, who had keys that let our little entourage through the various gates of Ellis. Both were clear violations that I later pointed out to the special master's offices."

The control model was becoming impossible to maintain. Total control at the lowest possible cost meant giving some inmates control over others. Total control meant having to answer to no one—not the legislature, not the governor, not the courts.

"With the slow decline of the BTs [building tenders], the absence of any guard authority (they were vastly understaffed) and the indifference of the TDC head honchos, a power vacuum developed at all the units," Klimko said. "And just like in politics, no power vacuum exists for long without opportunists seeking to take advantage. The gangs did just that. There were some units for a time that were virtually controlled by the gangs, who kept the other inmates in check, exacted justice and ran things right under the noses of the wardens, who preferred to look the other way."[1]

In the summer of 1982, before Eroy Brown's second trial, a former building tender from a prison in Sugar Land, just outside of Houston, explained the building tender system this way: "I jumped on inmates, I whipped ass for the bosses— that was my job. I didn't like that, I didn't like that at all. I mean, what about *my* rights? I'm being asked to whup some guy real bad, to violate his rights, and it hurt my own respect for myself sometimes; it hurt me with the other brothers inside. I was *glad* when that Judge Justice came along. Bam. Overnight I lost all my privileges, but at least I wasn't somebody's monster anymore."[2]

With the phasing out of the building tenders in 1983, the gangs that had plagued California prisons gained ascendance in Texas prisons. Organized by race, the Crips, the Bloods, the Mexican Mafia, the Aryan Brotherhood, and other gangs began competing for power. An unprecedented series of inmate killings and knifings took place.

"The question we always got at the newspaper," Klimko recalled, "was 'how do they get knives into prison?' The average Texan at that time didn't understand that weapons trafficking occurred in the prisons, often promoted by the BTs, who would arm their associates to keep control of the wings under their charge. The question should have been 'how do they keep anyone alive in the prisons?'"

The upsurge in prison violence and the continued revelations of the *Ruiz* case made things increasingly difficult for Jim Estelle. When Harry Whittington joined the TDC board in 1979, Estelle promised him that board meetings would last no more that two hours. Usually the votes were unanimous.[3]

Whittington was wary of unanimous votes and board members who became close friends of the chief executives. That made it difficult to question and even fire a manager. As the new member, Whittington bided his time. Estelle liked to say he worked for the TDC board, not the governor, and he bragged about his tight relationship with its members. Whittington's first run-in with Estelle came in July 1979 when Estelle proposed during a private board meeting that he could take on some outside work with a company that provided security in the Middle East. Several board members questioned the propriety of that. Estelle was already well compensated and the TDC was embroiled in a sweeping civil rights suit. Whittington thought the board had been clear, but three months later Estelle told him and the board chairman, James Windham, that he had accepted the outside job but would resign if it interfered with his work at the TDC. Whittington let Governor Clements know about the deal, and Estelle quickly learned that he *did* work for the governor. He ended his outside work.

"It was my first realization," Whittington wrote, "that Estelle would openly defy a majority of his board."

A 1978 TDC study predicted that the system would need two thousand more beds every two years.[4] According to the TDC mindset, two thousand beds required a maximum-security prison and several thousand acres of farmland to go with it. Under state law, inmates must work, and prisons must be as self-sustaining as possible. The head of the TDC board, James Windham, declared that a new prison site needed only two things: an adequate growing season and water. The board fastened its sights on two farms totaling more than 14,000 acres in the Rio Grande Valley, in Hidalgo County, the site of Brown's third trial. State officials extolled the 340-day growing season. They would be able to work inmates all year round.

Under state law the board was supposed to consider other sites, either near Huntsville or in West Texas, but Whittington learned that only the Valley sites would be considered. No land was available near Huntsville, he was told. He questioned TDC officials about the problems with the sites, including their cost and remoteness, and found the answers he received "incomplete, deceptive or untruthful."[5]

Prison reformers Charles and Pauline Sullivan questioned the choice, too, and sued the board for violating the Texas Open Meetings Act in March 1978. Soon the *Dallas Morning News* wrote that the previous owner of one of the tracts was a convicted criminal with ties to organized crime. Whittington and a state auditor found the land to be overpriced. A state board finally denied the purchase and the TDC board found that there was land available near Huntsville, after all, seven thousand acres of it adjacent to the Ellis farm, where Ellis II was eventually built.

In the ten years that Estelle had directed the TDC, the prison population more than doubled, from 16,000 inmates in 1972 to 36,000 in 1982. Five maximum-security prisons had been built, including the new Beto Unit near Tennessee Colony and the two Pack Units near Navasota.[6]

But the Texas legislature was taking a hard look at the TDC's habit of building only large, maximum-security prisons in rural areas. Justice had ordered the state to build small prisons holding no more than five hundred inmates close to urban areas, where families could visit. By building medium- and minimum-security prisons, the system could better classify inmates and help them make the transition back to the free world. Legislators liked the lower costs of transitional facilities. They were also questioning the costs of prison "perks" for prison managers that included free housing and inmate servants.[7]

Estelle's critics were not all liberals. Ray Keller, a conservative Republican from Duncanville, a bedroom community of Dallas, began questioning the costs as well. Along with Bill Hobby, the Democratic lieutenant governor who worked the levers of the state legislature, and Ray Farabee, a centrist Democrat, Keller came to see the TDC as a money pit. In declaring Keller one of the state's ten best legislators for 1983, *Texas Monthly* wrote:

As a law enforcement chairman, he refused to follow the traditional legislative script: give prison officials all the money they want and tell the folks back home that you're for law and order. When a rock-ribbed, tough-on-crime conservative like Keller decided that the business-as-usual approach cost far too much money and showed far too little success, he made prison reform respectable.

Jaws hit the floor the day Keller began talking in committee about a no-growth policy, sounding like an environmentalist who'd wandered into the wrong meeting by mistake. Not only would there be no new prisons but he also wanted to take $200 million from the prison system and spend it on halfway houses and better parole supervision. . . . The House passed the entire reform package without a single hostile question in floor debate and without a dissenting vote on six of the seven prison reform bills.

Jim Estelle had not taken stock of the revolution that was going on. Conservatives might be tough on criminals, but they were also looking at how the government's money was being spent. Estelle had admitted in the early 1970s that as many as 40 percent of Texas inmates didn't require maximum-security prisons. Such prisons had become a luxury the state couldn't afford anymore, Keller said. "The taxpayers are getting nothing out of it except a bunch of professional inmates."[8]

Unused to outside supervision or even dissension on his board, in September 1983 Jim Estelle announced his resignation. He had lost the confidence of his board, the legislature, and the governor's office. A federal judge and TDC inmates were questioning his civil rights practices, but even worse was the scrutiny of TDC's business and management practices.

In his resignation speech, Estelle said that perhaps the TDC would benefit from a different perspective. He offered to stay on for six months to allow the board time to find his successor and smooth the transition. But he was gone in three weeks, and the person behind that was the lead witness for the inmates in the *Ruiz* trial, Lawrence Pope.

Pope, a former banker turned bank robber, was obsessed with the insider business deals of the TDC and its officials. He found one in a $2 million construction contract to build a dairy farm at the Eastham prison and wrote Ray Keller about it.[9] The contract had gone to a Huntsville contractor, George Broxson, who was on the board of a landholding group called Ten-K. Pope had noticed in a magazine profile of Estelle that he owned stock in Ten-K. The board included not only Jim Estelle, but also Billy McMillan, who had been warden of Ellis before Pack took over, and James Williamson, the assistant warden who had captured and handcuffed Eroy Brown. Another shareholder had been convicted of embezzling $100,000 from the TDC employee's credit union.[10]

Nothing in the contract for the dairy farm pointed to a crime by Estelle or the other Ten-K board members, but the deal smelled so bad that Estelle left insisting that he had never profited from any deal. "I do not lie or steal," he declared. It was a humiliating way to leave.[11]

Estelle soon went to work for a Huntsville bank. Lawrence Pope, who had grown up in Huntsville, had always suspected that TDC officials and the Huntsville banks were involved in all sorts of wicked collusion. George Beto had been a bank director. Estelle could be sure that Pope would be combing through the public records of every deal he made. He stayed at the bank for six months and then moved back to California, where he worked for many years in its prison system. It was a shame, because Estelle believed in many of the reforms that the inmates were calling for.

Within a year, violence was overwhelming the TDC as inmate gangs grew out of control, and management could no longer use building tenders to intimidate and control the inmates. The guards reacted with more and more violence. In 1984, the year of Eroy Brown's third trial, approximately two hundred disciplinary actions were taken against TDC guards and other officials for using excessive force. It seemed that Brown was right, that high-ranking prison officials were capable of violence.

26

FREE AT LAST

As the summer wore on, the civil rights case to protect Brown's inmate witnesses became a miniature version of *Ruiz v. Estelle.* For *Brown v. Estelle,* Bruce Fort joined forces with Bill Habern. Habern recruited David Vanderhoof, a former Justice Department lawyer who had played a leading role in *Ruiz.* Vanderhoof was a familiar figure in Judge Justice's courtroom. He had represented the United States in the lawsuit to integrate Texas schools. When it became apparent to Judge Justice that mentally ill juveniles were being held in prison-like conditions in the state reform schools, he observed to Vanderhoof that there seemed to be a right-to-treatment case. "Vanderhoof jumped on this like a shark after live bait," Justice told his biographer.[1]

During *Ruiz,* Vanderhoof waved a 1924 Texas prison investigation like a bloody shirt, insisting that conditions were no better in 1978 than they had been fifty years earlier. He declared that he knew a man in Virginia who took better care of his charges and offered more spacious conditions than Texas prisons. The man ran a kennel.[2]

Vanderhoof soon lost his job under the Reagan administration. His marriage fell apart and he was broke. Habern bought him a plane ticket to Texas and got him a fee. Federal judge Norman Black feared a replay of the *Ruiz* case, with dozens of witnesses making charges and countercharges, followed by lengthy appeals. When Vanderhoof proposed compulsory arbitration, Black grabbed it.

Doug Becker, a private attorney hired by the state attorney general's office, had to go along. Habern believed it to be the first time that the TDC had ever let inmate claims be taken to arbitration rather than trial. The agreement, Becker said, didn't mean that the TDC admitted that the inmates had been harassed. He continued to argue that they were safe. Two arbitrators, Allen Breed, former director of the National Institute of Corrections, and Roy Gerard, a retired assistant warden of the Federal Bureau of Prisons, were chosen. The hearings for twenty inmates were set for the Criminal Justice Center at Sam Houston State University.

Judge Black believed the arbitration process would be much more effective than judicial intervention. The inmate witnesses would appear before the arbitrators and state their cases for transfer to federal protection.

In December Black and the arbitrators reached an agreement. Six TDC inmates were transferred to federal prison, including Robert Reed, who claimed someone had held him down and scratched Pack's name on his chest with a knife, and Robert Franks, who said an inmate was allowed to keep a knife to threaten him with. Six other inmates were moved within the system and had their "good time" restored. Four more were paroled.[3]

As for Eroy Brown, Black ruled that Brown should never be returned to TDC custody. If Brown were convicted of killing Billy Moore, or any other crime in Texas, he would serve his sentence in a federal prison. It was a protection that Brown would have for the rest of his life.[4]

Brown's trial for shooting Billy Moore had been heating up in the press. The defense obtained Moore's employment file from Texas Parks and Wildlife and shared it with reporters. Moore had worked as a game warden from 1961 to 1968, and resigned under pressure for taking a hundred dollars to let commercial fishermen run nets in a private lake. His supervisor complained that he had failed to return state-issued property. A note on his exit interview said Moore should not be rehired because "he cannot be depended on and he will not tell the truth."

Blazek retorted that it was typical of the defense to try the victim. "But I don't see anything in those employment records that indicate it was a good thing to kill him."[5]

Since the two sides couldn't agree on a site, Darrell Hester moved the trial to his backyard, the small town of Edinburg in the Rio Grande Valley. Edinburg was first named in 1908 for the town's developer, Dennis B. Chapin. Chapin shot and killed a Texas Ranger in a San Antonio saloon, and was acquitted, presumably by reason of self-defense. The embarrassed civic leaders renamed the town for the Scottish birthplace of one of its other developers.[6]

Edinburg was the county seat of Hidalgo County. A Democratic stronghold, it was 80 percent Hispanic and one of the poorest counties in Texas. Short of a big city, Eroy Brown could not have asked for a better town for his trial. The jury wouldn't have a black person on it, but neither would it consist of rural Anglos. It would likely be all Hispanic.

Habern had helped Brown win parole for the sentence that had put him in Ellis. Despite Washington's efforts, however, Eroy Brown was held without bail. Because the grant for the defense was only $50,000, and the charge was no longer a capital crime, Washington was allowed to bill the state for the services of only one lawyer. He could have a second lawyer, to be paid at the investigator's rate of $17.50 an hour. Habern was still broke from the second trial and owed back taxes. He had spent the last trial sleeping on the floor of a medical student's apartment. He wanted to go but he couldn't afford it. Kent Schaffer had earned his law degree and could afford to sit second chair for the investigator's fee. There would be no special prosecutor for Walker County. Frank Blazek would have to rely on his investigator, Walter Pinegar, to help him try the case. By then Craig Washington could try this case in his sleep, not that he would be getting much.

The image of TDC officials continued to be tarnished. One of Estelle's last acts as director was to fire a veteran warden, Robert Cousins. A bitter critic of Frances Jalet when he was warden at Ellis in the early 1970s, Cousins had been accused in one lawsuit of ordering a gang of building tenders to beat an inmate with ax handles. But nothing had ever stuck to him. When mounted guards at Coffield prison captured an escapee in September 1983, Cousins ordered them to "do something to his ass." The guards trampled the inmate with a horse and whipped him with their reins. Cousins made the mistake of ordering the beating on his car radio. He had been heard at three prisons in the Tennessee Colony area. Investigators found hoof prints and rein marks on the inmate.

A TDC board member gamely contended that this was an isolated incident,[7] but a week later the court-appointed monitor issued a report stating that brutality by high-ranking prison officials was a common occurrence. "In a great many instances, brutal, unprovoked beatings were inflicted upon inmates who were guilty of violating institutional rules but who posed no immediate threat to safety or security," the report stated.[8]

Mark White and Ray Keller called for a house-cleaning of TDC management. D. V. "Red" McKaskle, a veteran of the Beto and Estelle administrations, had been acting as director since Estelle had resigned, but his heart was not in investigating and punishing men he had worked with for years.

For months nothing but bad news had been coming out of the TDC. In early March the *Valley Morning Star* ran a wire-service story that said fifty-two TDC officers had been dismissed, demoted, or reprimanded for brutality against inmates. The two most recently fired were an assistant warden and a building captain at the Wynne prison, Wallace Pack's old stomping ground.[9]

On Thursday, April 19, 1984, Washington and Blazek quickly picked a Hispanic jury of seven men and five women. The trial was expected to last a week to ten days. The following Monday, Blazek surprised everyone by announcing that he would call only four witnesses. Those included James Williamson, the assistant warden at Ellis who had captured Brown, and Evan Hodge, an FBI firearms expert who was supposed to provide new ballistics evidence. Although he hadn't participated in the autopsy, Dr. Aurelio Espinola, chief deputy medical examiner from Houston, was sent, presumably to appeal to the Hispanic jury. Washington had so thoroughly demolished Levi Duson in the last trial that Blazek could not put him on again. He would have only one inmate witness, James Soloman.

Williamson again told the story of how he had handcuffed Brown when he walked up out of Turkey Creek, covered in slime, with a bullet hole in one foot and a pair of handcuffs dangling from his wrist. Schaffer asked him about the prison's policy for carrying weapons on the farm, and Williamson said that it was permitted if they were kept locked in a car trunk.

Soloman told the story he had stuck with since the first trial, that Brown had been placed in the back of the car and had come out the other side, that Brown had grabbed Moore by the left shoulder and fired the gun, with his hand raising up and down, "throwing" the bullets.

"The only thing I could see was fire jumping from the pistol," Soloman said. He also threw in the line that Mike Hinton, the first special prosecutor, had added to his statement: as he was shooting, Brown said, "I'm tired of your shit."[10]

Blazek tried to support Soloman's account that Brown had fired at close range—less than a foot—by questioning his firearms expert, Hodge. Blazek put on a photograph of Moore's wound that showed some red spots. Hodge said that burning gunpowder from a bullet fired at close range could cause the spots. But he was not a medical expert and could not say what the red spots were.

Espinola testified that the gun appeared to have been fired from a distance of six inches, judging by the red burns in the photograph. But he had to acknowledge that he had not performed the autopsy. Joseph Jachimczyk had, and Jachimczyk had not noted gunpowder burns or other signs that the gun had been fired at close range. Blazek asked whether the spatters on Eroy Brown's shirt could have come from Moore's wound. Washington demonstrated that if Moore was kneeling when he was shot, as Soloman said, it wasn't possible for the blood to spatter on Brown's upper shirt and collar.

"You don't even know if that's blood, do you?" Washington asked Espinola. The prosecution had never tested Brown's clothes.[11]

The prosecution's case had never been lengthy, and it had always depended on the inmate witnesses. Blazek finished his first set of witnesses in four hours and rested. Washington and Schaffer weren't sure what Blazek was up to. Perhaps he would put on a string of rebuttal witnesses. But Blazek assured them that if they could finish with all the witnesses, the jury could have the case before the weekend. Washington didn't want to rush.

It was as though Blazek was trying to separate the case from its history. It was Washington and Schaffer who introduced the police reports, witness statements, tape recordings, and other evidence that the prosecution had used in the first two trials. Then they put on their own medical expert from Dallas, Dr. Patrick Besant-Matthews, who noted that nowhere in the autopsy report did Jachimczyk say that Moore had been shot at close range. Besant-Matthews quoted Jachimczyk's autopsy report, which said that he had found no gunpowder around the wound. The microscopic black particles near the wound might have been dirt or some other matter from the bullet. Another defense medical expert, Irving C. Stone, chief of the crime lab for Dallas County, strongly disagreed with Blazek that the wound might have bled so profusely that it washed away gunpowder. It was as though the prosecution was trying to undo the medical examiner's report and replace it with evidence that matched Soloman's account.[12]

Washington had reserved his cross-examination of Soloman until after the prosecution rested. On the morning of the fourth day of the trial, he brought Soloman's ex-wife, Regina Bell, into the courtroom. Early in his investigation, Schaffer had heard from an inmate that Soloman was agitated about her. While Soloman was in Ellis, Bell had moved in with another man and then left him. Shortly after the April 1982 mistrial, Soloman was paroled, returned to Dallas, and convinced her he had reformed. The two began living together.

She told the defense investigator how in October 1982 prosecutors sent Soloman a round-trip plane ticket to Galveston so he would be available for the second trial. But he missed the plane, so Bell drove him to Galveston and stayed for a couple of days. She recalled Duson and Soloman sitting on the hotel bed in Galveston going over the transcripts of their testimony in the first trial, laughing and joking, and making sure they had their stories straight. She said a white man came to the hotel room and gave each of the men $300, and that they would receive more after the trial. One of the men, she said, declared that if they hadn't testified for the prosecution, prison officials would have killed them. Washington couldn't put all this on, for it was hearsay.[13] But Bell was more than happy to testify about her ex-husband's reputation for truthfulness.

After Brown was acquitted, Soloman flew back to Dallas, and about three weeks later, he shot Bell and paralyzed her from the waist down. Soloman was back in prison serving a life sentence. Neither the defense nor the prosecution had invoked the rule that witnesses could be present in the courtroom only during their own testimony. After Bell testified, she was wheeled to the aisle, where she sat and glared at Soloman while Washington cross-examined him.

Washington focused his cross-examination on what Soloman had said about the gun. In one of his tape-recorded interviews, he talked about Pack holding the gun. But when he testified, Soloman denied he had ever seen Pack holding the gun. Washington asked Soloman to help reenact the shooting by holding Pack's pistol. "I don't want that pistol in my hand," Soloman said. Sitting in her wheelchair, his ex-wife let out a soft "hmmp."

Washington took Soloman through all the inconsistencies in his testimony: about where he had stood, what he could possibly see from a hundred yards through the rolled-up window of a car, and whether Brown had fought with Moore. That afternoon Washington spent four hours ripping Soloman to pieces.

But the strain was beginning to tell on both Washington and his client. After Washington took Soloman through his contradictions, he pushed him about lying about Brown. Soloman insisted he was telling the truth.

"I haven't lied on him, and I wouldn't hurt any convict and give him a hard time," he said.

That was too much for Eroy Brown. He jumped up from his chair.

"But you hurt me!" he shouted at Soloman. "I have been hurt, too, seven years. They are trying me for my life." He began weeping as Washington and Schaffer worked to calm him. Then Washington himself got up, walked out of the courtroom, and sat down on the hall floor, crying. Schaffer and friends from the courtroom came out to calm him, too.

"I can't take it," he said, angrily. "I'm not going back there anymore." Brown was on the verge of undoing a trial that had been going well for him. "All he has to do is sit there and let me do the work," Washington said. "I am the one staying up to two a.m. and getting back up at six a.m. I am the one carrying the bags up to the courtroom. I know those transcripts like I know my birth certificate. I know all the lies they are going to tell."

Once both men had calmed down, they returned to the courtroom.

"Mr. Brown," Judge Hester warned, "that outburst didn't help your case." He said he would gag him if there was another one. A few minutes later, Hester adjourned court. The next day, Friday, April 27, Brown would testify for the third time.

After Hester left, Washington asked his client to turn around and look at the half-filled courtroom, where Washington's Hispanic supporters were seated.

"Are you alone, Eroy?" Washington said.

"No, no," said several women. One began weeping.

For five more minutes, the two men sat praying, until a deputy took Eroy out of the room, and back to jail.[14]

Brown later said that the night before he was to testify, the guards at the Hidalgo county jail had kept him awake all night with inspections at two or three in the morning. He figured they were trying to agitate him into doing something rash that could be used against him in court. But he didn't bite.

As before, Brown told the same story. Since he was being tried for shooting Moore, not drowning Pack, Blazek pressured him about the gun. Closing his hand around the small pistol as Brown had described Pack doing, Blazek challenged Brown to pull the trigger. He could not.

"With just my thumb pressure," Blazek said, "the cylinder won't turn. How did you fire that gun?"

"You answer me that," Brown said softly. "I wish it would have never happened. . . . It was an accident. I wasn't trying to kill Major Moore or anybody else that day."

Blazek kept after Brown for an hour, but couldn't draw out any inconsistencies.[15]

The jury had the weekend to think things over. Monday morning, April 30, Blazek called Bill Adams, the farm supervisor who had hauled Brown to the reservoir for running his head. Once again Adams said Brown told him he had been smoking pot that day, and once again he admitted he hadn't written him up for it, he hadn't seen Moore strike Brown, and he had no idea why Brown was barefoot when he was arrested. He admitted that Brown had been a trusty and had never given him any trouble.

Blazek then brought in some prison officials, Moore's friends, and a parole commissioner who testified that Moore had a reputation as a peaceful man. Washington asked the parole commissioner, Kenneth Coleman, if he knew anything about Moore beating some hunters when he was a game warden, or an allegation that Moore had beaten some prisoners, or the incident in which Pack was supposed to have hung an inmate from the bars in a straitjacket or forced another one to lick his boots. It was a way of putting on allegations without bringing in witnesses.[16]

Washington also brought in an inmate witness, Hugh Urdy, who testified that Soloman had testified in exchange for early parole.

On Tuesday morning, May 1, 1984, Washington and Blazek made their final arguments. Blazek called Brown "a paranoid, rageful individual." "Eroy Brown drowned the life out of Wallace Pack and brutally shot the life out of Billy Max Moore knowingly and deliberately," Blazek said. "He is guilty of murder and I urge you to return a verdict of guilty of murder based on the evidence."

Craig Washington took aim squarely at the state's key witness, James Soloman, and made a passionate appeal for his client's freedom. Washington said his afternoon-long cross-examination had showed them all how many ways Soloman could find to lie. "Soloman somehow thinks the world looks better," he said, "that he can see the sunset, the trees, and flowers by standing on someone else's shoulders."

Brown sat at the defense table, quietly weeping.

Brown had no choice but to act, Washington said, with one handcuff on and Pack pointing a pistol to his head. For the third time, Washington asked twelve jurors to put themselves in Eroy Brown's shoes.

"There you are, a convict from Waco serving a twelve-year sentence for robbery," Washington said, his voice breaking, "standing there, having less than a minute to decide whether or not to fight for your life.

"Who's gonna believe you even if you live? Who's gonna take your word against the officials? You know what the evidence is, and this man is not guilty, and you know it."

At the end of his argument, Washington, like Brown, was in tears.

At about 12:30 the jury retired to deliberate. Rather than try to bring all the physical evidence into the tiny jury room, Hester cleared the courtroom, and let the jurors have access to the state's scale model of the scene, the photographs, and the police and autopsy reports. He had ruled earlier that the lawyers would not be allowed to tell the jurors that Brown had been acquitted of drowning Pack.

It took them two hours to come to a verdict. The jury foreman, Hector de la Cruz, a twenty-eight-year-old construction foreman, said that once Soloman took the stand, the state's case fell apart. "Everybody knew he was lying all the way," he said.

The first vote, taken half an hour into the process, was twelve to none for acquittal. Several of the jurors embraced Brown after the verdict. One praised God.

"TDC inmates don't shoot prison guards and walk away," Washington said, "but God was with Eroy on April 4, 1981, and God was with him today."[17]

Once the jury had announced its verdict, Brown was a free man, but getting free involved a few technicalities. The county jailer needed a release from the TDC, and Brown's parole officer had to be informed. Then a court order from Judge Hester had to be delivered. It took three more hours to get Brown out of the Hidalgo county jail. Carrying his possessions in a couple of sacks, he emerged to face television cameras.

"He doesn't want his $200 gate money," Washington said. "He doesn't want his suit. He just wants to be free."

There was a party that night on the fourth floor of the Echo Hotel, with food and drinks. Brown smoked a cigarette and sipped a beer. The music of Marvin Gaye and Teddy Pendergrass played in the background. It had taken him three years to win his freedom. There was a lot of talk about God and the many people who had helped him.

Brown said that he had learned to enjoy doing legal research during the years his case stretched on. "I think God has been showing me the way," he said. "With only a ninth-grade education I've been able to understand what I've read on my own case and I've learned to enjoy using my head." He said he planned to get a high school certification and perhaps work for a law firm. He had a job lined up, but he wouldn't say where.

Washington and Schaffer had hired a body guard since the Galveston acquittal, and they were still worried that some flake would harm them or Brown. "It never stops," Brown said. "I don't think it ended in the courtroom. They'll still be trying the Wallace Pack and Billy Max Moore case from now on."

Kent Schaffer observed that fifteen prison employees had been fired and another ninety-two others had been disciplined for using excessive force since the first of the year. "I'm afraid TDC will stop at no expense to get Eroy Brown," Schaffer said. "They spent a million dollars to get him in court and they haven't. So now if some TDC employees knew where Eroy was living, he'd be dead tomorrow."

27

AFTERMATH

Winning the case for Eroy Brown was one thing—getting paid for the work was another. Walker County had $50,000 from the state to pay for Brown's defense, but five months after losing the case, Frank Blazek still refused to pay Washington. Blazek argued that because Washington had helped write the legislation to pay the attorneys of indigent clients, such payments were illegal.

Washington said Blazek was wrong. "The law says that I can't do contract labor for the state," Washington said, "but that I can be paid for legal work on an appointed case."

Even the judge of the Walker County commissioners court, Ralph A. Davis, seemed to think that not paying Washington was wrong. "We got the money to pay for Senator Washington," he said, "and it seems that we should pay him for the work he did."[1]

Washington successfully sued Walker County in February 1985, but Blazek continued to insist that paying Washington would be a conflict because he was a legislator. He was going to take it to the Texas Supreme Court.

"They would have paid me by return mail if I would have let them run over me and convict Eroy," Washington said. It took Washington another year of lawsuits to get Walker County to pay him.[2]

As for the nearly $200,000 he was owed for the second trial, Washington had to use political tactics. Washington was a state senator, and that summer the Texas senate added an amendment to the state highway bill to pay Brown's legal fees. Faced with a roadblock to a $1.7 billion highway bill, Governor Mark White agreed to pay Washington and Habern out of emergency funds.[3]

If nothing else, the trials of Eroy Brown led to a change in the way in which the state pays lawyers. Texas lawyers for the indigent are now paid on a weekly basis.

When Eroy Brown left Edinburg in the back seat of Craig Washington's Mercedes Benz, the Texas prison system was falling apart. Within a year of Estelle's departure, five wardens retired or resigned, and another five were removed for brutality and fabrication of evidence against *Ruiz* witnesses.[4]

In 1986 Mark White was still denouncing Judge Justice, "Cadillac prisons," and the *Ruiz* case. He refused to reappoint Harry Whittington to the TDC board. In 1986 Bill Clements ran for governor a third time, criticizing White for mismanaging the prisons. After Clements was re-elected, he called a meeting with Judge Justice, the inmates' attorney Bill Turner, and Jim Mattox, the Democratic attorney general. Clements settled all the basic elements of *Ruiz*: no more building tenders, limits to overcrowding, clearly stated policies on the use of force, and improved medical care. It was 1987. Clements could have reached that settlement in 1980 if he had wanted to.

Rather than reform prisons, Clements expanded them. Ignoring traditional pay-as-you-go financing, he funded new prisons through bonds. Budgets were still balanced and the fiscal pain was passed on to the future. There was no problem in keeping the beds filled. Clements created a statewide council of law enforcement officials that blamed illegal drugs and easy parole for crime. There was nothing to do about crime but warehouse as many criminals as possible for as long as possible.[5]

In 1990 the Texas Department of Corrections changed its name to the Texas Department of Criminal Justice. "Corrections" never did have much to do with Texas prisons. But Texas was determined to build more prisons. The TDCJ is now a sprawling complex of prisons to be found in every area of the state. It houses from 165,000 to 170,000 inmates, making Texas the most punitive state in the nation.

Politicians occasionally blame prison growth on population growth, but a public policy analyst, Scott Henson, points out that "from 1978 until 2004, the Texas prison population increased 573 percent (from 22,439 to 151,059), while the state's total population increased just 67 percent (from 13.5 million to 22.5 million)."[6]

In 2008 the Texas prison system peaked at 172,000 inmates, surpassing California. Texas is now looking to follow California's example by diverting more nonviolent offenders to probation, imposing shorter sentences, and providing drug and alcohol rehabilitation. Thirty years after *Ruiz*, Texas prisons seem to have reached a limit to their growth. They're too big to be allowed to fail, but too expensive to be allowed to grow.

The growth of Texas prisons wasn't altogether a bad thing for Bill Habern. The Brown trial left him broke for a time, but it also restored his taste for being a lawyer. He set out to become the state's expert on post-conviction law.

During the long wait in 1983 to see whether Eroy Brown would be tried a third time, and whether he and Washington would be paid, Habern filed a civil suit on behalf of two former inmates from the Wynne prison who had been "dog boys," or as Habern liked to say, "dog bait." The dog boys were given a two-hour start to run into the woods, climb a tree, and wait until the dogs followed their trail and found them. But once that happened, they were ordered to jump down from the tree and fight the dogs. Habern said that one of the former inmates had been bitten a hundred and twenty times in one incident while the other was bitten fifty-six times. "These kids were just chewed up," he said.

Without acknowledging any wrongdoing, the TDC settled out of court for $14,000.[7]

Habern closely studied the tougher sentencing and parole laws that the Texas legislature passed every two years to fill the rapidly expanding prison system. An inmate's parole is determined by what law was in effect at the time he was sentenced. It's hard to keep track of which laws apply. Habern conducted seminars and wrote papers to help other lawyers sort out the tangle of changes.

In October 2009 Habern was glowing from a recent court victory against the Texas Board of Pardons and Paroles. "My mission in life," he said, "is to change that parole board."

Something like half a million people in Texas are governed by parole law. All sorts of false and malignant information may exist in an inmate's file, which he and his lawyer are usually not allowed to see. Some of the most aggrieved by the process are the pariahs of state law: sex offenders. The eighteen members of the parole board hear seventy thousand cases a year. The board has about a thousand registered sex offenders on the streets and another seven thousand in the pipeline. The three members in Austin typically dispose of a case in five minutes.

Habern's client was a former convict who had found religion in prison and wanted to be a preacher. Thirty years ago he was accused, but not convicted, of raping a woman. The Texas parole board declared him a sex offender, with all the stigma and problems that come with the label.

The problem with the parole board has long been its secrecy. The Fifth Circuit Court of Appeals held that an inmate who has not been convicted of a sex offense cannot be categorized as a sex offender without a hearing. All Habern wanted was a parole hearing for his client so he could confront the allegations against him.

The state resisted all the way, so US District Judge Sam Sparks held a hearing before a jury in Austin. The state's basic approach seemed to be that a man convicted of crimes has no rights left. A young attorney for the state tried to explain that even though the parole board hadn't given the inmate a hearing, it had still offered him due process. That produced an explosion by Judge Sparks.

"A sixth-grader who's not doing well in school, who's a C student, can look at these undisputed facts and make a determination that due process was not followed," Sparks said. "The only things we know in this case are that there were no hearings and that for over a year and two-thirds nothing was done. Ten minutes. That's all it would have taken to hold a hearing."[8]

Sparks sounded a bit like William Wayne Justice chewing out the state in *Ruiz*. The state may be hoping for relief from the Fifth Circuit Court of Appeals. It's familiar territory to Habern. He still likes butting heads with authority.

Craig Washington scarcely took a breath after the Eroy Brown trial. In 1989 he was elected to Congress in a special election to replace Mickey Leland, who had died in a plane crash in Africa, working to feed starving children. Leland held Barbara Jordan's old inner-city seat in Houston, the 18th Congressional District. One of his supporters was Bob Lee, a community organizer in the Fifth Ward, the historically black neighborhood where both Jordan and Leland had grown up. In the barbershops and beauty shops and churches, Lee used a word-of-mouth campaign slogan to help voters remember Washington. He was the man who walked Eroy Brown.[9]

Washington's two terms in Congress did not go well. He went through bankruptcy. He put the mother of one of his children on his office payroll and paid rent to an ex-wife for Houston offices. Washington said he knew he was viewed in Houston as an ineffective Congressman "who had his baby mama on the payroll, and as kind of a sleaze ball."[10]

Washington did not play to stereotypes. He worked on Joe Biden's 1994 crime bill to put a hundred thousand cops on the streets. He vigorously opposed Clarence Thomas's nomination to the Supreme Court. He angered the Houston business community by opposing the North American Free Trade Agreement and increased funding for NASA, a major source of federal jobs in the Houston area. Summoned by the business leadership to discuss his votes, Washington was indignant that well-to-do business leaders thought they had more say-so than ordinary people.

After losing the Democratic primary in 1994, he married again and moved to Bastrop and tried to live the life of a quiet country lawyer, walking his children to school. But that marriage didn't last. In May 2003, as he was returning to

Houston from a trip to the Valley, he saw a crime scene at a truck stop near Victoria. A truck driver who was smuggling a load of illegal immigrants from Mexico had disconnected his trailer and left it. Nineteen people inside had died of asphyxiation. The driver, a Jamaican named Tyrone Williams, and thirteen people were indicted for the deaths in federal court. The sole defendant to be indicted for capital murder was Williams, the only black.

Washington worked passionately to save Williams's life, arguing the basic unfairness of singling out the truck driver, who by all indications had not known that his passengers were dying. In a trial in 2006, Washington's client was convicted of smuggling that led to the deaths, but the jurors could not agree on the death penalty. Washington had again saved a life.[11]

On July 20, 2009, Craig Washington went to a trial at the 208th Criminal Court in downtown Houston with his old colleague from the Eroy Brown case, Kent Schaffer. Schaffer wasn't Washington's colleague this time, though—he was Washington's lawyer. Washington was facing charges of aggravated assault and a possible sentence of two to twenty years.

The charge stemmed from an incident at Washington's law office in midtown Houston at 8:30 p.m. on New Year's Eve, 2008. Armed with a pistol, Washington confronted two white teenagers from the Houston suburbs who entered the fenced parking lot and carport. The driver, age eighteen, said that as he was driving away, Washington shot his Camaro twice. Washington swore the car was backing up, aiming to run him over. It was a matter of self-defense, he said.

The case was set to go to trial. A new district attorney, a woman and former prosecutor and judge named Pat Lykos, had been elected. Unlike past Harris County prosecutors, Lykos favors more innovative sentencing and more flexible probation. She offered Washington "pre-trial diversion," which is typically reserved for defendants with no previous convictions. In exchange for doing community service and staying out of trouble for two years, Washington's case would disappear.[12]

A small mob of reporters gathered around Schaffer in the courtroom hallway after the deal was announced. Wearing a dark suit and the customary black cowboy boots of a Texas trial lawyer, Schaffer said that it was a good agreement. Although he thought he could win the case if it went to trial, Schaffer said, "Acquittal is never guaranteed."

The reporters turned the cameras on Washington, who, at sixty-seven, shaves his head bare. His beard is gray. He wore a dark suit and navy bow tie with white polka dots. He wore lighter footwear than his lawyer: black suede, soft-soled, three-eyelet desert boots that resembled an elegant version of the shoes Eroy Brown wore almost thirty years earlier.

Schaffer said that Washington would do pro-bono legal work as his community service. He often did such work anyway.

Washington said that in the courtroom he had sat next to a scared young man
who was waiting for a hearing. He had no idea Washington was there as a defendant, not as a lawyer. In that deep, calm voice of his, Washington said, "I told him
not to be afraid. No one should be afraid of the system."

Once again he quoted Martin Luther King Jr.'s line from the steps of Montgomery's Capitol, the one he had used in Eroy Brown's case: "We shall overcome
because the arc of the moral universe is long, but it bends towards justice." Then
he stepped into the elevator and headed home.

After he was acquitted for shooting Billy Moore, Eroy Brown told an AP reporter, "For the sake of God and the thirty-five jurors who believed in me and for
all those people who hoped and prayed, I will never do anything to cause me to
go back to jail."[13]

It was a good promise, but one he did not keep. Habern and Washington tried
to get him a job installing air conditioning ductwork on the southwest side of
Houston. He said that his aunt, who had supported him during his boyhood and
trials, noticed a car parked outside her house in the Houston neighborhood of
Sunnyside. He got Craig Washington's office to run a license plate check, and the
car belonged to a state investigator. That was when he made what he calls his biggest mistake and left Houston.

He got his parole office changed to Fort Worth and lived with his mother's
youngest sister, Hazel, and worked as a janitor. But he relapsed into using heroin.

"I've been in denial for twenty-six years," Brown wrote in a letter to set the
record straight. He hooked up with his old crime partner, Charles Ray Johnson.
Johnson had helped in the holdup of a Fort Worth motel that landed Brown in
Ellis prison. Near the end of October 1984, they drove to Waco with a friend who
had his aunt's car, planning to steal a case of cigarettes from a convenience store.
One of Brown's old girlfriends knew the clerk, who had served time with her in
prison, and thought they could coerce her into giving them up. Brown went behind the counter to look for the cigarettes, but there weren't any.

"It was supposed to be an extortion," Brown wrote, but it turned into a robbery. They emptied the cash register of twelve dollars, took a couple of candy
bars, and left. They were headed back to Fort Worth the next morning when they
were arrested in a roadside park in Hillsboro, north of Waco.

The Waco police quickly realized they had a prize. The store clerk said two
men came into the store and one of them pulled a knife, placed it at her side,

and demanded the money in the cash register. The other one, she testified, came around the counter to see if the cash register was empty. She identified him as Eroy Brown.[14]

A court-appointed attorney, a former Waco prosecutor named Ken Ables, represented Brown. The two accomplices got off lightly in exchange for testifying against Brown. Johnson, who held the knife, was out on parole on a thirty-year sentence. Prosecutors agreed not to enhance his sentence in exchange for his testimony. Charges against the other man were dropped. Pointing out how lightly the other two had been treated, Ables argued for a sentence of twenty-five years for Brown.

This was Brown's fourth felony conviction and his sentence could be enhanced. In March 1985 the jury gave him ninety years as a habitual criminal. No lawyer could bring up Brown's murder acquittals to the jury, but Brown's face and story had been spread all over the local newspaper.

For the last twenty-five years Eroy Brown has been kept in a series of federal prisons. I talked to him in Beaumont in 1999 for a couple of hours before he was moved to another prison in Colorado. After I talked to him in Victorville, California, in the late summer of 2010 he was transferred to Leavenworth prison in Kansas.

In 2000 he had come up for parole, and in one of their hasty, five-minute-long reviews of his record, two Texas parole commissioners approved him. Eroy Brown hadn't been a security problem and hadn't gotten into any major trouble. He was about fifty years old. Surely the criminal impulse had been just about "timed" out of him. But word got to the parole commission about Brown. The recommendation was revoked.

Habern has filed an affidavit that he will serve as Eroy Brown's advocate in his next parole hearing. "His continued incarceration is a political act," Habern said. "Why not release him now while he still has some family and he might have a chance of leading a few productive years, and not be a burden to the state? What is the purpose of keeping Eroy Brown in prison?"

Politics is one answer, of course. But another word comes to mind: retribution. Facts will never matter to the state in the case of Eroy Brown. The opinion of thirty-five jurors will never matter. It will be hard for Texas criminal justice officials ever to understand why Washington and Habern defended Eroy Brown so passionately.

"They never understood," Habern said, "how much we believed he was innocent."

NOTES

PROLOGUE

1. Steve Martin and Sheldon Ekland-Olson, *Texas Prisons: The Walls Came Tumbling Down*, p. 151; Ben Crouch and James Marquart, *An Appeal to Justice: Litigated Reform of Texas Prisons*, pp. 137–138; Robert Perkinson, *Texas Tough: The Rise of America's Prison Empire*, p. 280.
2. Jim Willett and Ron Rozelle, *Warden: Prison Life and Death from the Inside Out*, pp. 133–135.
3. Lon Bennett Glenn, *The Largest Hotel Chain in Texas: Texas Prisons*, pp. 141–142.
4. "TDC Official Opposes Proposal to Pay Wages to Inmates for Working," *Houston Post*, Aug. 26, 1982.

CHAPTER I

1. Crouch and Marquart, *Appeal to Justice*, p. 51; Martin and Ekland-Olson, *Texas Prisons*, p. 69; Chad Trulson and James W. Marquart, *First Available Cell: Desegregation of the Texas Prison System*, p. 9; Glenn, *Largest Hotel Chain in Texas*, p. 96.
2. Rinker Buck, unpublished manuscript, 1982, pp. 14–15.
3. Buck, pp. 25A–29A.
4. Interview with Ray Hill, June 2007.
5. The details of the morning have been drawn from Richard Pustka's testimony at Brown's second trial (Oct. 28, 1982).
6. Glenn, *Largest Hotel Chain in Texas*, p. 371.
7. "Frustrations of Prison Work Leave Ellis Unit Warden Ready to Retire," *Houston Post*, March 22, 1981.

CHAPTER 2

1. Details of the fishing trip are drawn from trial testimony of Richard Pustka (Oct. 28, 1982).
2. Details of the morning and capture of Brown are drawn from trial testimony of James Williamson (Feb. 2, 1982, and Nov. 1, 1982) and Robert DeYoung (Feb. 3, 1982, and Oct. 31–Nov. 1, 1982).
3. The description of the beatings is based on interviews with Eroy Brown and investigative interviews with inmates by Brown's lawyers.
4. Willet and Rozelle, *Warden*, pp. 133–135.
5. Interview with Eroy Brown, 1999.
6. "TDC Admits Strip Cells Used for 'Really Disruptive' Cases," *Houston Chronicle*, April 16, 1981; and "Convict Enters Innocent Plea in Slayings of 2 TDC Officials," *Houston Chronicle*, May 19, 1981.

CHAPTER 3

1. "TDC Ellis Warden, Head of Farm Slain," *Houston Post*, April 5, 1981.
2. "Slayings Shake Estelle," *Dallas Morning News*, April 6, 1982.
3. "TDC Chief Strengthens Death Penalty Stance," *Houston Chronicle*, April 6, 1981.
4. "Texas Inmate Cites Alleged Right Denials," *Houston Chronicle*, Oct. 3, 1978.
5. Perkinson, *Texas Tough*, p. 277.
6. 503 F. Supp. 1265; 1980 US Dist. LEXIS 17383, section 97.
7. 503 F. Supp. 1265; 1980 US Dist. LEXIS 17383, section 1391.
8. William Barrett, "Lifer," *Houston City Magazine*, April 1982, p. 75.
9. Martin and Ekland-Olson, *Texas Prisons*, pp. 149–151.
10. "TDC Chief Strengthens Death Penalty Stance," *Houston Chronicle*, April 6, 1982.
11. Barrett, "Lifer."
12. "New Prison Head Views Dr. Beto as 'the Master,'" *Houston Post*, Aug. 6, 1972.
13. Estelle Papers, "Introduction to Corrections."
14. David Horton and George Nielson, *Walking George: The Life of George John Beto and the Rise of the Modern Texas Prison System*, p. 165.
15. Robert Chase, *Civil Rights on the Cell Block: Race, Reform, and Violence in Texas Prisons and the Nation, 1945–1990*, p. 7.
16. Chase, *Civil Rights on the Cell Block*, p. 318, and *Handbook of Texas*, "Texas Legislature," www.tshaonline.org/handbook/online/articles/mkt02.
17. Chase, *Civil Rights on the Cell Block*, p. 327.
18. No criminal charges were filed, but in the federal civil rights case that followed, *McMillan v. Estelle*, the court concluded that the rights of the inmates had been flagrantly violated. In 1978 the state settled for attorneys' fees and $11,000 in damages to the inmates.

19. *Hays County Citizen*, Jan. 9, 1975. The conservative was Walter "Mad Dog" Mengden, a state senator from Houston. He earned his nickname because members on the floor sometimes howled when he spoke, to egg him on.
20. Chase, *Civil Rights on the Cell Block*, p. 304.
21. "Final Report of Joint Committee on Prison Reform," p. 47.
22. "Carrasco Seen as Block, Leland Says Shootout Will Hinder Reform," *Austin American-Statesman*, Jan. 11, 1975.
23. See for instance, *Houston Post* columnist Lynn Ashby, "The TDC Flap," Oct. 4, 1978: "But I, for one, am getting fed up with axe murderers complaining that they get blisters on their hands while picking cotton. I've about had my fill of sadists and rapists complaining about their constitutional rights."
24. "Estelle Says Suspect Kept Naked in Isolation Prior to Sanity Tests," *Dallas Morning News*, April 15, 1981.
25. "Prisoner Is Charged in Slayings," *Fort Worth Star-Telegram*, April 7, 1981.
26. "Now the Other Story," *Dallas Morning News*, April 16, 1981.
27. Texas Department of Corrections, *1981 Annual Report*, pp. 70–71.

CHAPTER 4
1. Descriptions of Rick Berger's work at the crime scene are based on his investigative reports and trial testimony.
2. The tape recordings were transcribed and entered into evidence at Brown's second trial.
3. Walter Pinegar's investigative report.
4. Bill Adams's witness statement.

CHAPTER 5
1. Chase, *Civil Rights on the Cell Block*, p. 118.
2. Ellis file, Beto Papers.
3. Joseph Hallinan, *Going up the River: Travels in a Prison Nation*, p. 21.
4. John DiIulio, a critic of litigated prison reform, calls the use of inmate guards the "rotten crutch" of Beto's system. *Governing Prisons: A Comparative Study of Correctional Management*, p. 210.
5. See for instance, "Once Low-Rated, Texas Prisons Now Rank among the Finest," *Houston Chronicle*, Feb. 4, 1968. And "Texas Prison System One of the Best in US," *Houston Post*, July 7, 1977, which extols Beto.
6. http://www.folkstreams.net/film,122.
7. Jackson folder, Beto Archives, Sam Houston State University.
8. William Bennett Turner upbraided Jackson in court for stretching the truth about Texas prisons. See Martin and Ekland-Olson, *Texas Prisons*, pp. 164–167.
9. Bruce Jackson, *Wake Up Dead Man: Hard Labor and Southern Blues*, p. 162.
10. Jackson, *Wake Up Dead Man*, p. 11–12.
11. Jackson, *Wake Up Dead Man*, p. 306.
12. Danny Lyon, *Like a Thief's Dream*, p. 11.

13. In 1969 he published *The Destruction of Lower Manhattan.*
14. Interview with Danny Lyon, May 2009.
15. Many TDC officials had copies of the photo. Former guard Lon Glenn includes the Redwine picture from his personal collection in his book, *The Largest Hotel Chain in Texas.*
16. Chase, *Civil Rights on the Cell Block,* p. 59.
17. Lyon, *Like a Thief's Dream,* pp. 21–22.
18. Interview with Danny Lyon, May 2009.
19. Danny Lyon, *Conversations with the Dead,* p. 13.

CHAPTER 6

1. In June 1968 Beto wrote Illinois warden Joe Ragen: "I recall that several years ago you were worried about the 'bleeding hearts' taking over. I am of the opinion that they have taken over. The permissiveness, not only in prison but in society generally, is rapidly bringing this country to ruin. In fact, the general attitude is such that people with a philosophy similar to yours and mine have extreme difficulty working in prisons." Beto Archive, Sam Houston State University.
2. http://www.lib.utexas.edu/taro/utcah/00348/cah-00348.html.
3. In his old age, McAdams was interviewed for a documentary video, *Writ Writer,* by Susanne Mason (2007), mentioned below.
4. Martin and Ekland-Olson, *Texas Prisons,* p. 29.
5. Atul Gawande, "Hellhole," *The New Yorker,* March 30, 2009.
6. For example, "Once Low-Rated, Texas Prisons Now Rank Among the Finest," *Houston Chronicle,* Feb. 4, 1968; and Paul Harvey, *Joliet Herald-News,* May 29, 1968. Harvey's story is in the Beto Archive, Sam Houston State University.
7. Cited in Chase, *Civil Rights on the Cell Block,* p. 195.
8. Jalet, "Ellis Report." Copy in author's possession courtesy of Robert Perkinson.
9. Beto's harassment of Jalet is detailed in Judge Carl Bue's opinion in *Dreyer v. Jalet,* 349 F. Supp. 452 (1972). Also Martin and Ekland-Olson, *Texas Prisons,* pp. 37–39.
10. Martin and Ekland-Olson, *Texas Prisons,* pp. 50–51.
11. For Beto's role in supporting the building tenders' lawsuit, see Martin and Ekland-Olson, *Texas Prisons,* p. 42.
12. *Dreyer v. Jalet,* 349 F. Supp. 452 (1972).
13. Quoted in "Another Planet," *Texas Observer,* July 7, 1972.
14. Susanne Mason, *Writ Writer.*
15. Beto's testimony is preserved in his archive at Sam Houston State University.
16. Former TDC warden Lon Glenn quotes a convict who confirms Ray Hill's theory that prison culture is a single, unified culture: "'Old Bear Tracks [sic] knows us so well that there is no difference between us. He can look down into that cell block or tank and tell you what you're thinking. Bear Tracks would make a perfect convict'" (*Largest Hotel Chain in Texas,* p. 67).
17. Interview with Ray Hill, Sept. 2008.

212 NOTES TO PAGES 57–68

CHAPTER 7

1. Bill Habern interview, Dec. 1998.
2. *Huntsville Item*, May 22, 1974, and Aug. 17 and 18, 1974.
3. "The Ten Best and the Ten Worst Legislators," *Texas Monthly*, July 1981, p. 106.
4. "Craig Washington, Known for Political, Courtroom Talents," *Houston Chronicle*, March 13, 1983.
5. CURE news release, Dec. 20, 1983.
6. "Maverick Craig Washington," *Houston Post*, Feb. 1, 1981.
7. http://www.lrl.state.tx.us/scanned/specialSessions/HRO_Special_67-1.pdf.
8. "Rep. Washington Says Pay Forcing Him to Quit," *Houston Chronicle*, May 23, 1973.
9. Eroy Brown interview, April 2010.
10. Interview with Timothy Sloan, Oct. 2000.

CHAPTER 8

1. "Beatings Administered at 'Bottoms,' Ex-trusty Says," *Dallas Morning News*, April 6, 1981.
2. "TDC Chief Strengthens Death Penalty Stance," *Houston Chronicle*, April 6, 1981.
3. Paragraph 97, *Ruiz v. Estelle*, F. Supp. 1265; 1980 U.S. Dist. LEXIS 17383.
4. "Convicts Had Accused Warden of Brutality," *Dallas Times Herald*, April 15, 1981.
5. Martin and Ekland-Olson, *Texas Prisons*, pp. 157–159.
6. One other prison official involved in Brown's case testified in *Ruiz*. James Williamson, the assistant warden who captured Brown, testified about the use of building tenders. In August 1979, Justice Department attorney David Vanderhoof got Williamson to admit that building tenders with a history of violence got little or no punishment. Williamson defended TDC employees who had allowed two prisoners with a history of violence to rape an eighteen-year-old inmate for three days in December 1978. The victim was starved for two days and burned with cigarettes. Too young to be a typical Ellis admission, he had been sent there for "shock probation." One of the rapists had seven years tacked onto his sentence, but the other was restored to the rank of first-class trusty. Williamson said, "This is the worst thing I have ever seen in the penitentiary," but he exonerated the guards who had made their rounds and failed to turn up the brutality. "Privileges, Abuses of Inmates Denied," *Houston Post*, Aug. 18, 1979.
7. Crouch and Marquart, *Appeal to Justice*, pp. 83–84.
8. Paul Schneider, *Bonnie and Clyde: The Lives behind the Legend*, p. 355.
9. John Neal Phillips, *Running with Bonnie and Clyde: The Ten Fast Years of Ralph Fults*, p. 279.
10. "Siege Inmate's Slaying Trials Leave Walloping Bills," *Austin-American Statesman*, June 5, 1983, and "Ward Recovering from Near-Fatal Crash," *Houston Chronicle*, Nov. 16, 1982.

11. "Governor, Inmates Arguing Over Who Should Be Released," *Houston Post*, Nov. 2, 1980.

12. "White Says Decision Likely to Cost State Millions," *Houston Post*, Dec. 13, 1980.

13. "Powell's Decision to Enter TDC Case 'Encourages' White," *Houston Post*, Aug. 5, 1981.

14. "Capital Bickering, White Says Clements No Help in Fighting US Suits," *Houston Post*, March 21, 1981.

15. "Clements Requests $18 Million for TDC Plans," *Houston Post*, April 25, 1981.

16. "Tents up, TDC Officials Uncertain How Long Inmates to Remain under Canvas," *Houston Post*, May 22, 1981.

17. "Put 1,500 Inmates in Borrowed Tents, Clements Proposes," *Houston Post*, May 8, 1981.

18. "Prisoners Spending 2nd Winter in Tents," *Houston Chronicle*, Jan. 10, 1983.

19. "Texas' Toughest Prison Unit Simmers with Fear, Tension," *Dallas Morning News*, April 26, 1981.

20. "Prison Inmates Stage Protest," *Houston Chronicle*, April 30, 1981.

21. "TDC Witness Killed in Prison Knife Fight," *Dallas Morning News*, Oct. 24, 1981.

22. Martin and Ekland-Olson, *Texas Prisons*, pp. 149–151.

23. "*Ruiz* Witnesses for Plaintiffs," memorandum from Bruce C. Green, TDC legal counsel, to Walter Pinegar, Feb. 16, 1982. The inmate witness was Stephen D. Thompson.

CHAPTER 9

1. Interview with Eroy Brown, April 1999.

2. Most of the details for this section are drawn from Eroy Brown's juvenile records.

3. "Furlough Denial May Have Led to Killings," *Houston Chronicle*, April 12, 1981.

4. Interview with Eroy Brown, April 2010.

5. *Houston Chronicle*, April 12, 1981.

6. "Man Held in Slayings Once Sentenced Here," *Fort Worth Star-Telegram*, April 7, 1981.

7. "Inmate's Letter Hints of Anger Building Up in Him," *Dallas Times Herald*, April 12, 1981.

CHAPTER 10

1. Clinton had been an ACLU attorney before joining the court, and had filed a suit that led to the racial integration of the women's dormitories at the University of Texas in Austin. Cf. Dwonna Naomi Goldstone, *Integrating the 40 Acres*.

2. "Lawyers Ask for State Records of Inmate Accused of Killing TDC Officials," *Houston Chronicle*, Oct. 22, 1981.

3. Inmate witness statements made to Kent Schaffer.

4. Details have been drawn from the transcription of the Nov. 30, 1981, hearing.
5. Possibly the disturbed inmate was Billy McCune, who had been sentenced to death in the 1950s for rape. The Wynne warden, Howard "Mama" Sublett, helped get the sentence commuted to life. McCune cut off his penis and gave it to a guard in a cup. Danny Lyon was captivated by McCune's artwork and writing, which he featured in *Conversations with the Dead*. He saw to it that Mc-Cune's autobiography was published in 1973. McCune was paroled in 1976, two years before Lacy claimed he was celled with a sexually mutilated man.

CHAPTER 11

1. "Family of Slain Warden Hires Lawyer to Aid DA," *Houston Chronicle*, Nov. 24, 1981. The payment amount comes from trial records.
2. http://hintonbaileybond.com/hinton.asp.
3. "Man Accused of Killing Two TDC Officials to Have 2 Trials," *Houston Chronicle*, Jan. 12, 1982.
4. "Judge Rules Inmate Eroy Brown's Constitutional Rights Not Violated," *Houston Chronicle*, Jan. 22, 1982.
5. Interviews with Sloan, Oct. 2000, and Brown, April 2010.
6. Testimony of Bill Adams, Feb. 2, 1982.
7. Martin and Ekland-Olson, *Texas Prisons*, p. 69.
8. Testimony of Charles Spivey, Feb. 2, 1982.

CHAPTER 12

1. This section is based on the transcription of James Soloman's testimony, Feb. 2, 1982.
2. Walker County investigator Walter Pinegar attributed the phrase to Brown in a newspaper interview months before Hinton met with Soloman. See "Questions Surround Prison Farm Slayings at Huntsville," *Dallas Times Herald*, April 12, 1981.
3. Soloman testimony, Feb. 2, 1982, p. 40.
4. "Fellow Inmate Tells Court He Saw Brown Shoot Ellis Farm Manager," *Houston Post*, Feb. 4, 1982.
5. Robert DeYoung's testimony in the second trial, Oct. 29 and Nov. 1, 1982, p. 33.
6. DeYoung testimony, Feb. 3, pp. 13–14.
7. DeYoung testimony, Feb. 3, p. 29.
8. Joseph Jachimczyk testimony, Feb. 4, 1982, pp. 32–33.
9. Jachimczyk testimony, p. 91.
10. Jachimczyk testimony, p. 112.
11. Testimony of FBI fingerprint expert, Jerry Withers, Nov. 1, 1982, p. 9.
12. Testimony of William Kinard, Feb. 4, 1982, pp. 20–21.
13. Testimony of Ronald M. Loftin, Feb. 4, 1982, p. 17.

CHAPTER 13

1. "Attorney: Inmate 'Defending His Life' When TDC Officials Killed," *Houston Chronicle*, Feb. 9, 1982.
2. "Brown Says He Was Threatened by Warden," *Houston Post*, Feb. 10, 1982.
3. James Soloman's testimony, Feb. 9, 1982, pp. 131–132.
4. Assistant warden James Williamson testified that Brown said, "A man's got to do what a man's got to do." Williamson's statement of April 4, 1981, and testimony, Feb. 2, 1982, p. 25.
5. Soloman testimony, Feb. 9, 1982, p. 139.
6. "Lawyer for Ellis Inmate Outlines Self-Defense," *Dallas Times Herald*, Feb. 9, 1982.
7. "Attorney: Inmate 'Defending His Life' When TDC Officials Killed," *Houston Chronicle*, Feb. 9, 1982.

CHAPTER 15

1. Interview with Cinny Kennard, Oct. 2009.
2. Ward's cross-examination begins on p. 173 of the transcript of Brown's testimony on Feb. 9, 1982.
3. Brown testimony, Feb. 9, 1982, pp. 186–187.
4. Brown testimony, Feb. 9, 1982, pp. 191–192.
5. Brown testimony, Feb. 9, 1982, pp. 200–201.
6. Brown testimony, Feb. 9, 1982, pp. 200–201.
7. Brown testimony, Feb. 9, 1982, p. 211.
8. Brown testimony, Feb. 9, 1982, p. 212.
9. Brown testimony, Feb. 9, 1982, p. 214.
10. Brown testimony, Feb. 9, 1982, pp. 237–238.
11. Brown testimony, Feb. 9, 1982, pp. 243–245.
12. Brown testimony, Feb. 9, 1982, pp. 246–248.
13. Brown testimony, Feb. 9, 1982, pp. 249–251.
14. Brown testimony, Feb. 9, 1982, pp. 261–265.

CHAPTER 16

1. "Inmate Trial Is Recessing Till Monday," *Houston Post*, Feb. 6, 1982.
2. "8 Inmate Witnesses Declared in Contempt for Refusing to Testify at Brown Trial," *Houston Post*, Feb. 16, 1982.
3. "Inmates Afraid to Testify in Trial of Brown to Get Lawyer's Advice," *Houston Chronicle*, Feb. 12, 1982.
4. "Inmates Will Be Called; Some Reluctant to Testify," *Houston Chronicle*, Feb. 11, 1982.
5. "Ex-inmate Testifies in Brown Trial Warden 'Strict' but Not Abusive," *Houston Chronicle*, Feb. 23, 1982.

6. "Inmates Allege Beatings, Overcrowding in TDC Trial," *Houston Post*, Oct. 13, 1978.

7. Details drawn from Aubrey Komurke's testimony, Feb. 15, 1982.

8. Slaton died in 2005 (http://www.templerosegarden.org).

9. Barber followed McAdams to three different prisons. Martin and Ekland-Olson, *Texas Prisons*, pp. 47–48.

10. Kent Biffle, *A Month of Sundays*, pp. 152–155.

11. "Defense Witnesses Say Warden Had Reputation for Violence toward Inmates," *Houston Post*, Feb. 17, 1982. Suspicions about the cause of Bunt's death were brought up in *Dreyer v. Jalet*. See Martin and Ekland-Olson, *Texas Prisons*, pp. 48–49.

12. "Brown Witness Admits Mutilation, but Sticks to Story," *Dallas Times Herald*, Feb. 24, 1982.

13. "Ex-inmate Says Pack Tortured Him," *Houston Post*, Feb. 19, 1982; and "Ex-con Testifies He Saw Pack Help Kill Prisoner," *Houston Chronicle*, Feb. 19, 1982.

14. "Ex-con Testifies He Saw Pack Help Kill Prisoner," *Houston Chronicle*, Feb. 19, 1982. Austin's death was brought up in *Ruiz*. See Martin and Ekland-Olson, *Texas Prisons*, pp. 48 and 125.

15. "'Bottoms' Area for Unauthorized Punishment, Inmates Testify in Brown Trial," *Houston Chronicle*, Feb. 18, 1982.

CHAPTER 17

1. "Slain Warden Had Non-violent Reputation, Ex-prisoner Testifies," *Houston Chronicle*, Feb. 23, 1982.

2. "Witnesses Testify Pack Strict, but Non-violent," *Houston Chronicle*, Feb. 24, 1982.

3. "Brown Witness Admits Mutilation, but Sticks to Story," *Dallas Times Herald*, Feb. 24, 1982.

4. "TDC Officials Say Pack Not Violent," *Houston Post*, Feb. 24, 1982.

5. Martin and Ekland-Olson, *Texas Prisons*, p. 101.

6. "Witnesses Testify Pack Strict, but Non-violent," *Houston Chronicle*, Feb. 24, 1982.

7. "Assistant Warden Denied Prison Official Involved in Inmate's Hanging Death," *Houston Chronicle*, Feb. 25, 1982.

8. "Brown's Lawyers Obtain Tapes by Pack Slaying Eyewitnesses," *Houston Post*, Feb. 25, 1982.

9. "Final Arguments Set in Brown Trial," *Houston Post*, Feb. 26, 1982.

10. "Both Sides Agree Prison Is Violent," *Dallas Times Herald*, March 2, 1982.

11. "State Submits Final Arguments in Eroy Brown Murder Trial," *Houston Chronicle*, March 1, 1982. "Jury Resumes Deliberations in Brown Trial," *Houston Chronicle*, March 2, 1982. "Brown Jury Hears Final Arguments," *Dallas Times Herald*, March 1, 1982. "Jury Recesses; No Verdict in Brown Trial," *Dallas Times*

Herald, March 2, 1982. "Brown Case Jury Recesses after Asking for Exhibits," *Houston Post*, March 2, 1982. United Press International, stories by Barbara Canetti, March 1 and 2, 1982.

CHAPTER 18

1. The jury notes were preserved in the trial record.
2. "TDC Slaying Jury Hears Transcripts," *Dallas Morning News*, March 3, 1982.
3. "Brown Jury Interrupts Deliberations to Have Three Inmates' Testimony Read," *Houston Chronicle*, March 3, 1982.
4. "Prosecutor Vows to Take Brown to Trial Again," *Fort Worth Star-Telegram*, March 5, 1982.
5. United Press International, March 6, 1982.
6. Rinker Buck, "The Keepers and the Kept," *Life*, Oct. 1982, p. 38.
7. "Jury Deadlocked in Inmate's Trial," *Dallas Morning News*, March 4, 1982.
8. Testimony of Diana Baker, Nov. 8, 1982, pp. 17-18.
9. "Brown Case Ends in Mistrial," *Houston Chronicle*, March 5, 1982.
10. "The Keepers and Their Killer," *Life*, October 1982.
11. "Pack's Widow Maintains She's 'Confident We'll Win in the End,'" *Houston Post*, March 5, 1982.
12. "Jurors Say 'Inconsistencies' Lead to Deadlock," Associated Press, March 4, 1982.
13. "Prosecutor Vows to Take Brown to Trial Again," *Fort Worth Star-Telegram*, March 5, 1982.
14. "'We Were Climbing the Walls,' Reports Brown Case Juror," *Houston Post*, March 7, 1982.
15. Interview with Henry Dalehite, July 2007.

CHAPTER 19

1. "Texas to Seek Second Trial," *Dallas Morning News*, March 5, 1982.
2. Martin and Ekland-Olson, *Texas Prisons*, p. 183.
3. Martin and Ekland-Olson, *Texas Prisons*, pp. 186-189.
4. "Brown's Inmate Brother Files Suit against TDC," *Houston Chronicle*, March 16, 1982.
5. Martin and Ekland-Olson, *Texas Prisons*, pp. 189-192.
6. Martin and Ekland-Olson, *Texas Prisons*, p. 193.
7. "White Seeks Ouster of TDC Monitor," *Houston Chronicle*, Jan. 26, 1982.
8. Martin and Ekland-Olson, *Texas Prisons*, p. 197.
9. Martin and Ekland-Olson, *Texas Prisons*, p. 208.
10. Martin and Ekland-Olson, *Texas Prisons*, p. 209. Lon Bennett Glenn, a former TDC warden who wrote a book about Texas prisons, *The Largest Hotel Chain in Texas*, was skeptical that White and other state officials hadn't known what was going on. "At the time, there were about 22,000 inmates and roughly 4,000

officers in TDC," Glenn wrote, "all of whom clearly knew in graphic detail of the building-tender system. Nothing was kept secret. The claim that this fact was unknown to the highest elected officials in the state is, to say the least, disingenuous" (pp. 144–145). Glenn had nothing to say, however, about the dozens of TDC officials who lied in court about the use of inmate guards, which was one of the five major issues in *Ruiz*.

11. Martin and Ekland-Olson, *Texas Prisons*, p. 209.
12. Martin and Ekland-Olson, *Texas Prisons*, pp. 210–211.
13. "11 TDC Inmates Staging a Hunger Strike," *Houston Chronicle*, June 29, 1982.
14. "TDC Must Face Up to Questions Crisis Raised," *Houston Post*, May 23, 1982.
15. "TDC Compromise Averts Showdown," *Dallas Morning News*, May 16, 1982.
16. Martin and Ekland-Olson, *Texas Prisons*, p. 217.
17. "Clements and Prison Fiasco," *Dallas Morning News*, May 19, 1982.
18. "White, Clements Exchange Charges on Prison Problem," *Houston Post*, June 11, 1982.
19. "US and Texas Seek Settlement in Penal Reform," *New York Times*, Dec. 19, 1981.
20. "TDC Suggests Naming Units for Slain Warden," *Houston Post*, June 7, 1982.

CHAPTER 20

1. "Walker County DA Hurt in Crash," *Houston Chronicle*, April 9, 1982.
2. "Judge to Decide Monday on Brown Venue Change," *Houston Chronicle*, May 5, 1982. "Change of Venue Denied," *Houston Chronicle*, May 11, 1982.
3. "Benefit to Raise Funds for Eroy Brown Retrial," *Houston Chronicle*, July 23, 1982.
4. Interviews and e-mail exchanges with Frank Klimko, 2009–2010.
5. "Eroy Brown Taken from Jail to Hospital for Treatment of Hepatitis, Tuberculosis," *Houston Chronicle*, March 12, 1982. "Eroy Brown Refuses TDC Medical Treatment," *Houston Chronicle*, July 21, 1982.
6. "Clements' Fund-Raising Dinner to Set National Record," *Houston Chronicle*, June 13, 1982.
7. "Judge Resets Retrial of Eroy Brown in Prison Officials' Slayings for Aug. 30," *Houston Chronicle*, Aug. 2, 1982. "Judge Cites Dispute in Withdrawing from Eroy Brown Trial," *Houston Chronicle*, April 10, 1982.
8. "State Rests Case in Eroy Brown Trial; Defense's Opening Argument Today," *Houston Post*, Nov. 2, 1982.
9. Brown cross-examination, Nov. 2, 1982, p. 50.
10. "Brown Testifies He Drowned Warden in Self-Defense," *Houston Chronicle*, Nov. 3, 1982.
11. Brown cross-examination, Nov. 2, 1982, pp. 116–117.

CHAPTER 21

1. Testimony of Levi Duson, Nov. 2 and 3, 1982, pp. 51–52.
2. Duson testimony, Nov. 2 and 3, 1982, p. 121.
3. Duson testimony, Nov. 2 and 3, 1982, p. 77.
4. Duson testimony, Nov. 2 and 3, 1982, pp. 133–135.
5. Duson testimony, Nov. 2 and 3, 1982, pp. 184–185.
6. Duson testimony, Nov. 2 and 3, 1982, pp. 230–231.
7. "Questions Surround Prison Farm Slayings at Huntsville," *Dallas Times Herald*, April 12, 1981.
8. Duson testimony, Nov. 2 and 3, 1982, p. 235.
9. Duson testimony, Nov. 2 and 3, 1982, p. 247.
10. Duson testimony, Nov. 2 and 3, 1982, p. 249.
11. Duson testimony, Nov. 2 and 3, 1982, pp. 257–258.
12. Duson testimony, Nov. 2 and 3, 1982, pp. 261–262.
13. Duson testimony, Nov. 2 and 3, 1982, pp. 282–283.
14. Duson testimony, Nov. 2 and 3, 1982, pp. 295–296.
15. Duson testimony, Nov. 2 and 3, 1982, pp. 303–306.
16. Duson testimony, Nov. 2 and 3, 1982, pp. 228–230.
17. Duson testimony, Nov. 2 and 3, 1982, pp. 337–342.
18. Duson testimony, Nov. 2 and 3, 1982, p. 376.

CHAPTER 22

1. "Washington Gets Ill; Brown Trial Recesses," *Houston Post*, Nov. 6, 1982.
2. "Defense Team Rests in Retrial of Brown," *Houston Post*, Nov. 9, 1982.
3. "Eroy Brown Acquitted," *Huntsville Item*, Nov. 10, 1982.
4. "Eroy Brown Acquitted in Warden's Death," *Houston Chronicle*, Nov. 10, 1982.
5. "Brown Cleared in TDC Warden's Death," *Houston Post*, Nov. 10, 1982.
6. "Eroy Brown Acquitted in Warden's Death," *Houston Chronicle*, Nov. 10, 1982.
7. "Brown Cleared in TDC Warden's Death," *Houston Post*, Nov. 10, 1982.
8. "Eroy Brown Acquitted, Jurors Say They Didn't Believe State's Witness," *Huntsville Item*, Nov. 11, 1982.

CHAPTER 23

1. His name has been withheld to protect his privacy.
2. Interview with William Habern, Dec. 1998.
3. His name has been withheld to protect his privacy.
4. Interview with Ray Hill, Sept. 2008.
5. *Ruiz*, no. 76-1948, April 7, 1977.
6. "Brown Cleared in TDC Warden's Death," *Houston Post*, Nov. 10, 1982.
7. Interview with William Habern.
8. http://www.clarkprosecutor.org/html/death/US/brooks006.htm; http://en.aca demic.ru/dic.nsf/enwiki/1190557; and Charles Colson, "The Execution That Wasn't Painless," *Washington Post*, Dec. 11, 1982.

CHAPTER 24

1. "Official: State Funds Needed to Try Brown," *Houston Chronicle*, Nov. 11, 1982.
2. "Defense Fighting Change of Venue for Brown Trial," *Houston Chronicle*, Dec. 8, 1982.
3. John Hill and Ernie Stromberger, *John Hill for the State of Texas: My Years as Attorney General*, p. 139. http://www.tshaonline.org/handbook/online/articles/P/fpa36.html.
4. "Death Penalty Case That Highlighted Jury Bias Ends in Plea Deal," *Dallas Morning News*, March 20, 2008.
5. "Lack of Funds Slowing Eroy Brown Trial in 2nd Death," *Houston Post*, July 19, 1983.
6. "Hobby Knew about New Evidence in Brown Trial," *Huntsville Item*, July 24, 1983.
7. "White Suggests Team to Help Counties Try TDC Inmate Cases," *Houston Chronicle*, July 19, 1983.
8. "State Likely to Pay for Inmate's Defense," *Houston Chronicle*, Oct. 16, 1983.
9. "Charge Reduced against Inmate in Prison Farm Manager's Death," *Houston Post*, Oct. 26, 1983.
10. "Convict's Lawyer Sues White, State," *Houston Post*, Oct. 28, 1983.
11. "Judge Again Blocks Funds for Brown Trial," *Fort Worth Star-Telegram*, Nov. 4, 1983.
12. "Comptroller Swaps Barbs with Governor," *Houston Post*, Dec. 3, 1983.
13. "Inmate's Trial Spurs Funding Call," *Austin American-Statesman*, Dec. 10, 1983.
14. "State Told to Pay Brown's Trial Costs," *Houston Chronicle*, Dec. 10, 1983.

CHAPTER 25

1. Interviews and e-mail exchange with Frank Klimko, 2009–2010.
2. Rinker Buck, unpublished manuscript, pp. 38–39.
3. See Whittington's foreword to Martin and Ekland-Olson, *Texas Prisons*.
4. "Land Buys for Prisons Postponed," *Houston Post*, May 19, 1978.
5. Martin and Ekland-Olson, *Texas Prisons*, pp. xi–xii.
6. Perkinson, *Texas Tough*, p. 415.
7. "Prison Pay Fattened by Tax-Fed Benefits," *Austin American-Statesman*, Dec. 26, 1982.
8. Perkinson, *Texas Tough*, p. 425.
9. Keller file, Pope Archives, Dec. 17, 1983.
10. Martin and Ekland-Olson, *Texas Prisons*, pp. 235–236, and William Barrett, "Lifer," *Houston City Magazine*, April 1982.
11. Perkinson, *Texas Tough*, p. 285.

CHAPTER 26

1. Frank Kemerer, *William Wayne Justice: A Judicial Biography*, p. 151.
2. Martin and Ekland-Olson, *Texas Prisons*, pp. 117–118.
3. "Six Inmates Transferred to Federal Custody," *Houston Chronicle*, Dec. 15, 1983.
4. "6 Inmates Ordered Transferred," *Houston Post*, Dec. 15, 1983.
5. "Inmate Gets 3rd Trial as State Costs Mount," *Fort Worth Star-Telegram*, Oct. 28, 1983.
6. Edward Blackburn, *Wanted: Historic County Jails of Texas*, pp. 163–164.
7. Martin and Ekland-Olson, *Texas Prisons*, pp. 55–56 and 227. "Warden Fired for Telling Guards to Beat Prisoner," *Dallas Times Herald*, Oct. 12, 1983.
8. "White Vows Action If Report of Abuse in TDC Confirmed," *Houston Post*, Sept. 30, 1983.
9. "Prison Probes Lead to More Dismissals," *Valley Morning Star*, March 3, 1984.
10. "Inmate Says He Saw Brown Shoot Moore at Point-Blank Range," United Press International, April 23, 1984. "State to Rest in Brown Trial Today," *Houston Post*, April 24, 1984.
11. "State Rests Case in Eroy Brown Trial," *Houston Post*, April 25, 1984.
12. "Official Disputes Murder Testimony," *Houston Post*, April 26, 1984.
13. Investigator's interview with Regina Bell, April 20, 1984.
14. "Brown Lashes Out at Key Witness for Prosecution, Brings Trial to a Halt," *Houston Post*, April 27, 1984.
15. "Brown Describes Struggle, Deaths," *Houston Post*, April 28, 1984.
16. "Brown Reportedly Smoked Marijuana," *Houston Post*, May 1, 1984. "Eroy Brown Murder Trial Nears End," United Press International, April 30, 1984.
17. "Eroy Brown Free after Jury Finds Killing Self-Defense," *Houston Post*, May 2, 1984.

CHAPTER 27

1. "DA Blocks Lawyer's Fees to Washington," *Houston Chronicle*, Sept. 26, 1984.
2. "Walker County Fights Order to Pay Legal Fees," *Houston Chronicle*, April 9, 1986.
3. "Texas Legislature Approves Record Tax Increase Package," *Houston Chronicle*, July 4, 1984.
4. Martin and Ekland-Olson, *Texas Prisons*, p. 237.
5. Michael C. Campbell, "Agents of Change: Law Enforcement, Prisons, and Politics in Texas and California," pp. 162–166.
6. http://gritsforbreakfast.blogspot.com/2007/01/texas-incarceration-far-out-strips.html.
7. "Ex-inmates Win 'Dog Bait,'" *Houston Post*, Dec. 28, 1983. The lawsuit and the settlement didn't stop the practice. In 1989 a prison board member took several friends on a horseback ride to watch the dog boys at work. They wore padded suits now when they jumped down to fight the dogs. The board member, Jerry

Hodge, had a couple of jackets made up for his friends that were embroidered with the slogan "The Ultimate Hunt." Hodge, a Republican, frequently spoke for his party on criminal justice issues. A black member of the legislature denounced the practice as a slave sport. "Inmates Are Prey in 'Ultimate Hunt,'" *New York Times*, Aug. 16, 1990.

8. "US Judges Question Legality of Practices They Say Violate Due Process Rights of Prisoners," *Austin American-Statesman*, Aug. 31, 2009. In October 2009 a federal jury in Austin held the chair of the state parole board, Rissie Owens, personally liable for $21,000 in damages and $100,000 in attorney's fees.

9. Interview with Bob Lee, Aug. 2007.

10. http://groups.yahoo.com/group/Texasdeathpenaltynews/message/3197; Dave McNeeley, "Washington Played by His Own Rules," *Austin American-Statesman*, March 13, 1994.

11. "Legal Maverick Back in Spotlight," *Houston Chronicle*, March 6, 2005.

12. "Washington Gets Probation in Shooting," *Houston Chronicle*, July 21, 2009.

13. "Eroy Brown Fears Reprisal after Third Trial," *Huntsville Item*, May 3, 1984.

14. "Brown Identified in Robbery Case," *Waco Tribune-Herald*, Nov. 7, 1984.

A NOTE ON THE SOURCES

This book is drawn from the recorded testimony and documents for Eroy Brown's first two trials in 1982. I am grateful to Bill Habern for securing them. Many of these sources are posted at a website, TheTrialsofEroyBrown.com.

I found a great deal of information in the newspaper accounts of the trials. The coverage was rich and intensive, and made me regret the loss of two Texas dailies, the *Dallas Times Herald* and the *Houston Post*. Former *Dallas Times Herald* reporter William Barrett sent me his clips, which were extremely helpful. Barrett was also the author of the only magazine profile of Jim Estelle. Bob Lee gave me his copy of the *Houston Chronicle* coverage. I was especially grateful to have the unpublished manuscript of Rinker Buck, who wrote a seventy-five page treatment of Eroy Brown and *Ruiz* with inspired original reporting.

I reviewed the archives of George Beto at Sam Houston State University and W. J. Estelle at Texas A&M University. The mother lode of Texas prison research is to be found at the University of Texas, where the archives of Lawrence Pope and Frances Jalet, among others, repose.

Three books were extremely helpful on the *Ruiz* background. *Texas Prisons: The Walls Came Tumbling Down,* by Steve Martin and Sheldon Ekland-Olson, was indispensable. So was *An Appeal to Justice: Litigated Reform of Texas Prisons,* by Ben Crouch and James Marquart. Robert Perkinson's sweeping history of Texas prisons, *Texas Tough: The Rise of America's Prison Empire*, was invaluable. I was fortunate to have the doctoral dissertations of Robert Chase and Michael C.

Campbell by my side. Susanne Mason's PBS video *Writ Writer* (2007) should be seen by anyone who wants to understand the period. Albert Race Sample's autobiography, *Racehoss: Big Emma's Boy* (Ballantine, 1985), describes the plantation mentality of the TDC in the 1950s and '60s that was still active in 1981. I don't think anyone can understand Texas prisons without reading Lon Bennett Glenn's *The Largest Hotel Chain in Texas: Texas Prisons*, a lament by an old-school Texas warden about the changes produced by *Ruiz*. I don't often agree with Glenn, but as Jim Estelle said of Claude Brown's *Manchild in the Promised Land*, it is a point of view.

SELECTED BIBLIOGRAPHY

Abramsky, Sasha. *American Furies: Crime, Punishment, and Vengeance in the Age of Mass Imprisonment*. Boston: Beacon Press, 2007.

Alexander, Michelle. *The New Jim Crow: Mass Incarceration in the Age of Colorblindness*. New York: New Press, 2010.

Anderson, Lloyd C. *Voices from a Southern Prison*. Athens: University of Georgia Press, 2000.

Barrow, Blanche Caldwell. *My Life with Bonnie and Clyde*. Ed. John Neal Phillips. Norman: University of Oklahoma Press, 2004.

Bernstein, Patricia. *The First Waco Horror: The Lynching of Jesse Washington and the Rise of the NAACP*. College Station: Texas A&M University Press, 2005.

Biffle, Kent. *A Month of Sundays*. Denton: University of North Texas Press, 1985.

Blackburn, Edward. *Wanted: Historic County Jails of Texas*. College Station: Texas A&M University Press, 2006.

Brown, Gary. *Texas Gulag: The Chain Gang Years, 1875–1925*. Plano: Republic of Texas Press, 2002.

Buck, Rinker. Unpublished manuscript, 1982.

———. "The Keepers and Their Killer," *Life*, October 1982.

Campbell, Michael C. *Agents of Change: Law Enforcement, Prisons, and Politics in Texas and California*. Ph.D. diss., University of California, Irvine, 2009.

Chase, Robert. *Civil Rights on the Cell Block: Race, Reform, and Violence in Texas Prisons and the Nation, 1945–1990*. Ph.D. diss., University of Maryland, 2009.

Cook, Kerry Max. *Chasing Justice*. New York: Harper, 2005.

Crichton, Robert. *The Great Imposter*. New York: Random House, 1959.

Crouch, Ben M., and James W. Marquart. *An Appeal to Justice: Litigated Reform of Texas Prisons.* Austin: University of Texas Press, 1989.

Currie, Elliot. *Crime and Punishment in America.* New York: Metropolitan Books, 1998.

Davies, Nick. *White Lies: The True Story of Clarence Brandley, Presumed Guilty in the American South.* London: Chatto and Windus, 1991.

DiIulio, John J., Jr., ed. *Courts, Corrections, and the Constitution.* New York: Oxford University Press, 1990.

———. *Governing Prisons: A Comparative Study of Correctional Management.* New York: Free Press, 1987.

Foucault, Michel. *Discipline and Punish: The Birth of the Prison.* New York: Vintage, 1979.

Gilligan, James. *Violence: Our Deadly Epidemic and Its Causes.* New York: Putnam, 1996.

Glenn, Lon Bennett. *The Largest Hotel Chain in Texas: Texas Prisons.* Austin: Eakin Press, 2001.

Goldstone, Dwonna Naomi. *Integrating the 40 Acres: The Fifty-Year Struggle for Racial Equality at the University of Texas.* Athens: University of Georgia Press, 2006.

Gottschalk, Marie. *The Prison and the Gallows: The Politics of Mass Incarceration in America.* New York: Cambridge University Press, 2006.

Gourevitch, Philip, and Errol Morris. *The Ballad of Abu Ghraib.* New York: Penguin, 2009.

Guinn, Jeff. *Go Down Together: The True, Untold Story of Bonnie and Clyde.* New York: Simon and Schuster, 2009.

Hallinan, Joseph T. *Going up the River: Travels in a Prison Nation.* New York: Random House, 2001.

Harper, William T. *Eleven Days in Hell: The 1974 Carrasco Prison Siege at Huntsville, Texas.* Denton: University of North Texas Press, 2004.

Hill, John, and Ernie Stromberger. *John Hill for the State of Texas: My Years as Attorney General.* College Station: Texas A&M University Press, 2008.

Horton, David M., and George R. Nielsen. *Walking George: The Life of George John Beto and the Rise of the Modern Texas Prison System.* Denton: University of North Texas Press, 2005.

House, Aline. *The Carrasco Tragedy.* Waco: Texian Press, 1975.

Jackson, Bruce. *Disorderly Conduct.* Urbana: University of Illinois Press, 1992.

———. *Wake Up Dead Man: Hard Labor and Southern Blues.* Athens: University of Georgia Press, 1999.

Jacobs, James J. *Stateville: The Penitentiary in Mass Society.* Chicago: University of Chicago Press, 1977.

Joint Committee on Prison Reform. "Final Report of the Joint Committee on Prison Reform of the Texas Legislature." 63rd Legislature. December 1974.

———. "Report from the Citizens' Advisory Committee to the Joint Committee on Prison Reform." 63rd Legislature. December 1974.

Kauffman, Kelsey. *Prison Officers and Their World.* Cambridge, Mass.: Harvard University Press, 1988.

Kemerer, Frank R. *William Wayne Justice: A Judicial Biography.* Austin: University of Texas Press, 1991.

Lyon, Danny. *Conversations with the Dead.* New York: Holt, Rinehart, and Winston, 1971.

———. *The Destruction of Lower Manhattan.* New York: Macmillan, 1969.

———. *Like a Thief's Dream.* Brooklyn: powerHouse Books, 2007.

Martin, Steve J., and Sheldon Ekland-Olson. *Texas Prisons: The Walls Came Tumbling Down.* Austin: Texas Monthly Press, 1987.

McCall, Brian. *The Power of the Texas Governor.* Austin: University of Texas Press, 2009.

McCune, Billy. *The Autobiography of Billy McCune.* San Francisco: Straight Arrow Books, 1973.

Morris, Robert. *The Devil's Butcher Shop: The New Mexico Prison Uprising.* Albuquerque: University of New Mexico Press, 1983.

Murton, Thomas. *Accomplices to the Crime.* New York: Grover Press, 1969.

Oshinsky, David M. *"Worse Than Slavery": Parchman Farm and the Ordeal of Jim Crow Justice.* New York: Free Press, 1996.

Palmer, John W. *Constitutional Rights of Prisoners.* 2nd ed. Cincinnati: Anderson, 1977.

Perkinson, Robert. *Texas Tough: The Rise of America's Prison Empire.* New York: Metropolitan Books, 2010.

Phillips, John Neal. *Running with Bonnie and Clyde: The Ten Fast Years of Ralph Fults.* Norman: University of Oklahoma Press, 1996.

Potts, James L., and Alvin J. Bronstein. *Prisoners' Self-Help Litigation Manual.* Lexington, Mass.: Lexington Books, 1976.

Ragen, Joseph E., and Charles Finston. *Inside the World's Toughest Prison.* Springfield, Ill.: Bannerstone House, 1962.

Robinson, Ronald W. *Prison Hostage: The Seige of the Walls Prison in Huntsville, Texas.* Lewiston, N.Y.: Edward Mellen Press, 1997.

Rudovsky, David. *The Rights of Prisoners.* New York: American Civil Liberties Union, 1973.

Sample, Albert Race. *Racehoss: Big Emma's Boy.* New York: Ballantine, 1984.

Schneider, Paul. *Bonnie and Clyde: The Lives behind the Legend.* New York: Holt, 2009.

Simmons, Lee. *Assignment Huntsville.* Austin: University of Texas Press, 1957.

Simon, Jonathan. *Governing through Crime.* Oxford: Oxford University Press, 2007.

———. *Poor Discipline: Parole and the Social Control of the Underclass, 1890–1990.* Chicago: University of Chicago Press, 1993.

Sykes, Gresham M. *The Society of Captives: A Study of a Maximum Security Prison.* Princeton: Princeton University Press, 1958.

Taylor, William Banks. *Down on Parchman Farm*. Columbus: Ohio State University Press, 1999.

Texas Committee on Prison and Prison Labor. *A Summary of the Texas Prison Survey*, vol. I, 1924.

Texas Department of Corrections. *1981 Annual Report*.

Thomas, Jim. *Prisoner Litigation: The Paradox of the Jailhouse Lawyer*. New Jersey: Rowman and Littlefield, 1988.

Trulson, Chad R., and James W. Marquart. *First Available Cell: Desegregation of the Texas Prison System*. Austin: University of Texas Press, 2009.

Walker, Donald R. *Penology for Profit: A History of the Texas Prison System, 1867–1912*. College Station: Texas A&M University Press, 1988.

Willett, Jim, and Ron Rozelle. *Warden: Prison Life and Death from the Inside Out*. Albany, Tex.: Bright Sky Press, 2004.

Wilson, Steven Harmon. *The Rise of Judicial Management in the U.S. District Court, Southern District of Texas, 1955–2000*. Athens: University of Georgia Press, 2002.

Yackle, Larry W. *Reform and Regret: The Story of Federal Judicial Involvement in the Alabama Prison System*. New York: Oxford University Press, 1989.

Zimbardo, Philip. *The Lucifer Effect: Understanding How Good People Turn Evil*. New York: Random House, 2007.

ACKNOWLEDGMENTS

I began this book in 2000 with a grant from the Open Society Institute, for which I am deeply indebted. I returned to it after becoming an assistant professor of journalism at the Valenti School of Communication at the University of Houston in 2006. The Valenti School provided a semester's teaching leave, which enabled me to write the first draft. In 2010 I became chair of journalism at Texas Southern University, which generously underwrote the indexing and photography costs.

Many people helped me and encouraged me over the years. I am especially grateful to Bill Habern, Tim Sloan, and Kent Schaffer, who opened their files and their memories to me.

To my great regret, I never persuaded Craig Washington to talk to me for the book. He says he might write his own some day.

Alex Parsons read the first draft and gave me helpful advice on how to revise it. David McHam, a friend and mentor for many years in all things journalistic, helped me edit the revision. Jennifer Peebles created the map of Huntsville prisons and gave time and advice on promoting this book. Catherine Stevenson provided unmatchable encouragement.

Lynn Randolph, my wife, drew the crime scene diagram and, more importantly, has loved and supported me and my daughter, Elizabeth, during this work. She closely read the manuscript and saved me from many errors. I couldn't have done it without her.

INDEX

Page numbers in *italics* indicate illustrations.

Clinton, Sam Houston, 81–82, 213n1 (ch. 10)
Coffield prison, 5, 100, 194
Cohen, Robert, 152
Cole, Doyle, 137, 138
Coleman, Kenneth, 198
Colson, Charles, 180
community-based corrections programs, 25, 31, 62
Conversations with the Dead (Lyon), 47, 55, 214n5 (ch. 10)
Cooper v. Pate, 52
Costilow, Don, 138
Cousins, Robert, 194
Criminal Justice Division, 183, 184
Criminal Justice Planning Fund, 185
Crocker, Kerry, 88
Crouch, Ben, 223
Crowson, Major, 68
Cruz, Fred, 50, 53, 56
Cruz, Hector de la, 199
Cuevas, Ignacio, 68, 88, 183
CURE (Citizens United for Rehabilitation of Errants), 28, 172

Dalehite, Henry, 89, 149, 182; hearing held by, to discuss protective custody for inmate witnesses, 82–84, 86–87, 176; presiding of, at Brown's first trial, 81, 94, 98, 103, 106, 121, 122, 124, 127, 130, 131, 133, 134, 139, 140, 145, 146, 147
Dallas Times Herald, 66, 98, 223
Darrington Unit, 12, 77, 151, 152, 178
Davis, Cullen, 82
Davis, Ralph A., 201
death penalty, 62, 67, 68, 85, 89, 205
Death Row, 42, 80, 88
Degrate, Simmie, 74
DeYoung, Robert, 15–18, 33, 100–101, 120, 159–160
Diagnostic Unit at Huntsville, 85, 86, 87, 133, 164

Dial, Steve, 183
Dickerson, Wendell, 87
DiIulio, John, 210n4 (ch. 5)
"dog boys," 203, 221–222n7
Dreyer, Freddie, 52
Dreyer v. Jalet, 52–56, 211n9, 216n11 (ch. 16)
drugs: addiction to, 99, 206; as basis for crime, 202; dealing, 83. *See also* marijuana
Duson, Levi, 34, 35, 38–39, 86–87; in Brown's testimony, 110, 115; as a witness at Brown's first trial, 99–101, 106, 107, 108, 139, 141–143, 144–145, 148, 149, 159; as a witness at Brown's second trial, 160, 162–170, 171–172, 174, 195

Eastham Unit, 7, 67–68, 83, 118, 152, 191
Eckles, James E., 66
Ekland-Olson, Sheldon, 152, 223
Ellis, O. B., 42–43, 53
Ellis Report, 50–51
Ellis II, 189
Ellis Unit: aerial view of, *91*; the bottoms at, 65, 117; Brown's time in, 12–13, 78, 79–80; Bruce Jackson's research on, 43–46, 47; building tenders at, 53–54, 151, 187; Caldwell cutters at, 110–111; Danny Lyon's photographs of, 46–48; difficulties at, after Pack and Moore killings, 82–83, 87; farm at, 7, 44; fish fries at, 123; history of, 42–43; inmates living in tents at, 69–70; reactions to Brown mistrial at, 150; reputation of, and conditions at, 10, 174, 212n6 (ch. 8); scale model of, 144; singing at, 6, 7, 44; wardens at, 11, 191, 194; work stoppages at, 70-71, 152; writ writers at, 49–56
Espinola, Aurelio, 195, 196
Estelle, Ward James "Jim," 8, 10, 19, 65, 69, 150, 154, 155, 173, 175; archives of, 223; background of, 24–26; bitterness

Urdy, Hugh, 198
US House of Representatives, 27
US Justice Department, 22, 116, 117, 152
US Supreme Court, 19, 22, 27, 51, 52, 58, 82, 151, 182, 204

Vanderhoof, David, 192, 212n6 (ch. 8)
Vara, Richard, 148
Vietnam War, 34

Wade, Henry, 182
Walker County (Texas), 68, 82, 88–89, 136, 156, 158, 181–186, 194, 201; district attorney's office, 34, 39, 57, 83, 121, 156, 177; Grand Jury, 85; medical examiner, 67; sheriff's department, 11, 19, 101, 139
Wallace Pack-Billy Moore Fund, 157
"Walls, the," 19, 29, 59, 70, 80, 120, 134, 177
Wanstrath, Diana, 102
Ward, Mark, 39, 68, 83–85, 88, 121–130, 139–140, 142, 156, 181
Warden, Joetta, 144, 146, 147
Washington, Craig, 108, 194, 207; attempts of, to get paid for defending Brown, 184–186, 201, 203; biography and legal experience of, 61–63; and Brown's first trial, 89, 92–95, 100–104, 106–109, 120–122, 124, 127, 129, 130–133,

135–140, 142–143, 145, 146; and Brown's second trial, 156, 157–158, 160, 161, 162–169, 171–175; and Brown's third trial, 182, 183, 184, 195–200; career, post-Brown, 204–206; as one of "the People's Five," 27; political supporters of, 68–69; pretrial maneuvering of, 81, 82, 86, 87; threats on life of, 178, 180
Watergate tapes, 82
White, Mark, 69, 81, 151–155, 183–185, 194, 201–202, 217–218n10
Whittington, Harry, 152, 153, 154, 188–189, 202
Wiley, Kathy, 76, 77–78
Willett, Jim, 2
Williams, Tyrone, 205
Williamson, James, 15, 16, 39, 98, 101, 107, 120, 160, 171, 191, 195, 212n6 (ch. 8), 215n4 (ch. 13)
Windham, James, 189
work-furlough programs, 25, 28, 69
Writ Writer (Mason), 50, 224
writ writing, 49–56, 58, 59, 66, 67, 82, 132
Wynne Unit, 195, 203, 214n5 (ch. 10); "the bottoms" at, 117; building tenders at, 53–56; Pack's time at, 10, 12, 57, 66, 84, 118, 132–135, 137, 139, 141, 173; violent deaths at, 138, 139, 141